FIFTY EIGHT

JUN 2 7 2017

On the day **Thor Odinson** learned a long-kept secret, he dropped the mystic hammer **MJOLNIR** to the surface of the moon. Try as he might, Thor could not lift his once-faithful weapon. Unable to possess the power of his birthright, the thunder god relinquished the name of Thor now simply calls himself Odinson. Now he searches for redemption, but until he finds it, he will remain...

THE UNWORTHY THOR

JASON AARON
WRITER

ISSUES #1-2
OLIVIER COIPEL
ARTIST

MATTHEW WILSON
COLOR ARTIST

ISSUE #3
KIM JACINTO &
OLIVIER COIPEL
ARTISTS

MATTHEW WILSON
COLOR ARTIST

ISSUE #4
OLIVIER COIPEL
WITH **KIM JACINTO** (PRESENT DAY),
FRAZER IRVING (YOUNG THOR),
ESAD RIBIC (WORTHY THOR) &
RUSSELL DAUTERMAN (UNWORTHY THOR)
ARTISTS

MATTHEW WILSON,
MATT MILLA &
FRAZER IRVING
COLOR ARTISTS

ISSUE #5
OLIVIER COIPEL,
KIM JACINTO &
PASCAL ALIXE
ARTISTS

MAT LOPES &
JAY DAVID RAMOS
COLOR ARTISTS

VC's JOE SABINO
LETTERER

OLIVIER COIPEL WITH **MATTHEW WILSON** (#2-5)
COVER ART

CHARLES BEACHAM
ASSISTANT EDITOR

SARAH BRUNSTAD
ASSOCIATE EDITOR

WIL MOSS
EDITOR

THOR CREATED BY STAN LEE, LARRY LIEBER & JACK KIRBY

COLLECTION EDITOR **JENNIFER GRÜNWALD** † ASSISTANT EDITOR **CAITLIN O'CONNELL**
ASSOCIATE MANAGING EDITOR **KATERI WOODY** † EDITOR, SPECIAL PROJECTS **MARK D. BEAZLEY**
VP PRODUCTION & SPECIAL PROJECTS **JEFF YOUNGQUIST**
SVP PRINT, SALES & MARKETING **DAVID GABRIEL** † BOOK DESIGNER **JAY BOWEN**

EDITOR IN CHIEF **AXEL ALONSO** † CHIEF CREATIVE OFFICER **JOE QUESADA**
PRESIDENT **DAN BUCKLEY** † EXECUTIVE PRODUCER **ALAN FINE**

THE UNWORTHY THOR. Contains material originally published in magazine form as THE UNWORTHY THOR #1-5. First printing 2017. ISBN# 978-1-302-90667-2. Published by MARVEL WORLDWIDE, INC., a subsidiary of MARVEL ENTERTAINMENT, LLC. OFFICE OF PUBLICATION: 135 West 50th Street, New York, NY 10020. Copyright © 2017 MARVEL No similarity between any of the names, characters, persons, and/or institutions in this magazine with those of any living or dead person or institution is intended, and any such similarity which may exist is purely coincidental. **Printed in the U.S.A.** DAN BUCKLEY, President, Marvel Entertainment; JOE QUESADA, Chief Creative Officer; TOM BREVOORT, SVP of Publishing; DAVID BOGART, SVP of Business Affairs & Operations, Publishing & Partnership; C.B. CEBULSKI, VP of Brand Management & Development, Asia; DAVID GABRIEL, SVP of Sales & Marketing, Publishing; JEFF YOUNGQUIST, VP of Production & Special Projects; DAN CARR, Executive Director of Publishing Technology; ALEX MORALES, Director of Publishing Operations; SUSAN CRESPI, Production Manager; STAN LEE, Chairman Emeritus. For information regarding advertising in Marvel Comics or on Marvel.com, please contact Vit DeBellis, Integrated Sales Manager, at vdebellis@marvel.com. For Marvel subscription inquiries, please call 888-511-5480. Manufactured between 3/31/2017 and 5/2/2017 by QUAD/GRAPHICS WASECA, WASECA, MN, USA.

10 9 8 7 6 5 4 3 2 1

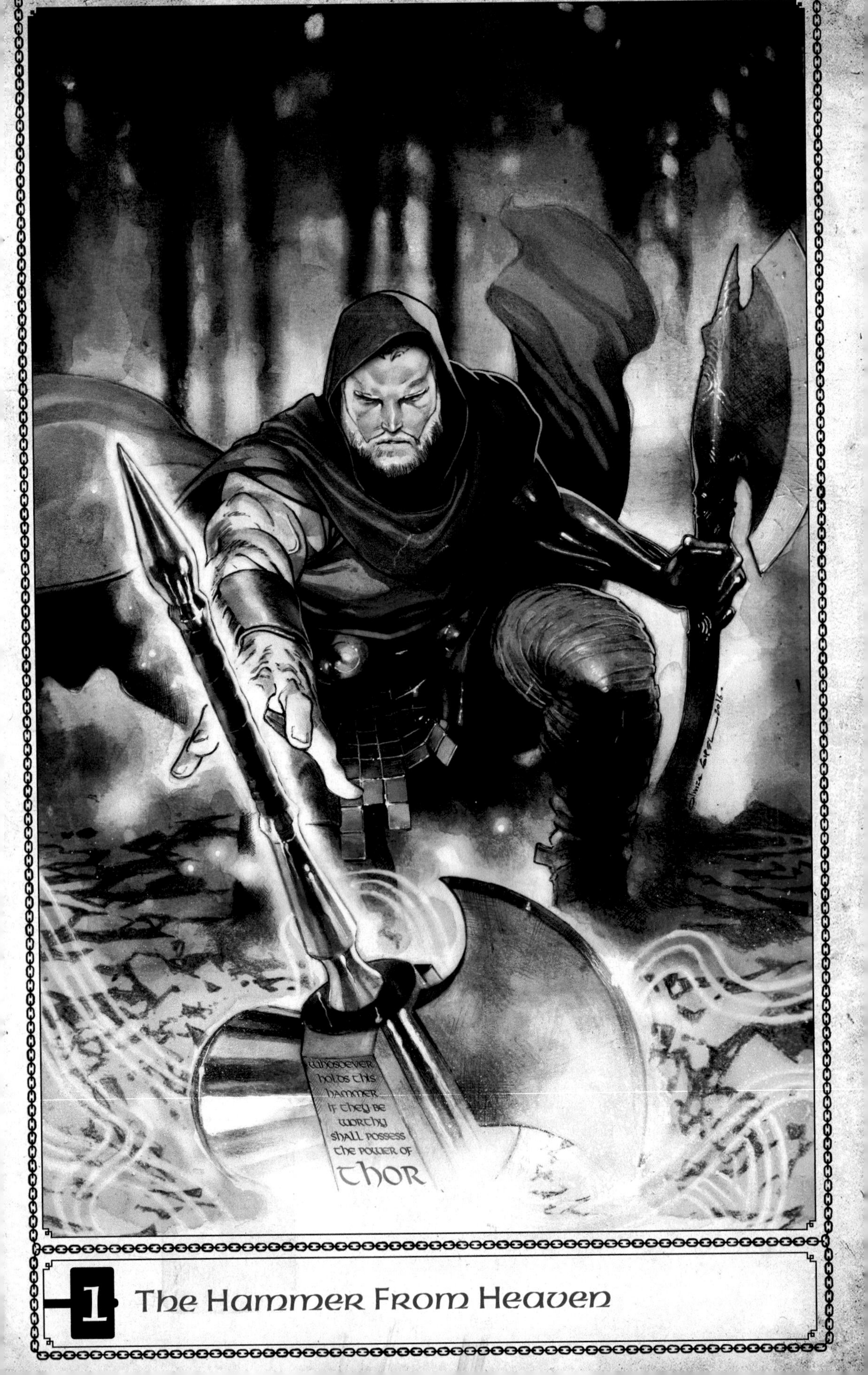
Whosoever
holds this
hammer
if they be
worthy
shall possess
the power of
Thor

1 The Hammer From Heaven

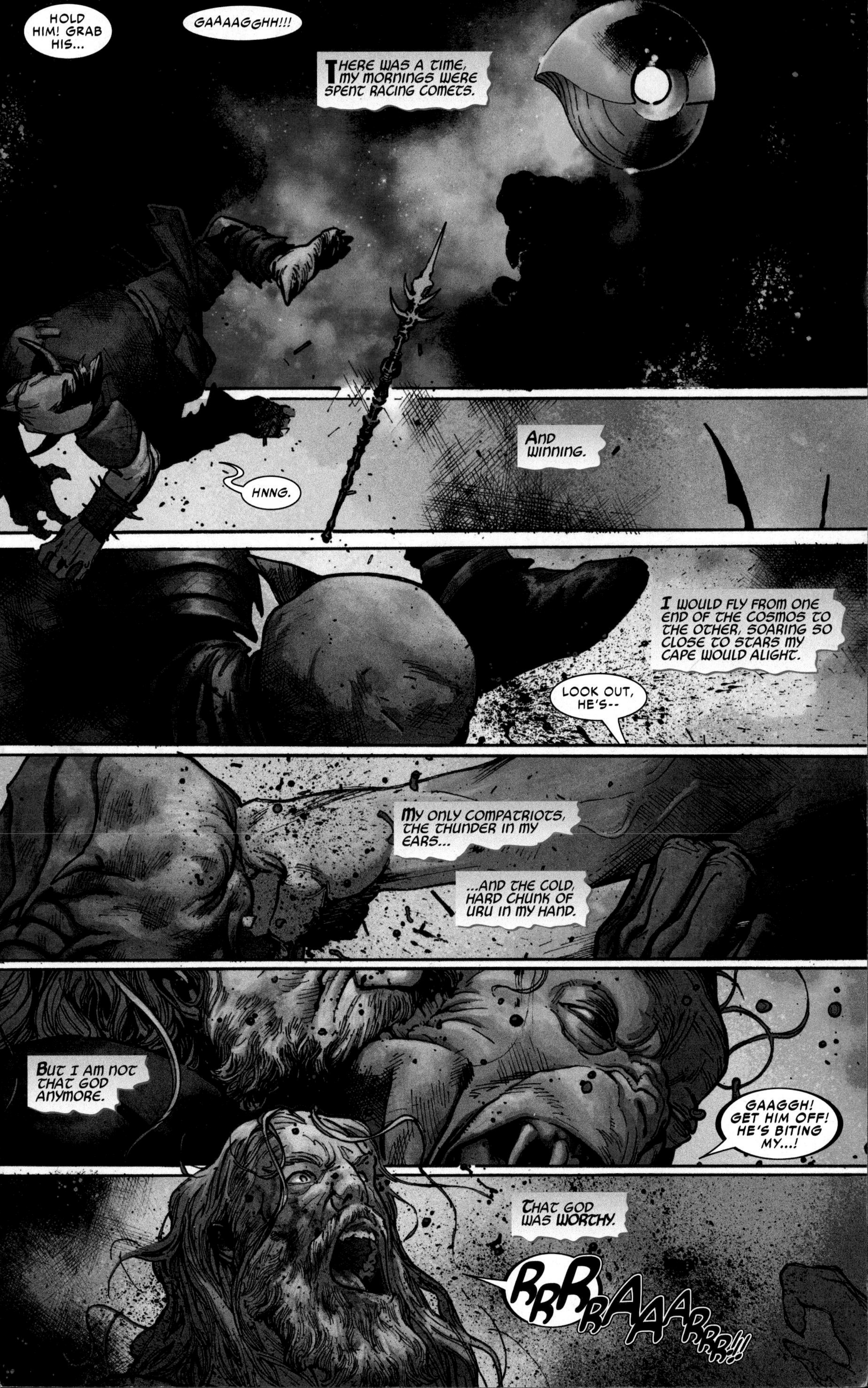
HOLD HIM! GRAB HIS...
GAAAAGGHH!!!
THERE WAS A TIME, MY MORNINGS WERE SPENT RACING COMETS.
AND WINNING.
HNNG.
I WOULD FLY FROM ONE END OF THE COSMOS TO THE OTHER, SOARING SO CLOSE TO STARS MY CAPE WOULD ALIGHT.
LOOK OUT, HE'S--
MY ONLY COMPATRIOTS, THE THUNDER IN MY EARS...
...AND THE COLD, HARD CHUNK OF URU IN MY HAND.
BUT I AM NOT THAT GOD ANYMORE.
GAAGGH! GET HIM OFF! HE'S BITING MY...!
THAT GOD WAS WORTHY.
RRRRAAAARRRR!!!

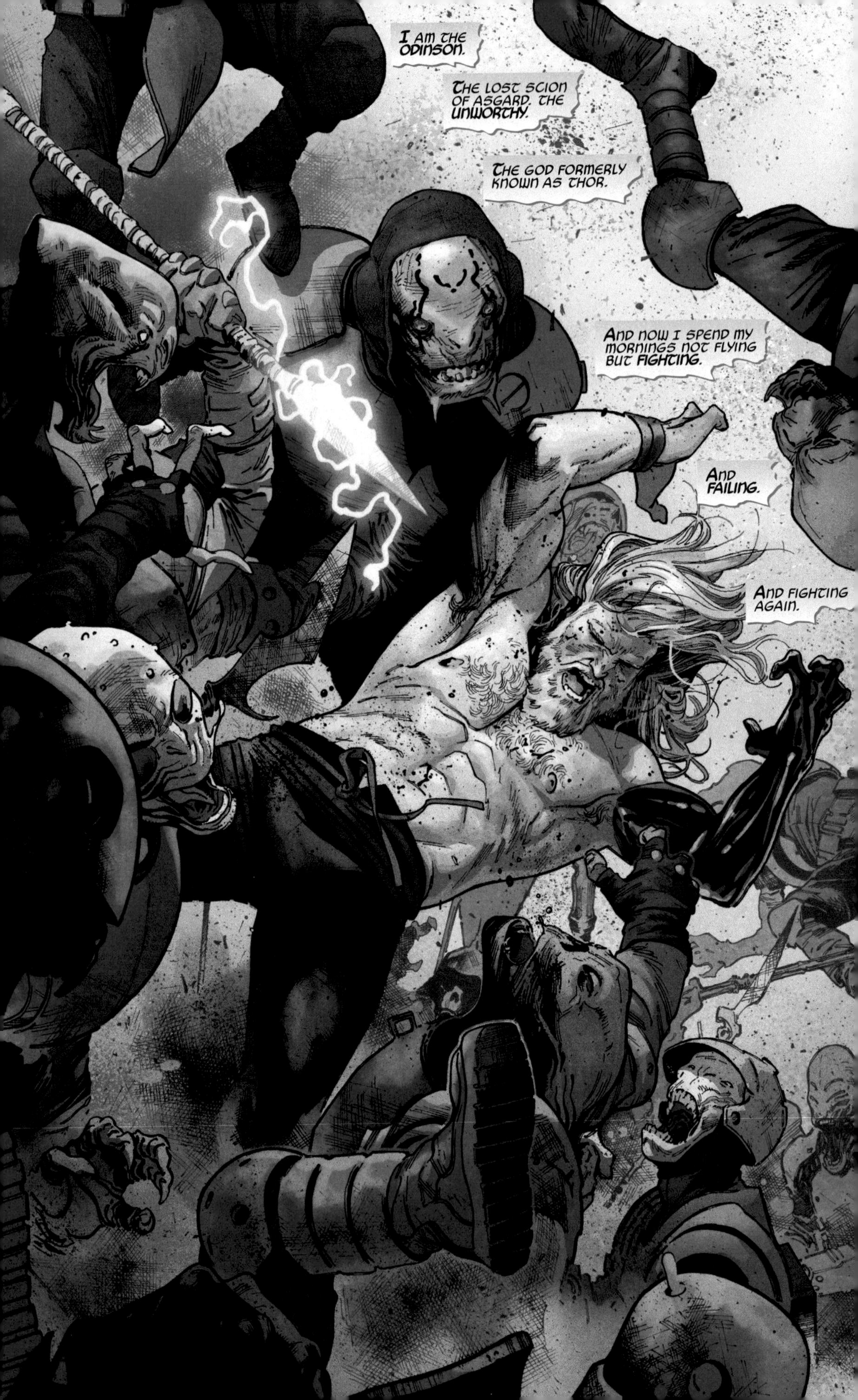
I AM THE ODINSON.
THE LOST SCION OF ASGARD. THE UNWORTHY.
THE GOD FORMERLY KNOWN AS THOR.
AND NOW I SPEND MY MORNINGS NOT FLYING BUT FIGHTING.
AND FAILING.
AND FIGHTING AGAIN.

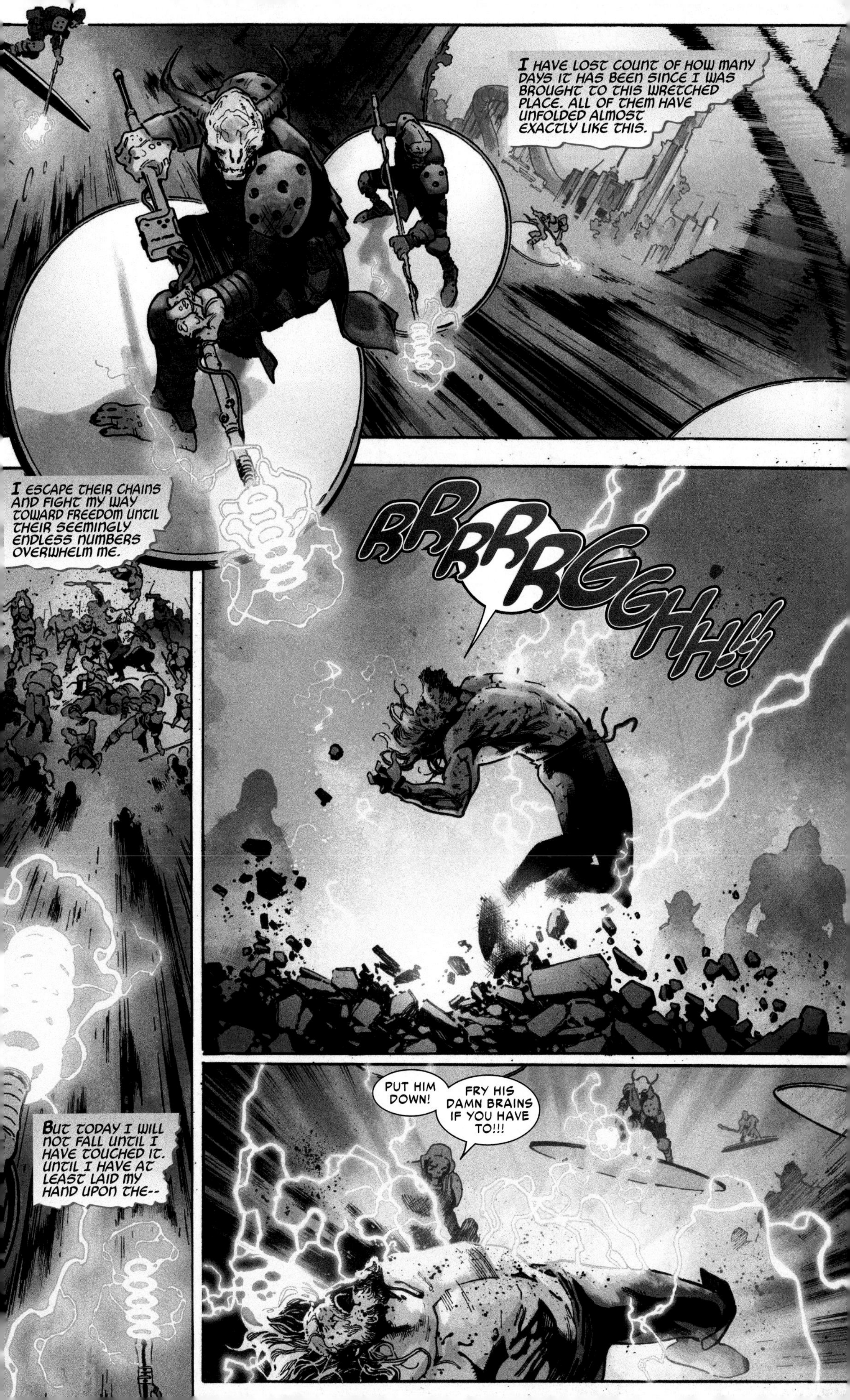
I HAVE LOST COUNT OF HOW MANY DAYS IT HAS BEEN SINCE I WAS BROUGHT TO THIS WRETCHED PLACE. ALL OF THEM HAVE UNFOLDED ALMOST EXACTLY LIKE THIS.
I ESCAPE THEIR CHAINS AND FIGHT MY WAY TOWARD FREEDOM UNTIL THEIR SEEMINGLY ENDLESS NUMBERS OVERWHELM ME.
RRRRRGGHH!!!
BUT TODAY I WILL NOT FALL UNTIL I HAVE TOUCHED IT. UNTIL I HAVE AT LEAST LAID MY HAND UPON THE--
PUT HIM DOWN!
FRY HIS DAMN BRAINS IF YOU HAVE TO!!!

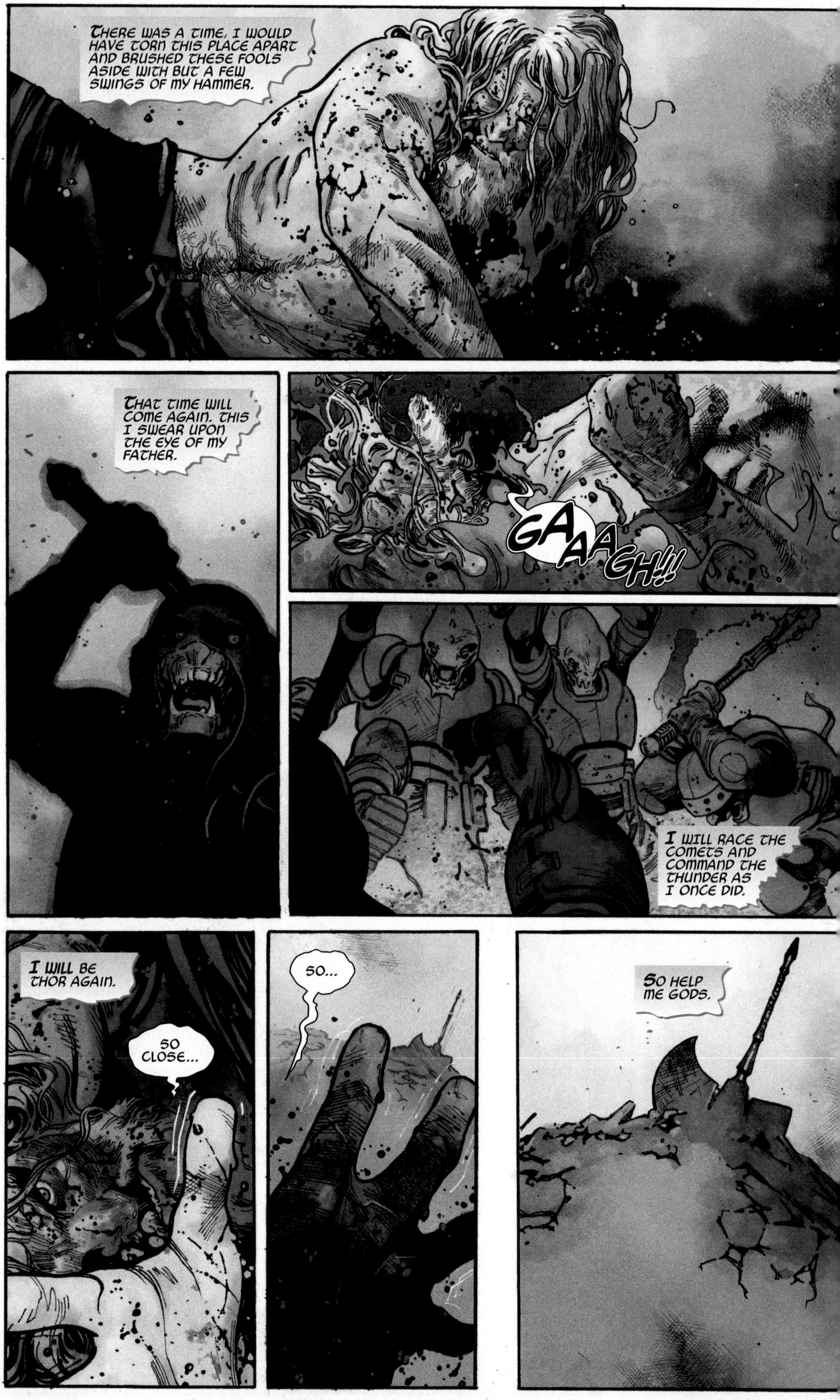
There was a time, I would have torn this place apart and brushed these fools aside with but a few swings of my hammer.
That time will come again. This I swear upon the eye of my father.
GAAAAGH!!!
I will race the comets and command the thunder as I once did.
I will be Thor again.
So close...
So...
So help me gods.

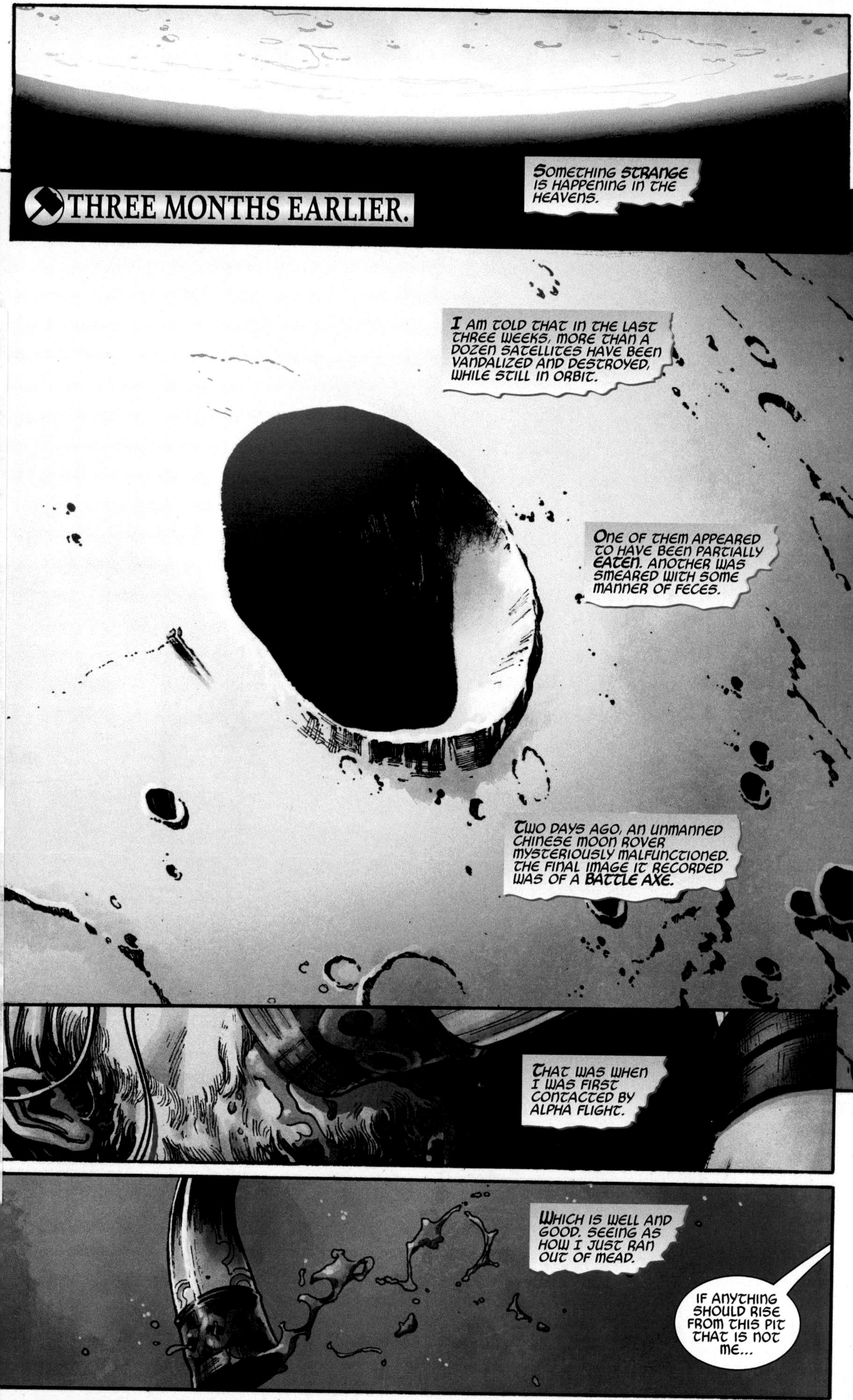
THREE MONTHS EARLIER.
SOMETHING STRANGE IS HAPPENING IN THE HEAVENS.
I AM TOLD THAT IN THE LAST THREE WEEKS, MORE THAN A DOZEN SATELLITES HAVE BEEN VANDALIZED AND DESTROYED, WHILE STILL IN ORBIT.
ONE OF THEM APPEARED TO HAVE BEEN PARTIALLY EATEN. ANOTHER WAS SMEARED WITH SOME MANNER OF FECES.
TWO DAYS AGO, AN UNMANNED CHINESE MOON ROVER MYSTERIOUSLY MALFUNCTIONED. THE FINAL IMAGE IT RECORDED WAS OF A BATTLE AXE.
THAT WAS WHEN I WAS FIRST CONTACTED BY ALPHA FLIGHT.
WHICH IS WELL AND GOOD, SEEING AS HOW I JUST RAN OUT OF MEAD.
IF ANYTHING SHOULD RISE FROM THIS PIT THAT IS NOT ME...

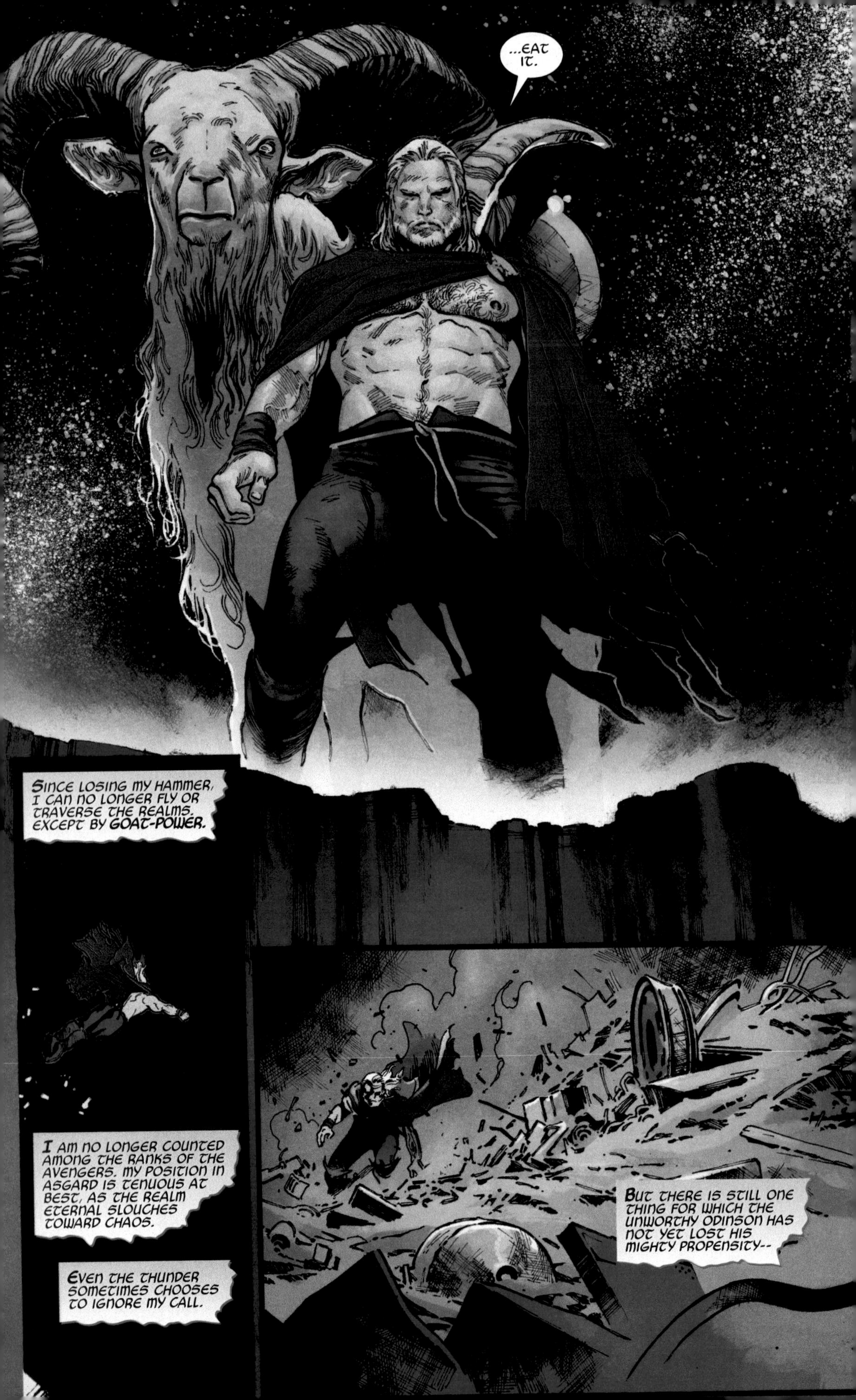
...EAT IT.
SINCE LOSING MY HAMMER, I CAN NO LONGER FLY OR TRAVERSE THE REALMS. EXCEPT BY GOAT-POWER.
I AM NO LONGER COUNTED AMONG THE RANKS OF THE AVENGERS. MY POSITION IN ASGARD IS TENUOUS AT BEST, AS THE REALM ETERNAL SLOUCHES TOWARD CHAOS.
EVEN THE THUNDER SOMETIMES CHOOSES TO IGNORE MY CALL.
BUT THERE IS STILL ONE THING FOR WHICH THE UNWORTHY ODINSON HAS NOT YET LOST HIS MIGHTY PROPENSITY--

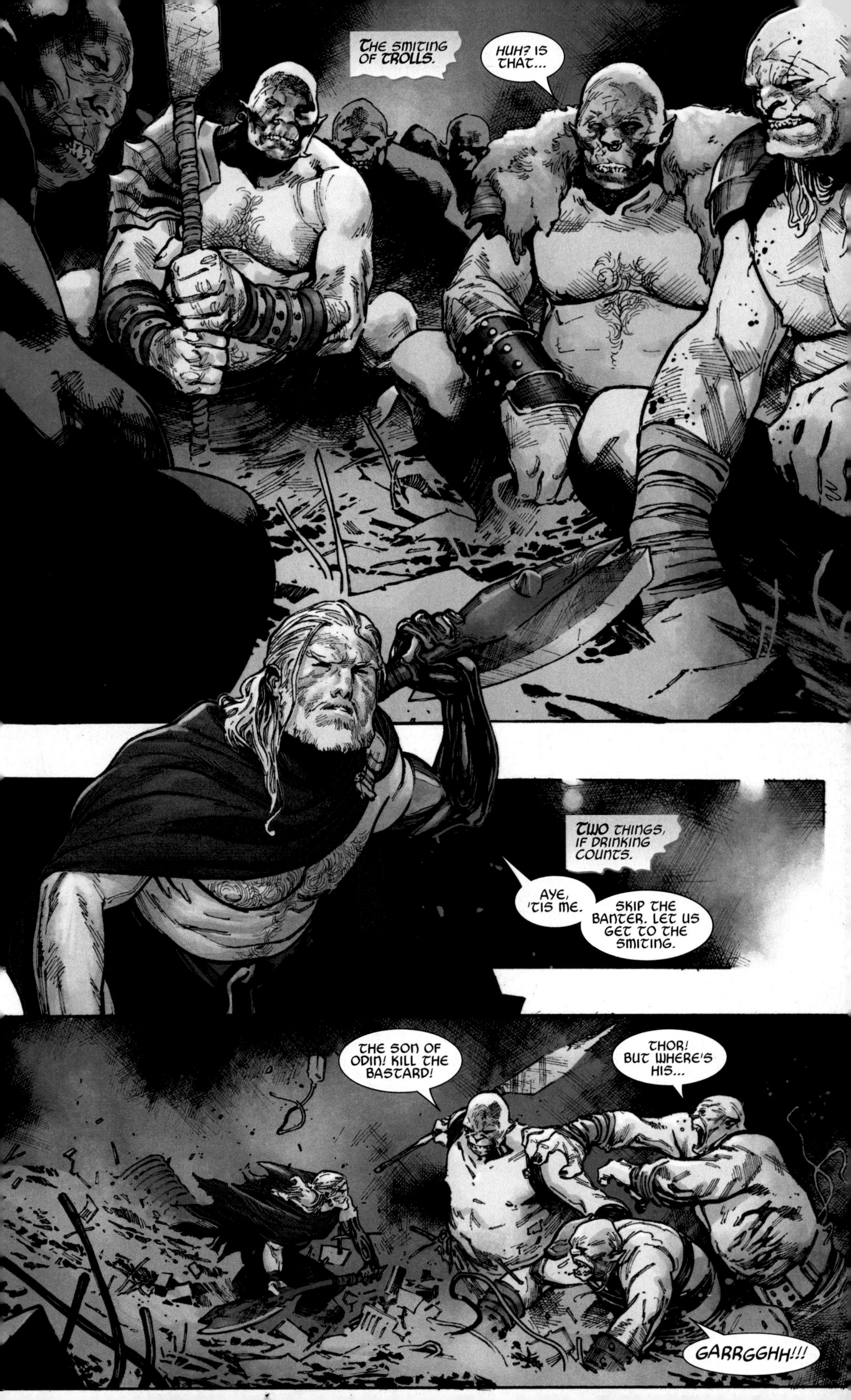
THE SMITING OF TROLLS.
HUH? IS THAT...
TWO THINGS, IF DRINKING COUNTS.
AYE, 'TIS ME.
SKIP THE BANTER. LET US GET TO THE SMITING.
THE SON OF ODIN! KILL THE BASTARD!
THOR! BUT WHERE'S HIS...
GARRGGHH!!!

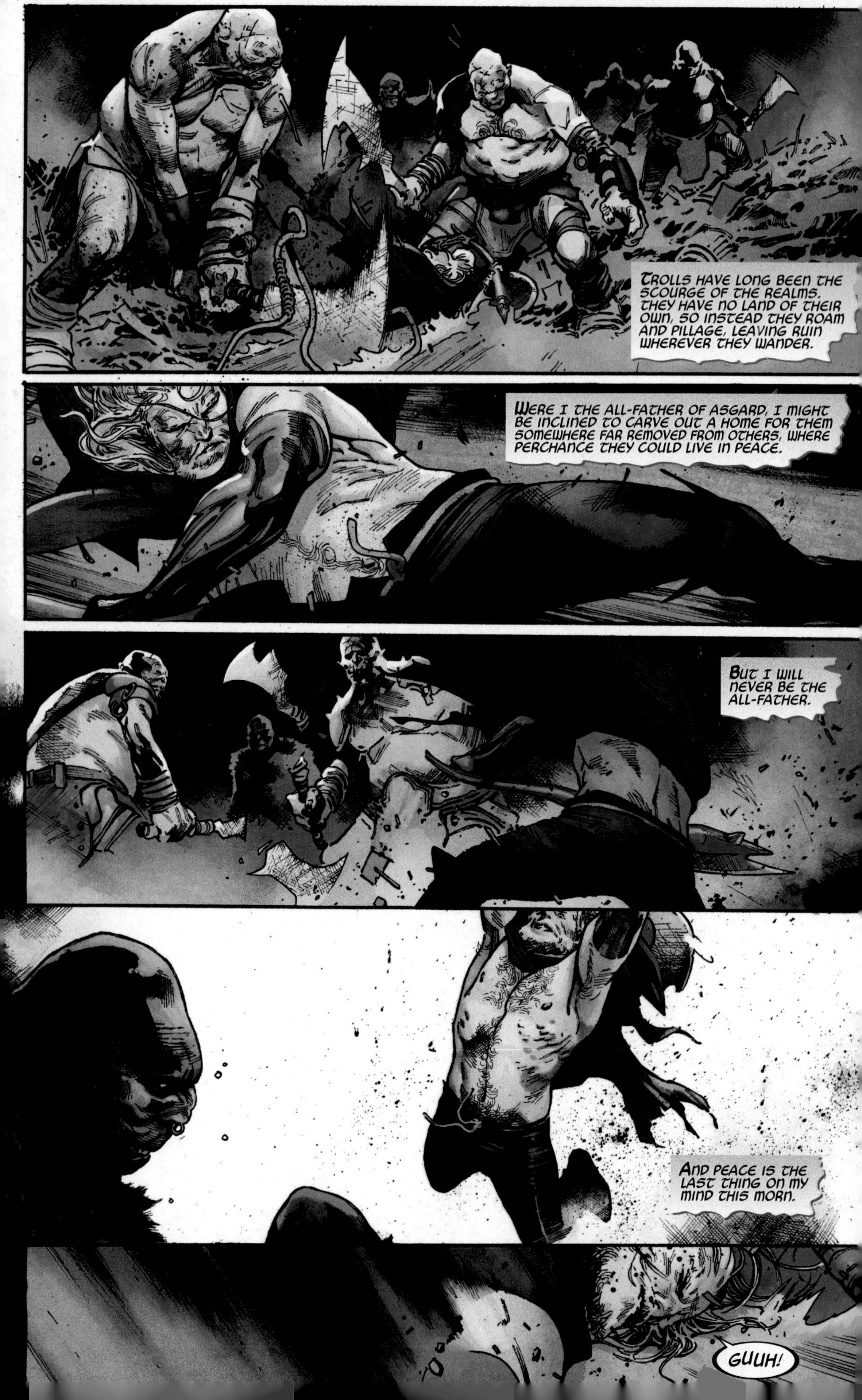

TROLLS HAVE LONG BEEN THE SCOURGE OF THE REALMS. THEY HAVE NO LAND OF THEIR OWN, SO INSTEAD THEY ROAM AND PILLAGE, LEAVING RUIN WHEREVER THEY WANDER.
WERE I THE ALL-FATHER OF ASGARD, I MIGHT BE INCLINED TO CARVE OUT A HOME FOR THEM SOMEWHERE FAR REMOVED FROM OTHERS, WHERE PERCHANCE THEY COULD LIVE IN PEACE.
BUT I WILL NEVER BE THE ALL-FATHER.
AND PEACE IS THE LAST THING ON MY MIND THIS MORN.
GUUH!

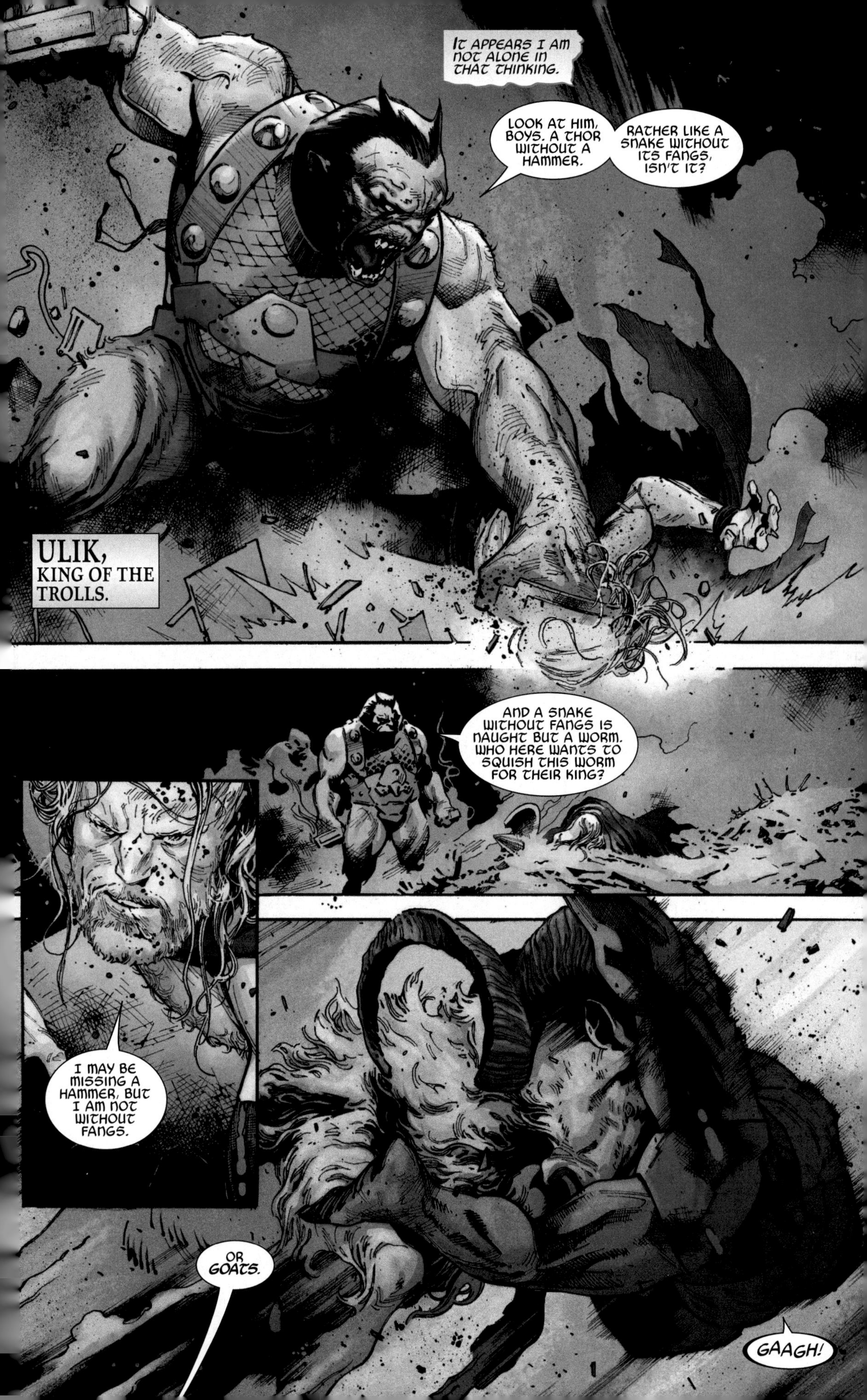

IT APPEARS I AM NOT ALONE IN THAT THINKING.
LOOK AT HIM, BOYS. A THOR WITHOUT A HAMMER.
RATHER LIKE A SNAKE WITHOUT ITS FANGS, ISN'T IT?
ULIK, KING OF THE TROLLS.
AND A SNAKE WITHOUT FANGS IS NAUGHT BUT A WORM. WHO HERE WANTS TO SQUISH THIS WORM FOR THEIR KING?
I MAY BE MISSING A HAMMER, BUT I AM NOT WITHOUT FANGS.
OR GOATS.
GAAGH!

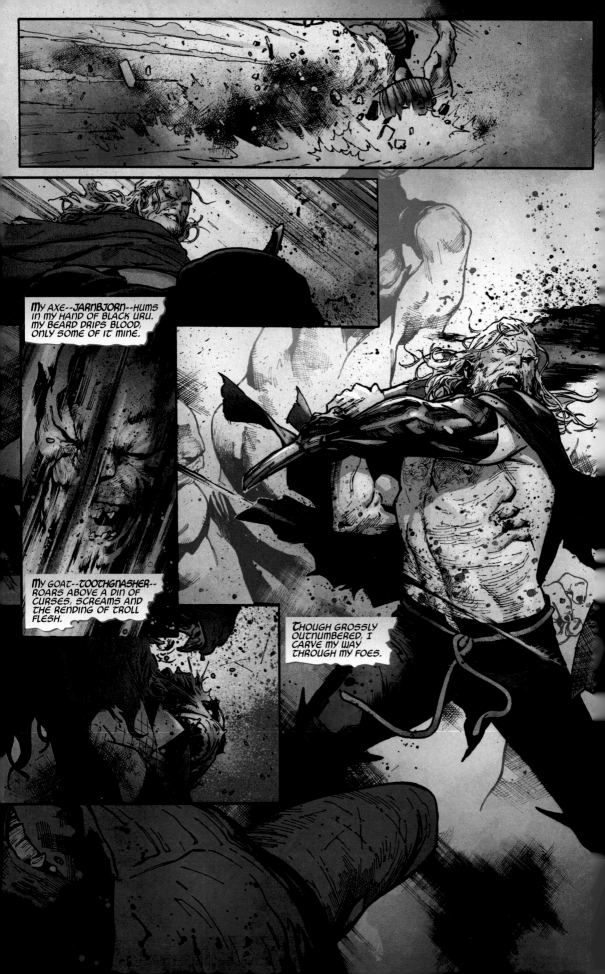

MY AXE--JARNBJORN--HUMS IN MY HAND OF BLACK URU. MY BEARD DRIPS BLOOD, ONLY SOME OF IT MINE.

MY GOAT--TOOTHGNASHER--ROARS ABOVE A DIN OF CURSES, SCREAMS AND THE RENDING OF TROLL FLESH.

THOUGH GROSSLY OUTNUMBERED, I CARVE MY WAY THROUGH MY FOES.

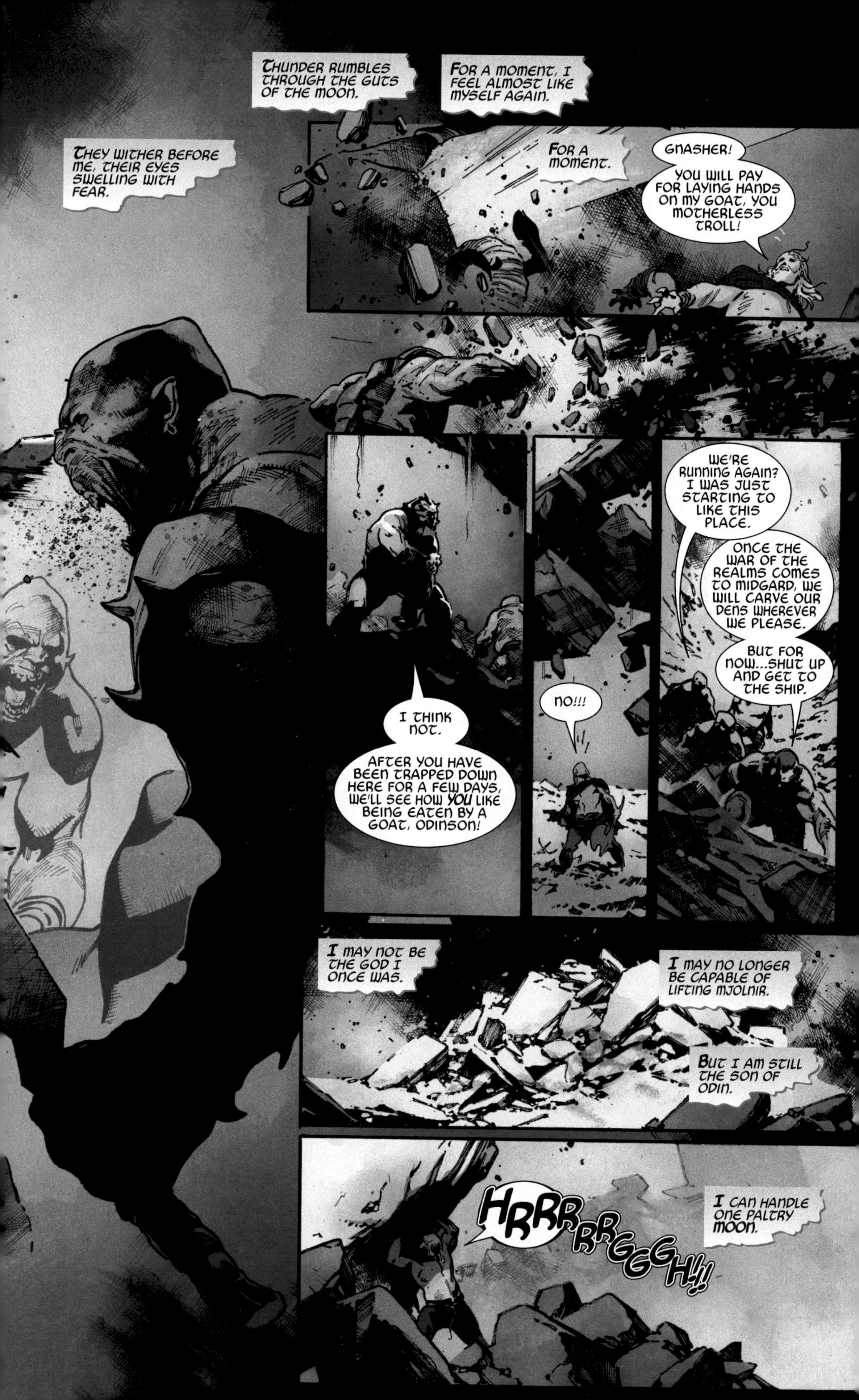
THEY WITHER BEFORE ME, THEIR EYES SWELLING WITH FEAR.
THUNDER RUMBLES THROUGH THE GUTS OF THE MOON.
FOR A MOMENT, I FEEL ALMOST LIKE MYSELF AGAIN.
FOR A MOMENT.
GNASHER!
YOU WILL PAY FOR LAYING HANDS ON MY GOAT, YOU MOTHERLESS TROLL!
I THINK NOT.
AFTER YOU HAVE BEEN TRAPPED DOWN HERE FOR A FEW DAYS, WE'LL SEE HOW YOU LIKE BEING EATEN BY A GOAT, ODINSON!
NO!!!
WE'RE RUNNING AGAIN? I WAS JUST STARTING TO LIKE THIS PLACE.
ONCE THE WAR OF THE REALMS COMES TO MIDGARD, WE WILL CARVE OUR DENS WHEREVER WE PLEASE.
BUT FOR NOW...SHUT UP AND GET TO THE SHIP.
I MAY NOT BE THE GOD I ONCE WAS.
I MAY NO LONGER BE CAPABLE OF LIFTING MJOLNIR.
BUT I AM STILL THE SON OF ODIN.
HRRRRRRGGGGH!!!
I CAN HANDLE ONE PALTRY MOON.

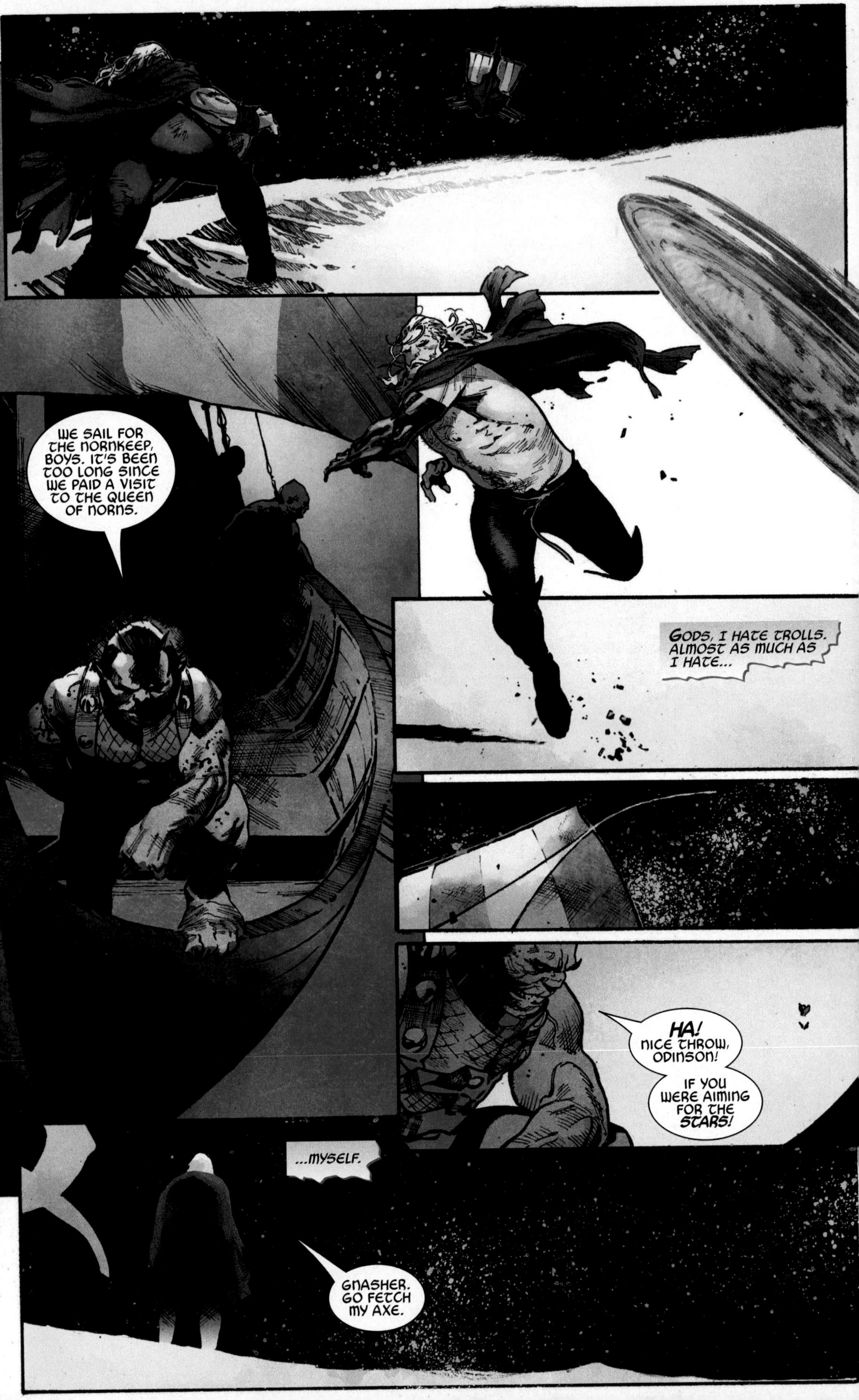
WE SAIL FOR THE NORNKEEP, BOYS. IT'S BEEN TOO LONG SINCE WE PAID A VISIT TO THE QUEEN OF NORNS.
GODS, I HATE TROLLS. ALMOST AS MUCH AS I HATE...
HA! NICE THROW, ODINSON!
IF YOU WERE AIMING FOR THE STARS!
...MYSELF.
GNASHER. GO FETCH MY AXE.

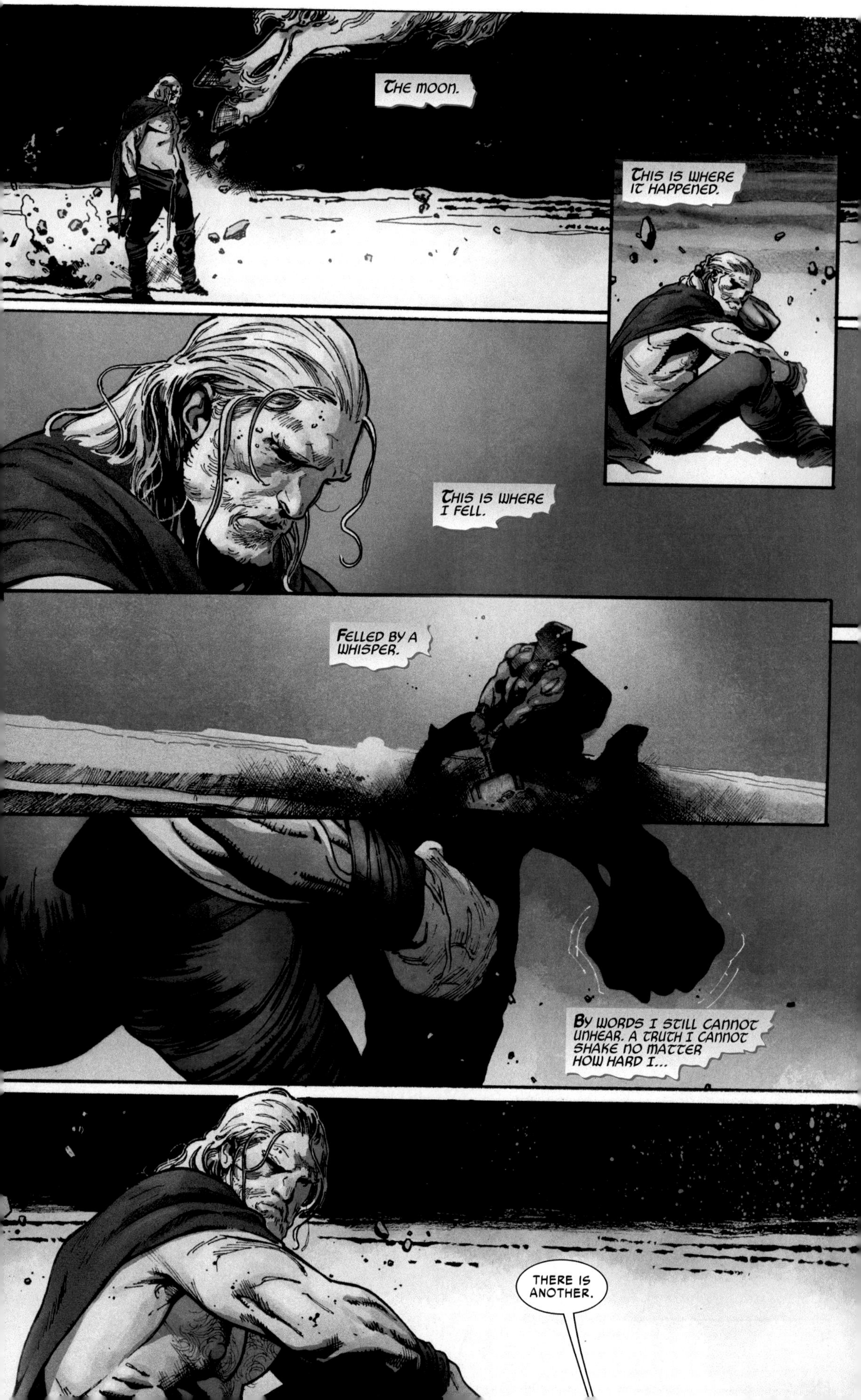
THE MOON.
THIS IS WHERE IT HAPPENED.
THIS IS WHERE I FELL.
FELLED BY A WHISPER.
BY WORDS I STILL CANNOT UNHEAR. A TRUTH I CANNOT SHAKE NO MATTER HOW HARD I...
THERE IS ANOTHER.

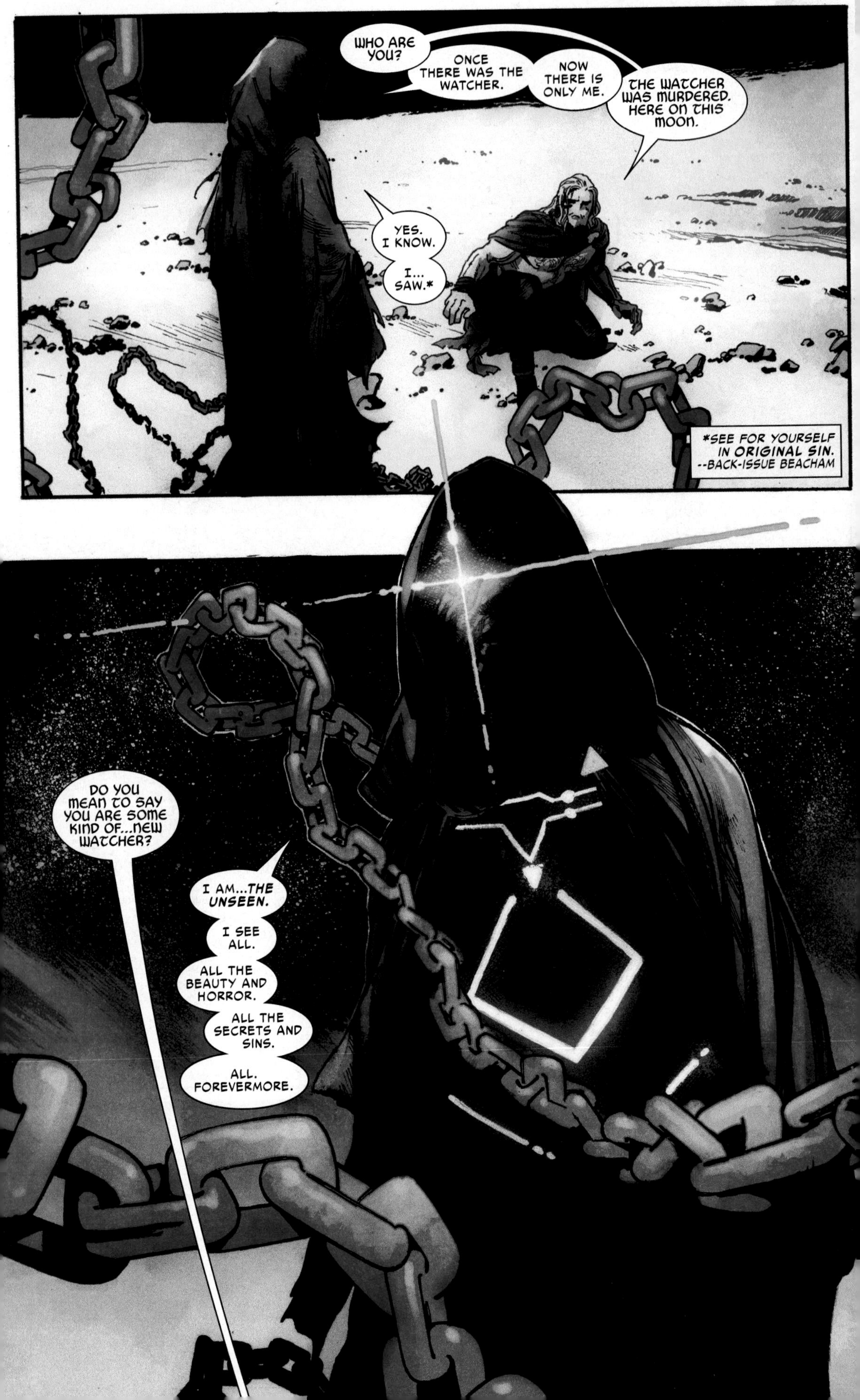
WHO ARE YOU?
ONCE THERE WAS THE WATCHER.
NOW THERE IS ONLY ME.
THE WATCHER WAS MURDERED. HERE ON THIS MOON.
YES. I KNOW.
I... SAW.*
*SEE FOR YOURSELF IN ORIGINAL SIN. --BACK-ISSUE BEACHAM
DO YOU MEAN TO SAY YOU ARE SOME KIND OF...NEW WATCHER?
I AM...THE UNSEEN.
I SEE ALL.
ALL THE BEAUTY AND HORROR.
ALL THE SECRETS AND SINS.
ALL. FOREVERMORE.

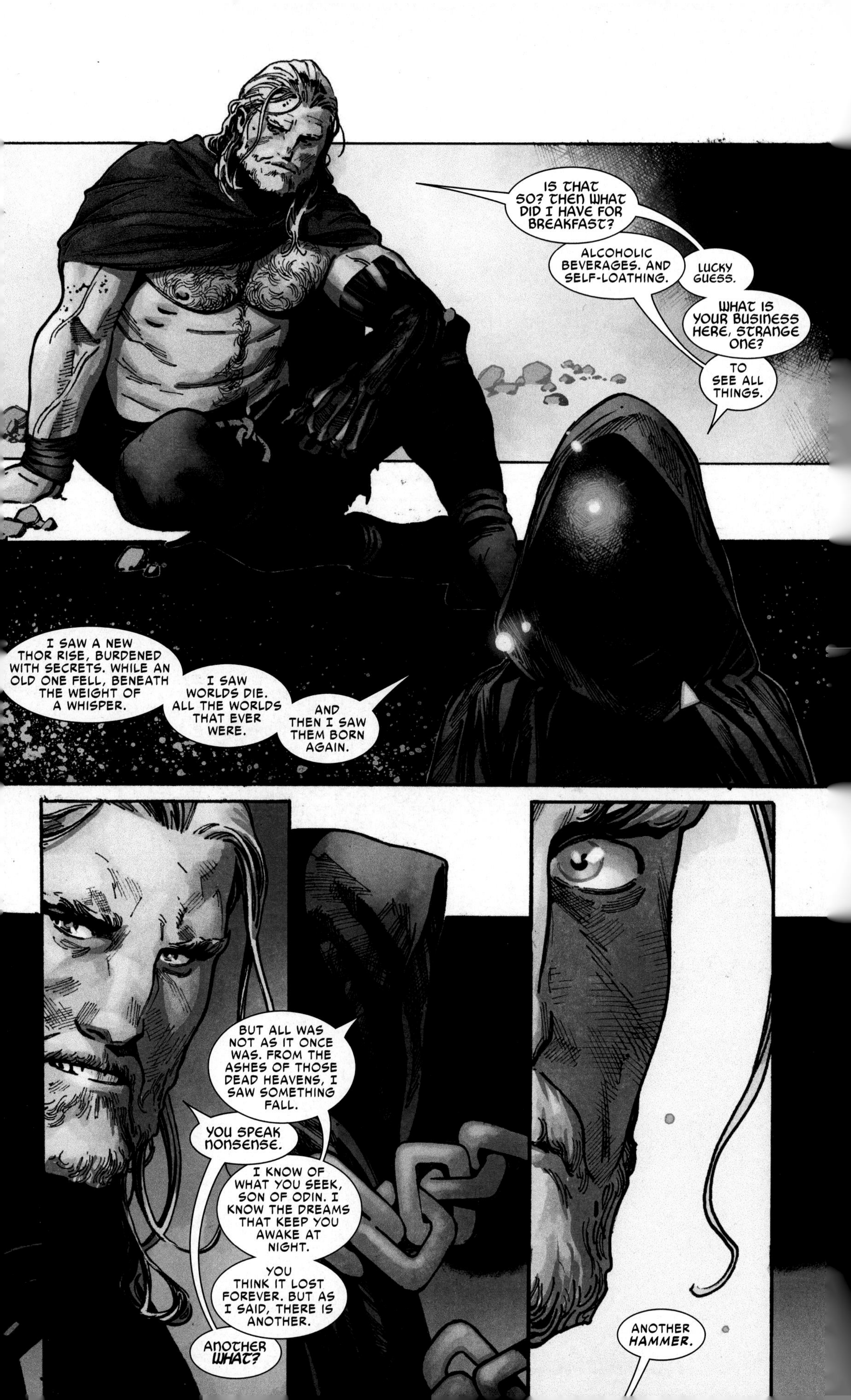
IS THAT SO? THEN WHAT DID I HAVE FOR BREAKFAST?
ALCOHOLIC BEVERAGES. AND SELF-LOATHING.
LUCKY GUESS.
WHAT IS YOUR BUSINESS HERE, STRANGE ONE?
TO SEE ALL THINGS.
I SAW A NEW THOR RISE, BURDENED WITH SECRETS. WHILE AN OLD ONE FELL, BENEATH THE WEIGHT OF A WHISPER.
I SAW WORLDS DIE. ALL THE WORLDS THAT EVER WERE.
AND THEN I SAW THEM BORN AGAIN.
BUT ALL WAS NOT AS IT ONCE WAS. FROM THE ASHES OF THOSE DEAD HEAVENS, I SAW SOMETHING FALL.
YOU SPEAK NONSENSE.
I KNOW OF WHAT YOU SEEK, SON OF ODIN. I KNOW THE DREAMS THAT KEEP YOU AWAKE AT NIGHT.
YOU THINK IT LOST FOREVER. BUT AS I SAID, THERE IS ANOTHER.
ANOTHER WHAT?
ANOTHER HAMMER.

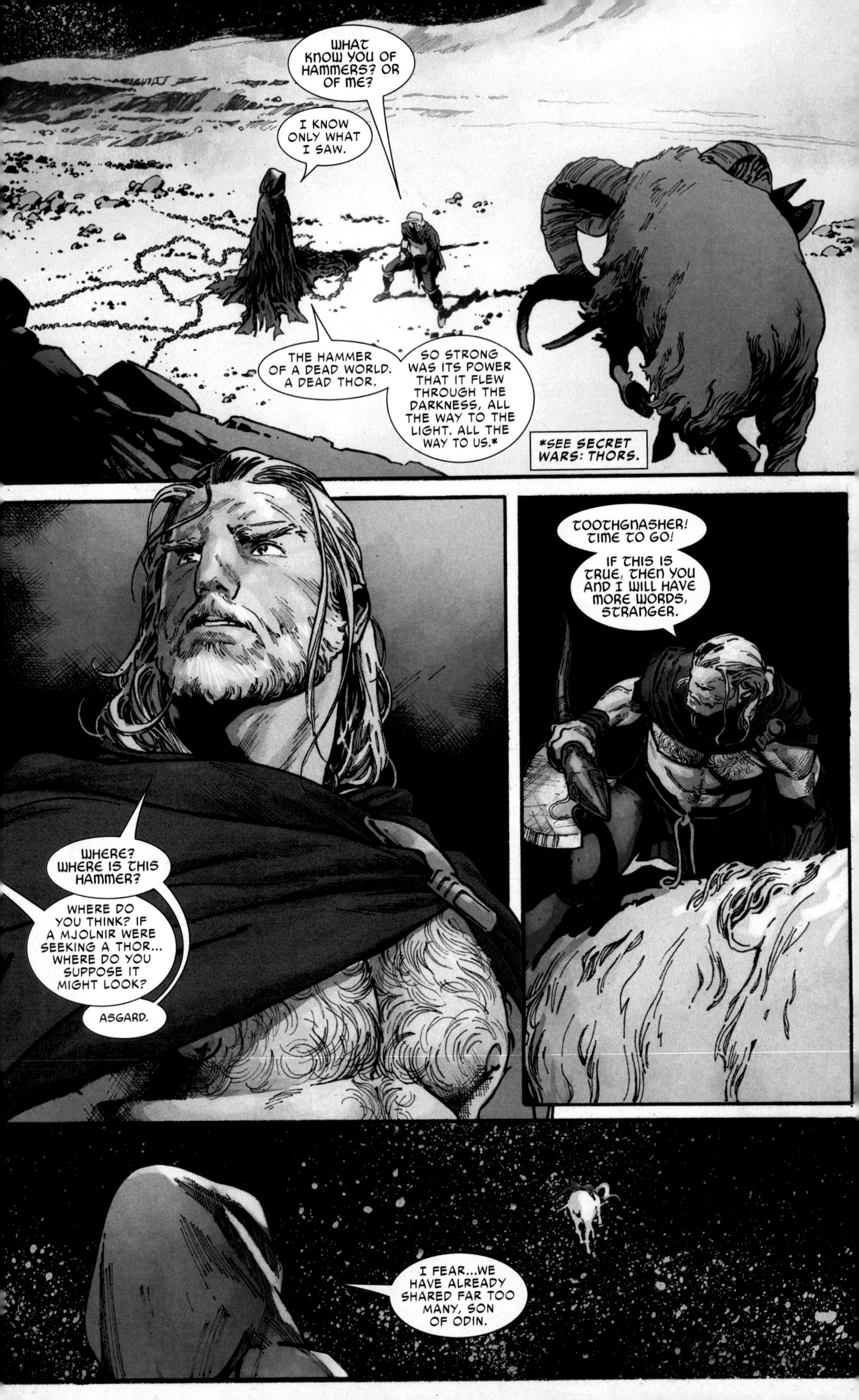
WHAT KNOW YOU OF HAMMERS? OR OF ME?
I KNOW ONLY WHAT I SAW.
THE HAMMER OF A DEAD WORLD. A DEAD THOR.
SO STRONG WAS ITS POWER THAT IT FLEW THROUGH THE DARKNESS, ALL THE WAY TO THE LIGHT. ALL THE WAY TO US.*
*SEE SECRET WARS: THORS.
WHERE? WHERE IS THIS HAMMER?
WHERE DO YOU THINK? IF A MJOLNIR WERE SEEKING A THOR... WHERE DO YOU SUPPOSE IT MIGHT LOOK?
ASGARD.
TOOTHGNASHER! TIME TO GO!
IF THIS IS TRUE, THEN YOU AND I WILL HAVE MORE WORDS, STRANGER.
I FEAR...WE HAVE ALREADY SHARED FAR TOO MANY, SON OF ODIN.

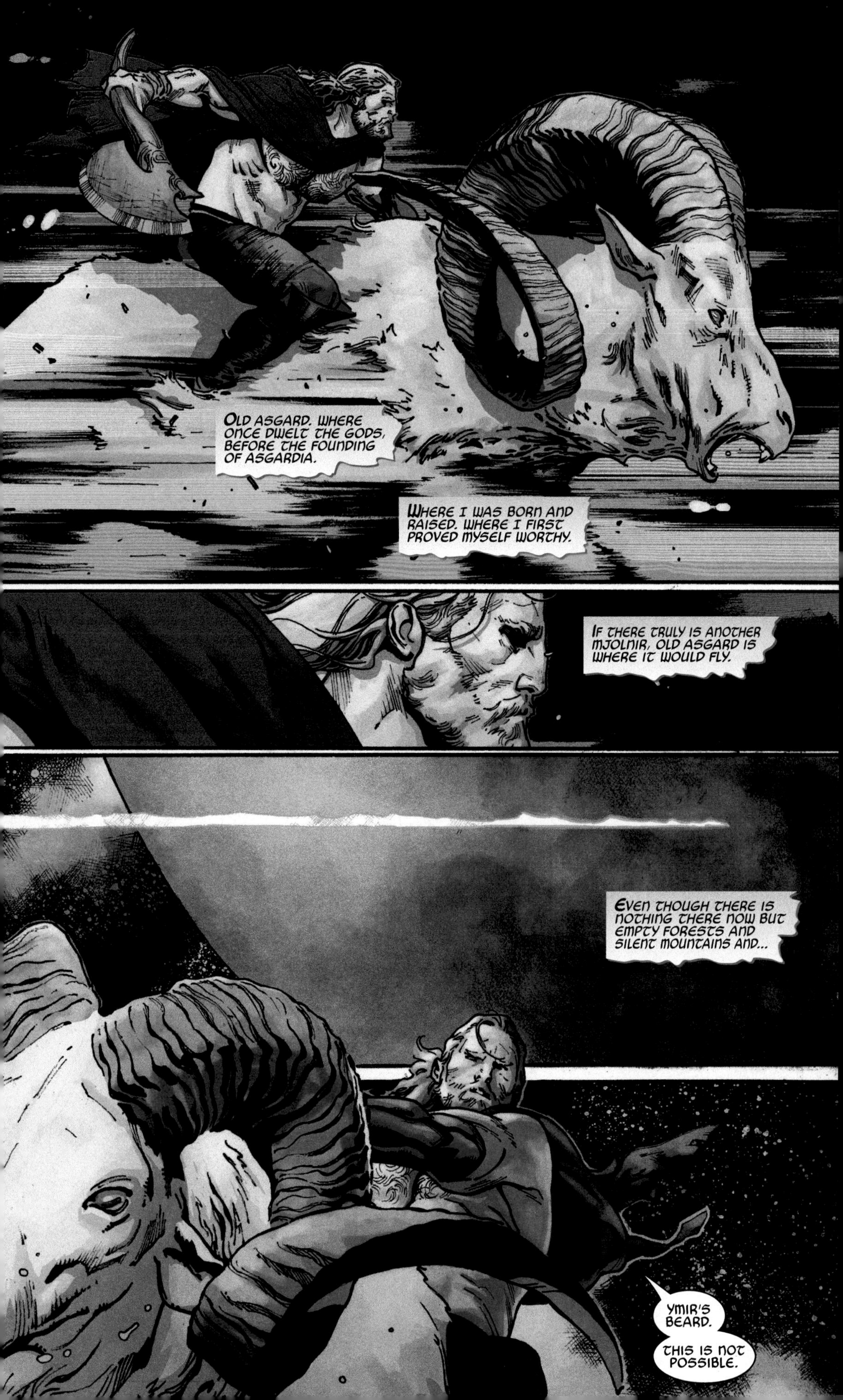

OLD ASGARD. WHERE ONCE DWELT THE GODS, BEFORE THE FOUNDING OF ASGARDIA.
WHERE I WAS BORN AND RAISED. WHERE I FIRST PROVED MYSELF WORTHY.
IF THERE TRULY IS ANOTHER MJOLNIR, OLD ASGARD IS WHERE IT WOULD FLY.
EVEN THOUGH THERE IS NOTHING THERE NOW BUT EMPTY FORESTS AND SILENT MOUNTAINS AND...
YMIR'S BEARD.
THIS IS NOT POSSIBLE.

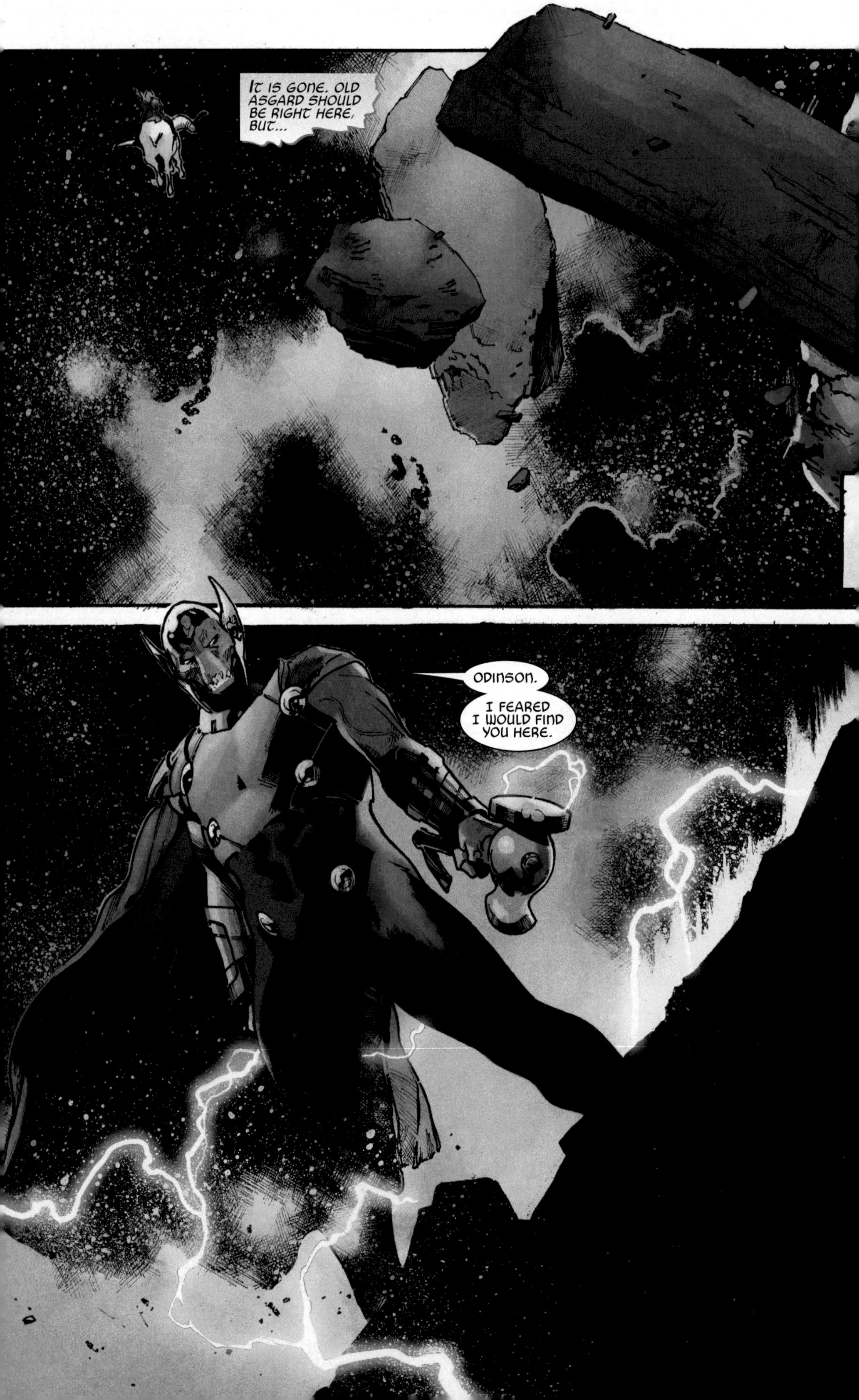
IT IS GONE. OLD ASGARD SHOULD BE RIGHT HERE, BUT...
ODINSON.
I FEARED I WOULD FIND YOU HERE.

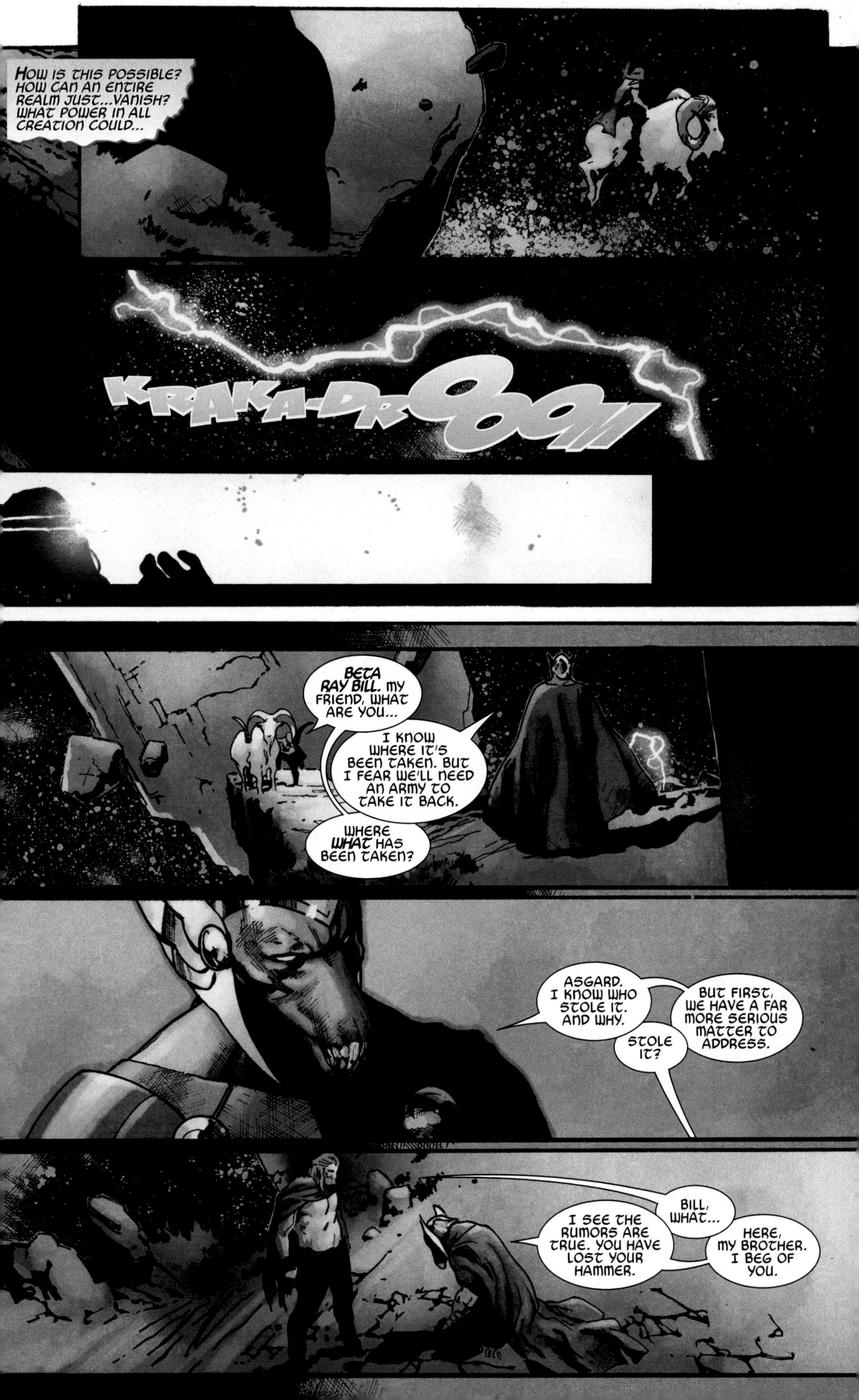

HOW IS THIS POSSIBLE? HOW CAN AN ENTIRE REALM JUST...VANISH? WHAT POWER IN ALL CREATION COULD...
KRAKA-DROOOM
BETA RAY BILL. MY FRIEND, WHAT ARE YOU...
I KNOW WHERE IT'S BEEN TAKEN. BUT I FEAR WE'LL NEED AN ARMY TO TAKE IT BACK.
WHERE WHAT HAS BEEN TAKEN?
ASGARD. I KNOW WHO STOLE IT. AND WHY.
STOLE IT?
BUT FIRST, WE HAVE A FAR MORE SERIOUS MATTER TO ADDRESS.
BILL, WHAT...
I SEE THE RUMORS ARE TRUE. YOU HAVE LOST YOUR HAMMER.
HERE, MY BROTHER. I BEG OF YOU.

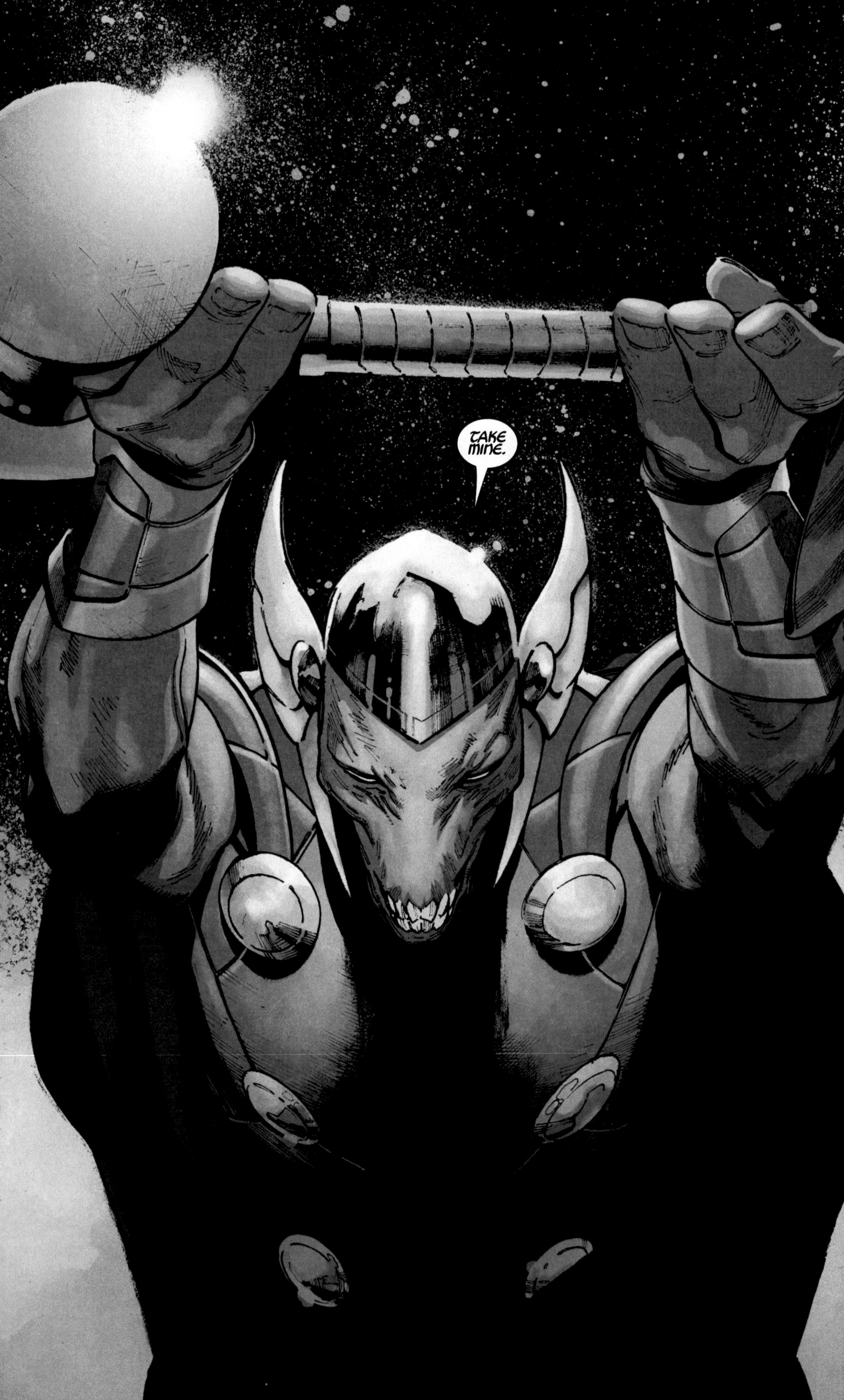
TAKE MINE.

UNWORTHY THOR #1 VARIANT BY **JOHN CASSADAY** & **LAURA MARTIN**

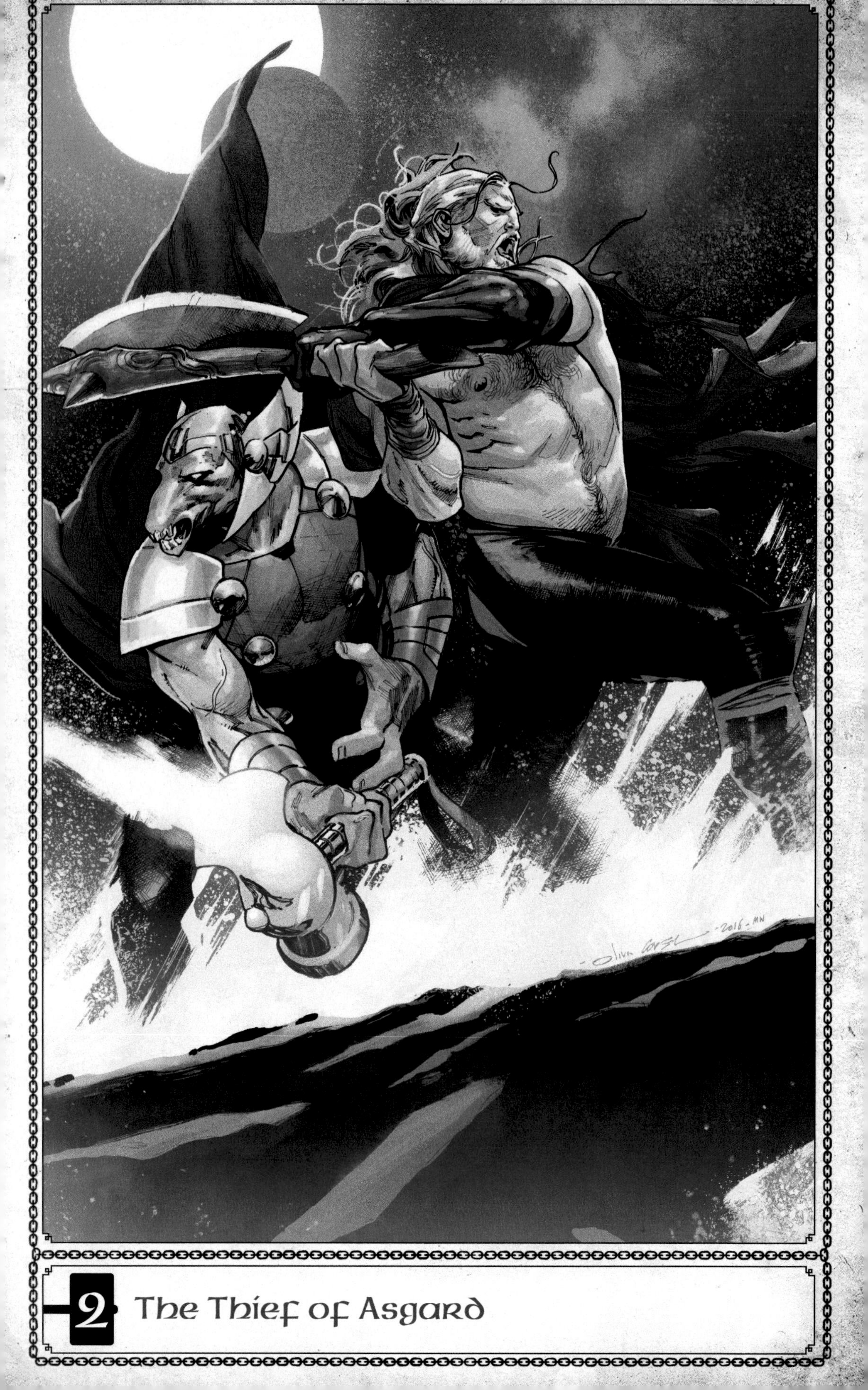

2 The Thief of Asgard

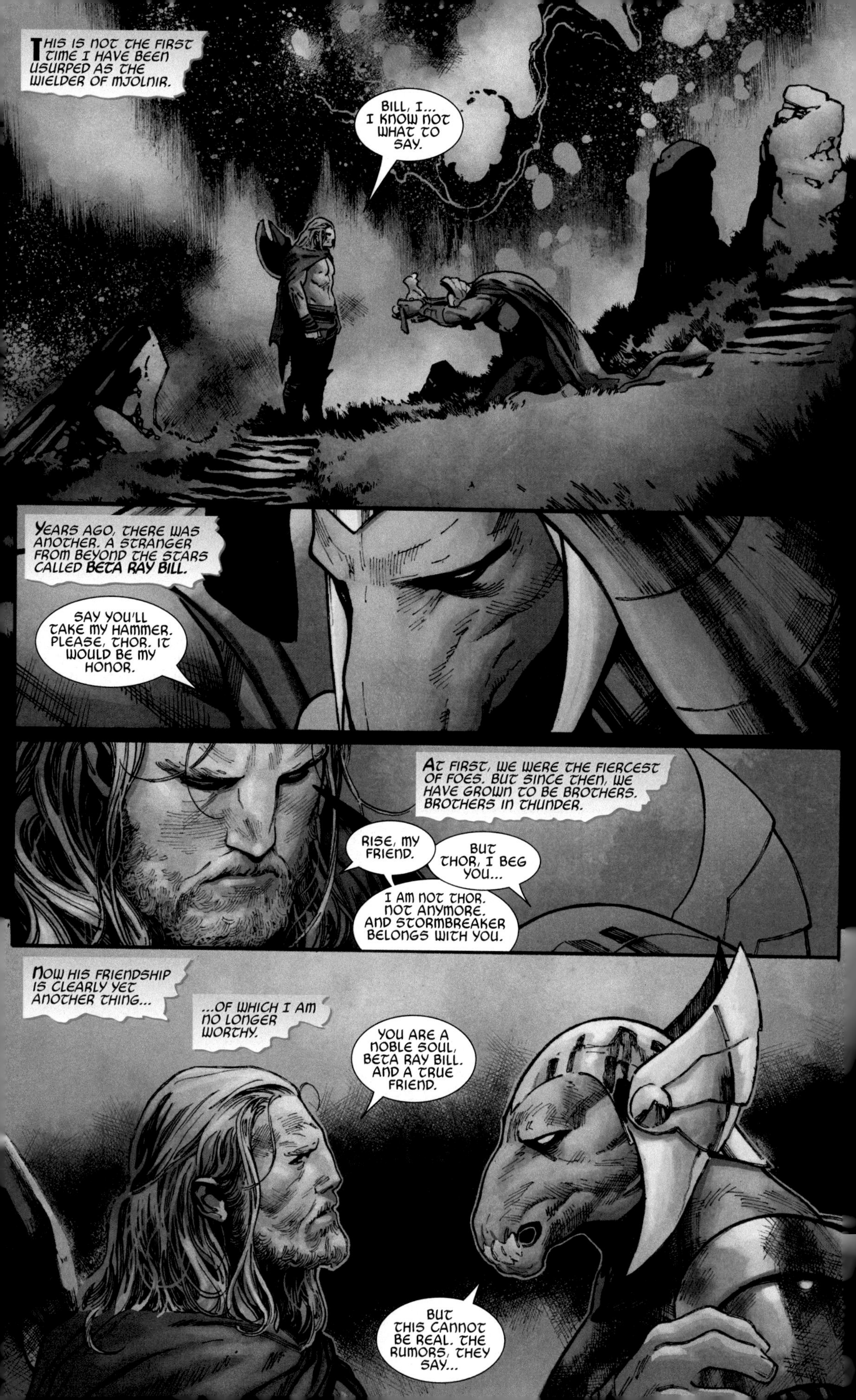
THIS IS NOT THE FIRST TIME I HAVE BEEN USURPED AS THE WIELDER OF MJOLNIR.
BILL, I... I KNOW NOT WHAT TO SAY.
YEARS AGO, THERE WAS ANOTHER. A STRANGER FROM BEYOND THE STARS CALLED BETA RAY BILL.
SAY YOU'LL TAKE MY HAMMER. PLEASE, THOR. IT WOULD BE MY HONOR.
AT FIRST, WE WERE THE FIERCEST OF FOES. BUT SINCE THEN, WE HAVE GROWN TO BE BROTHERS. BROTHERS IN THUNDER.
RISE, MY FRIEND.
BUT THOR, I BEG YOU...
I AM NOT THOR. NOT ANYMORE. AND STORMBREAKER BELONGS WITH YOU.
NOW HIS FRIENDSHIP IS CLEARLY YET ANOTHER THING...
...OF WHICH I AM NO LONGER WORTHY.
YOU ARE A NOBLE SOUL, BETA RAY BILL. AND A TRUE FRIEND.
BUT THIS CANNOT BE REAL. THE RUMORS, THEY SAY...

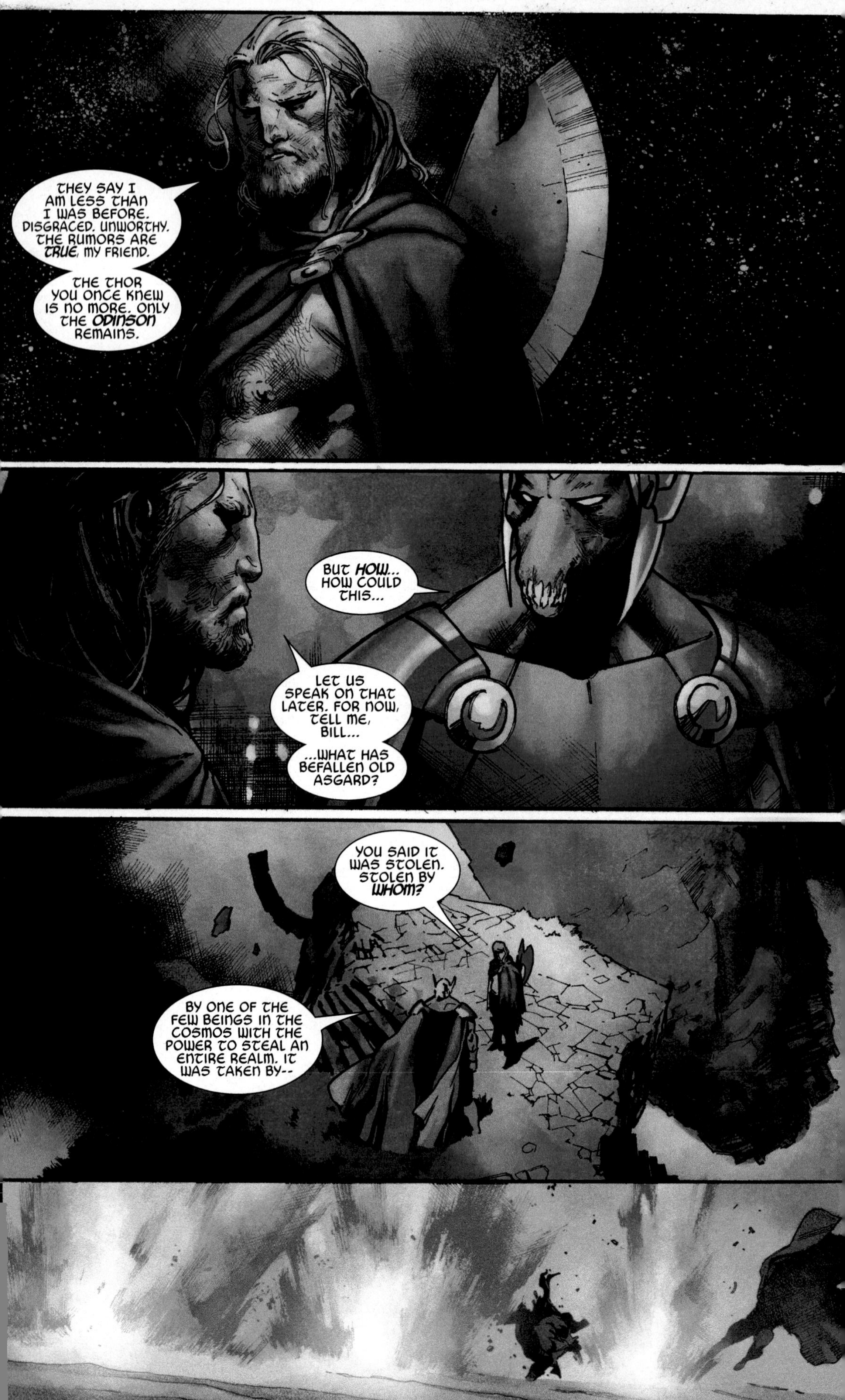
THEY SAY I AM LESS THAN I WAS BEFORE. DISGRACED. UNWORTHY. THE RUMORS ARE TRUE, MY FRIEND.
THE THOR YOU ONCE KNEW IS NO MORE. ONLY THE ODINSON REMAINS.
BUT HOW... HOW COULD THIS...
LET US SPEAK ON THAT LATER. FOR NOW, TELL ME, BILL...
...WHAT HAS BEFALLEN OLD ASGARD?
YOU SAID IT WAS STOLEN. STOLEN BY WHOM?
BY ONE OF THE FEW BEINGS IN THE COSMOS WITH THE POWER TO STEAL AN ENTIRE REALM. IT WAS TAKEN BY--

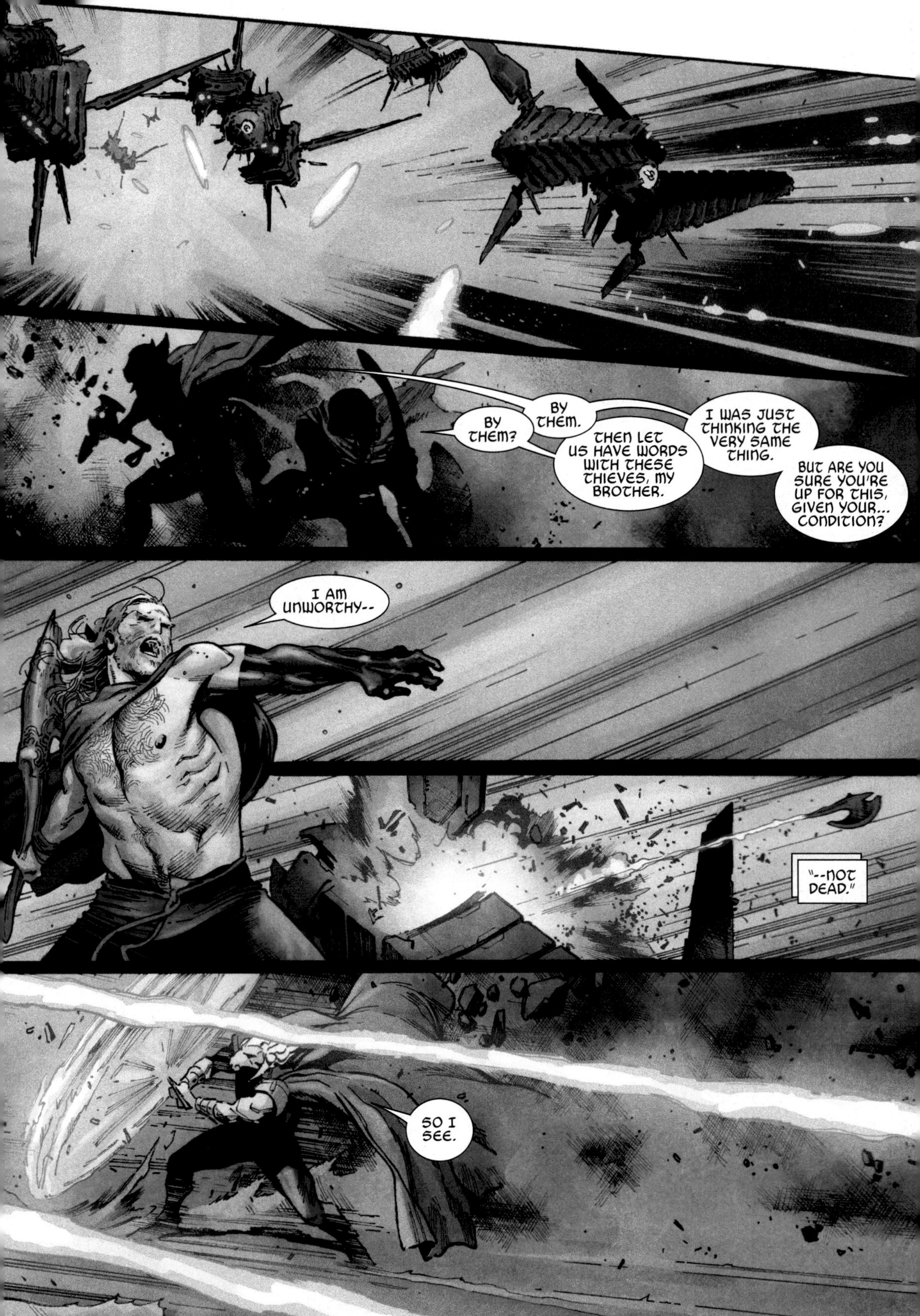
BY THEM.
BY THEM?
THEN LET US HAVE WORDS WITH THESE THIEVES, MY BROTHER.
I WAS JUST THINKING THE VERY SAME THING.
BUT ARE YOU SURE YOU'RE UP FOR THIS, GIVEN YOUR... CONDITION?
I AM UNWORTHY--
"--NOT DEAD."
SO I SEE.

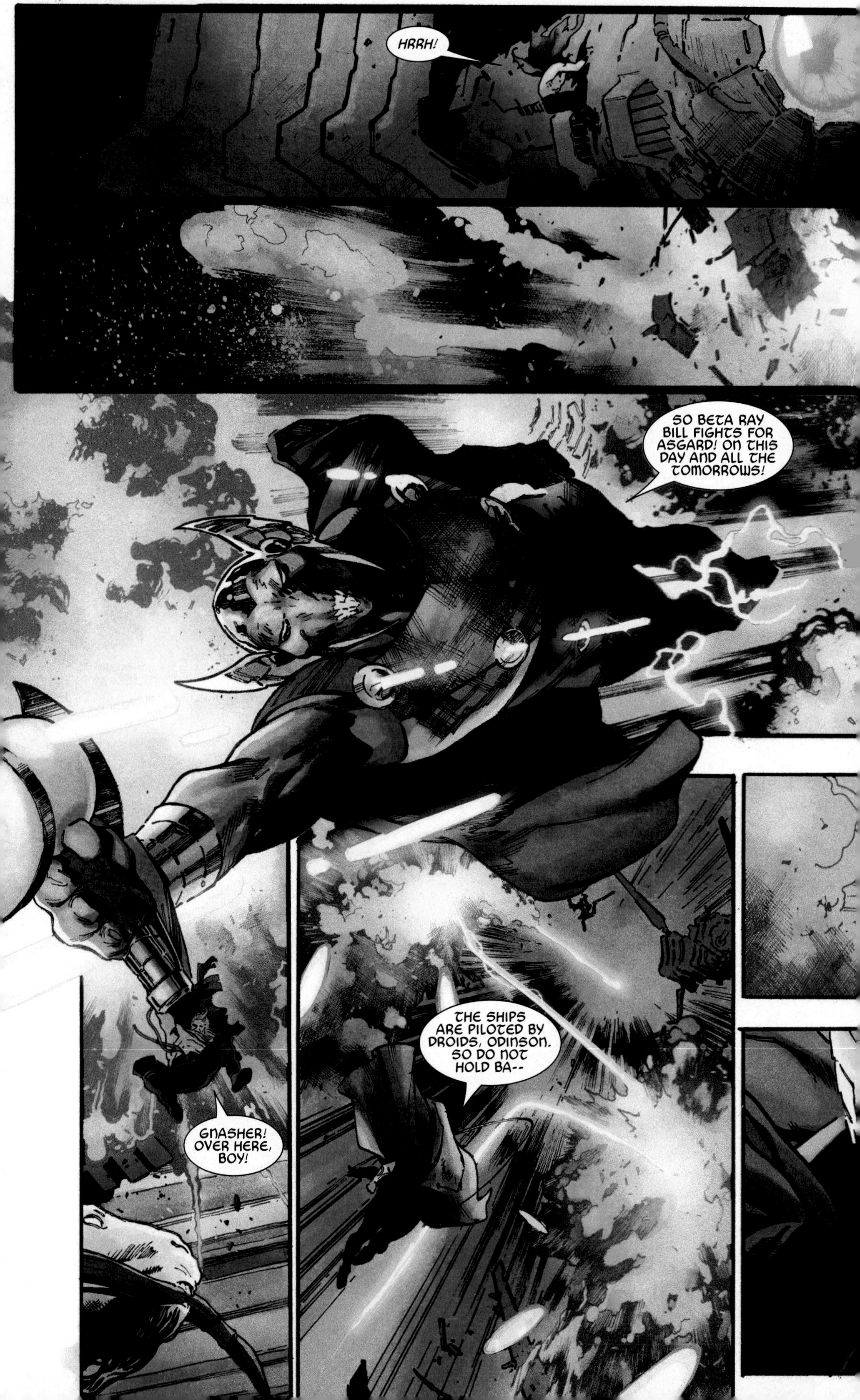
HRRH!
SO BETA RAY BILL FIGHTS FOR ASGARD! ON THIS DAY AND ALL THE TOMORROWS!
THE SHIPS ARE PILOTED BY DROIDS, ODINSON. SO DO NOT HOLD BA--
GNASHER! OVER HERE, BOY!

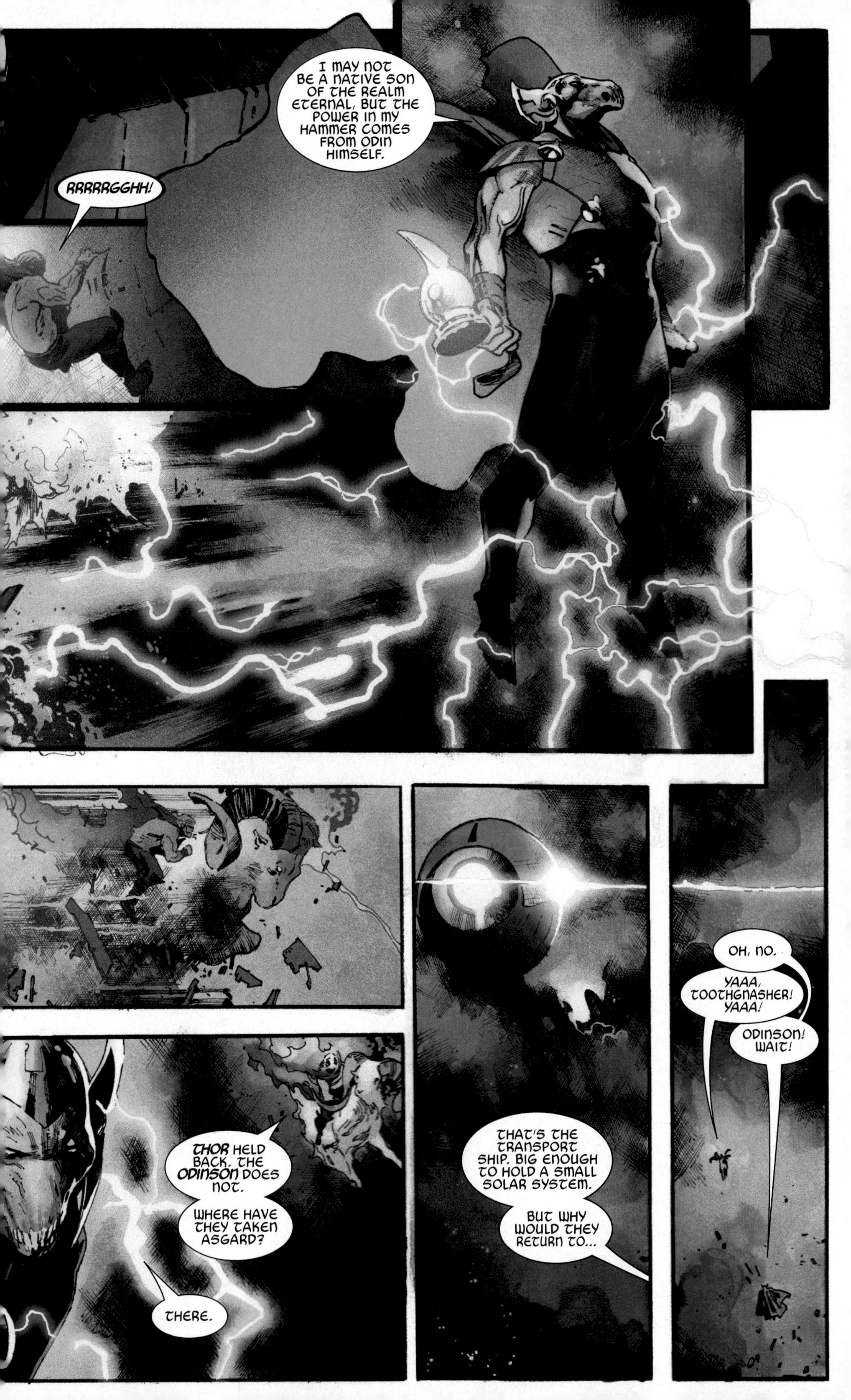
I MAY NOT BE A NATIVE SON OF THE REALM ETERNAL, BUT THE POWER IN MY HAMMER COMES FROM ODIN HIMSELF.
RRRRRGGHH!
THOR HELD BACK. THE ODINSON DOES NOT.
WHERE HAVE THEY TAKEN ASGARD?
THERE.
THAT'S THE TRANSPORT SHIP. BIG ENOUGH TO HOLD A SMALL SOLAR SYSTEM.
BUT WHY WOULD THEY RETURN TO...
OH, NO.
YAAA, TOOTHGNASHER! YAAA!
ODINSON! WAIT!

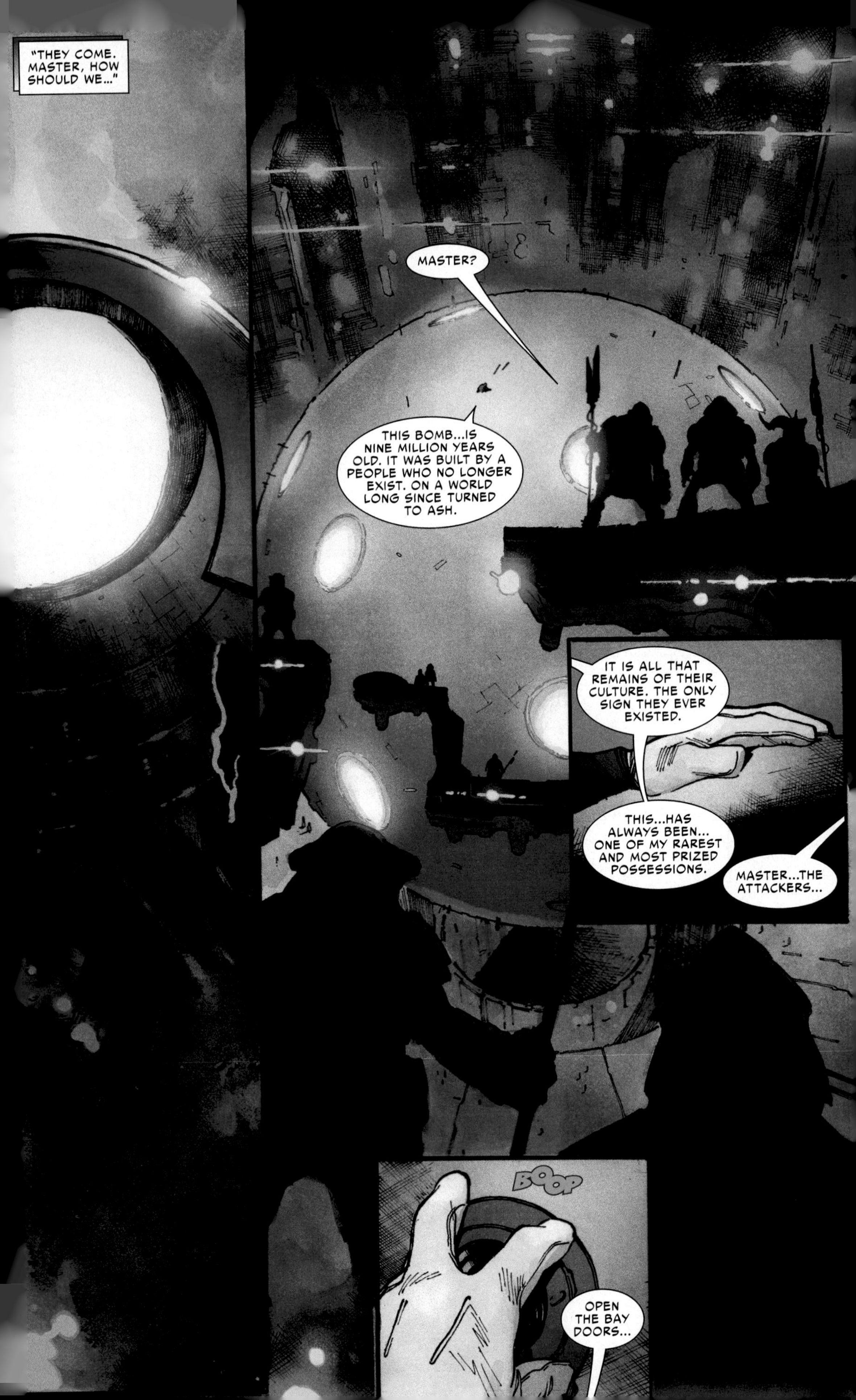
"THEY COME. MASTER, HOW SHOULD WE..."
MASTER?
THIS BOMB...IS NINE MILLION YEARS OLD. IT WAS BUILT BY A PEOPLE WHO NO LONGER EXIST. ON A WORLD LONG SINCE TURNED TO ASH.
IT IS ALL THAT REMAINS OF THEIR CULTURE. THE ONLY SIGN THEY EVER EXISTED.
THIS...HAS ALWAYS BEEN... ONE OF MY RAREST AND MOST PRIZED POSSESSIONS.
MASTER...THE ATTACKERS...
BOOP
OPEN THE BAY DOORS...

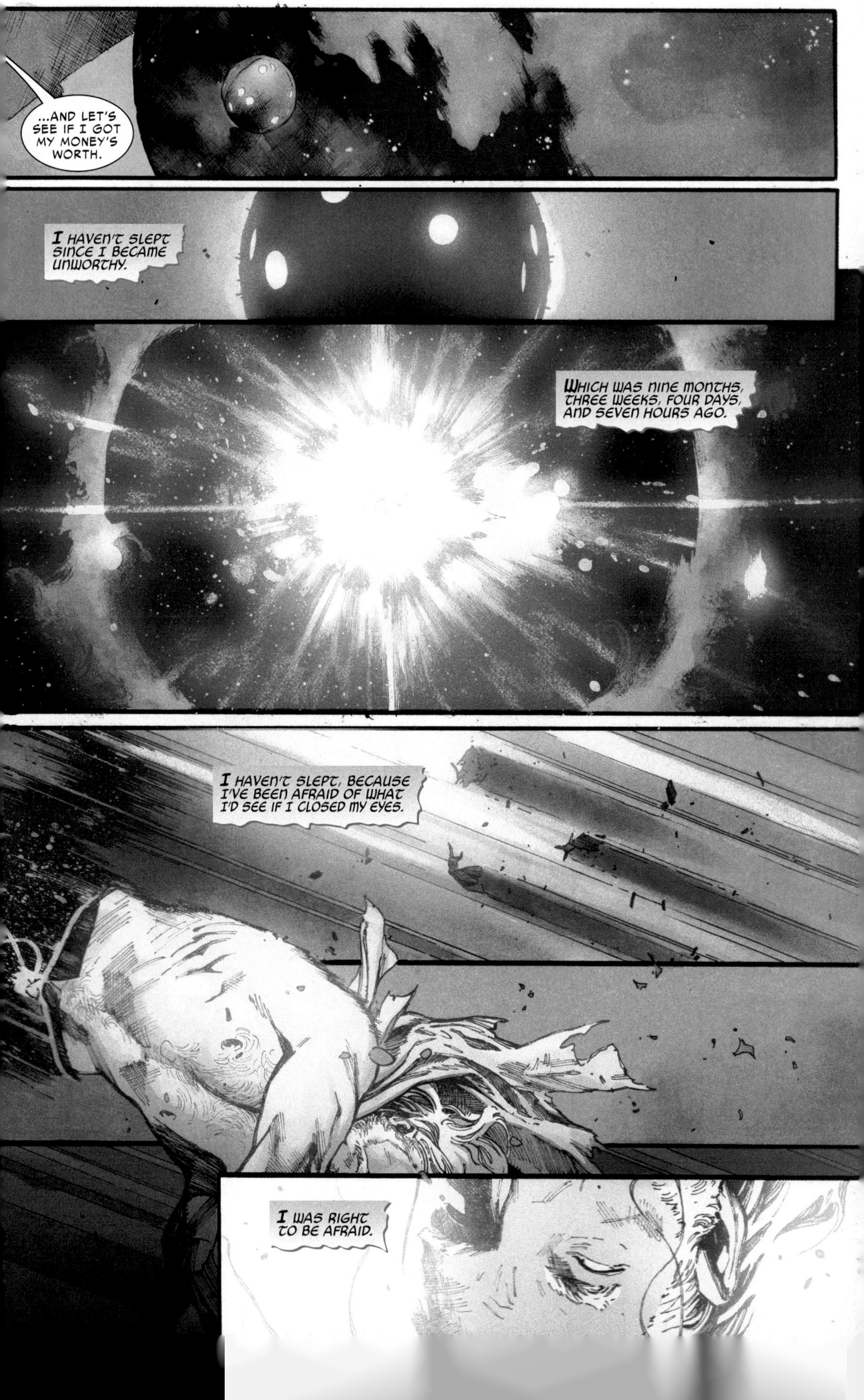
...AND LET'S SEE IF I GOT MY MONEY'S WORTH.
I HAVEN'T SLEPT SINCE I BECAME UNWORTHY.
WHICH WAS NINE MONTHS, THREE WEEKS, FOUR DAYS, AND SEVEN HOURS AGO.
I HAVEN'T SLEPT, BECAUSE I'VE BEEN AFRAID OF WHAT I'D SEE IF I CLOSED MY EYES.
I WAS RIGHT TO BE AFRAID.

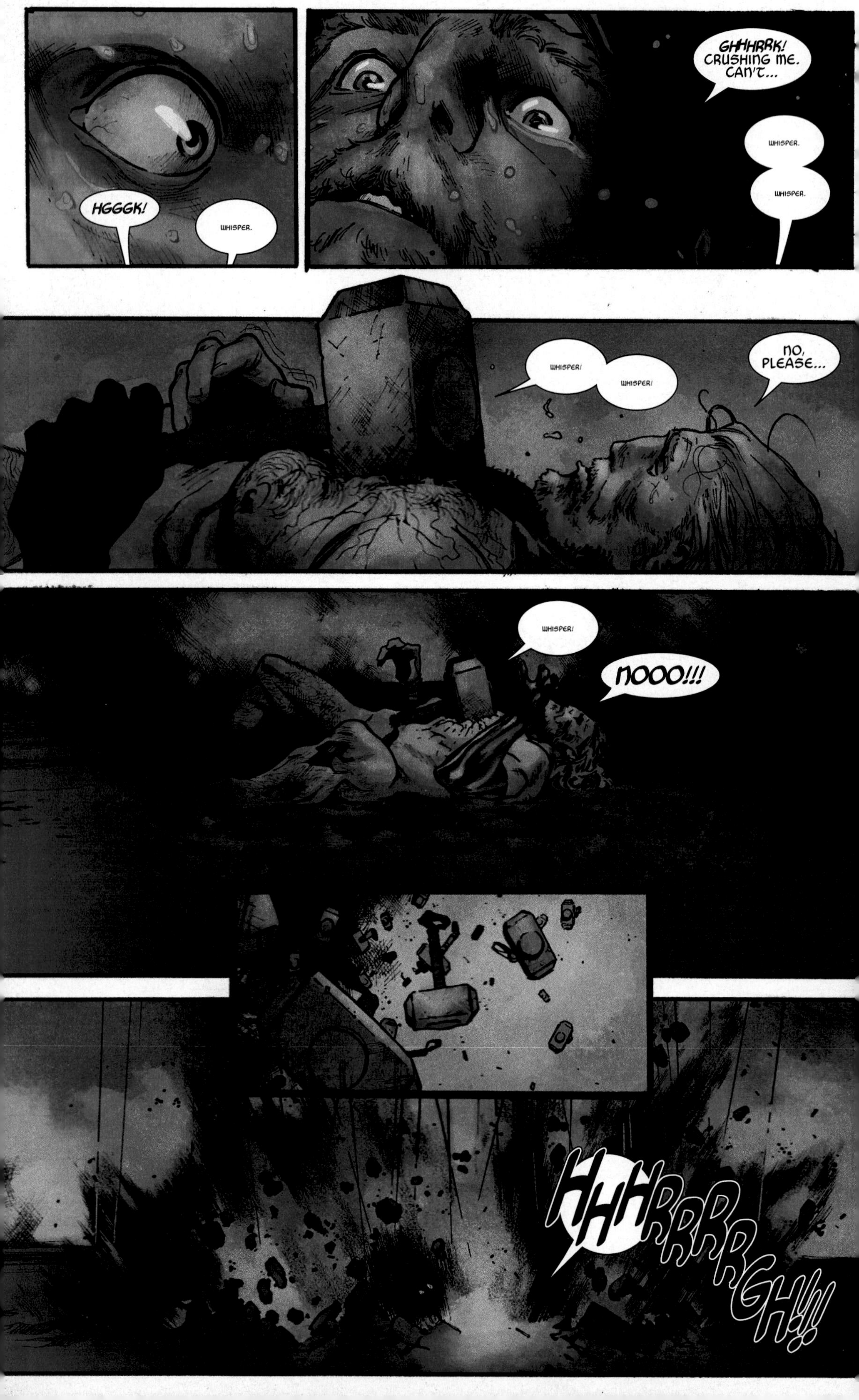
HGGGK!
WHISPER.
GHHHRRK! CRUSHING ME. CAN'T...
WHISPER.
WHISPER.
WHISPER!
WHISPER!
NO, PLEASE...
WHISPER!
NOOO!!!
HHHRRRRGH!!!

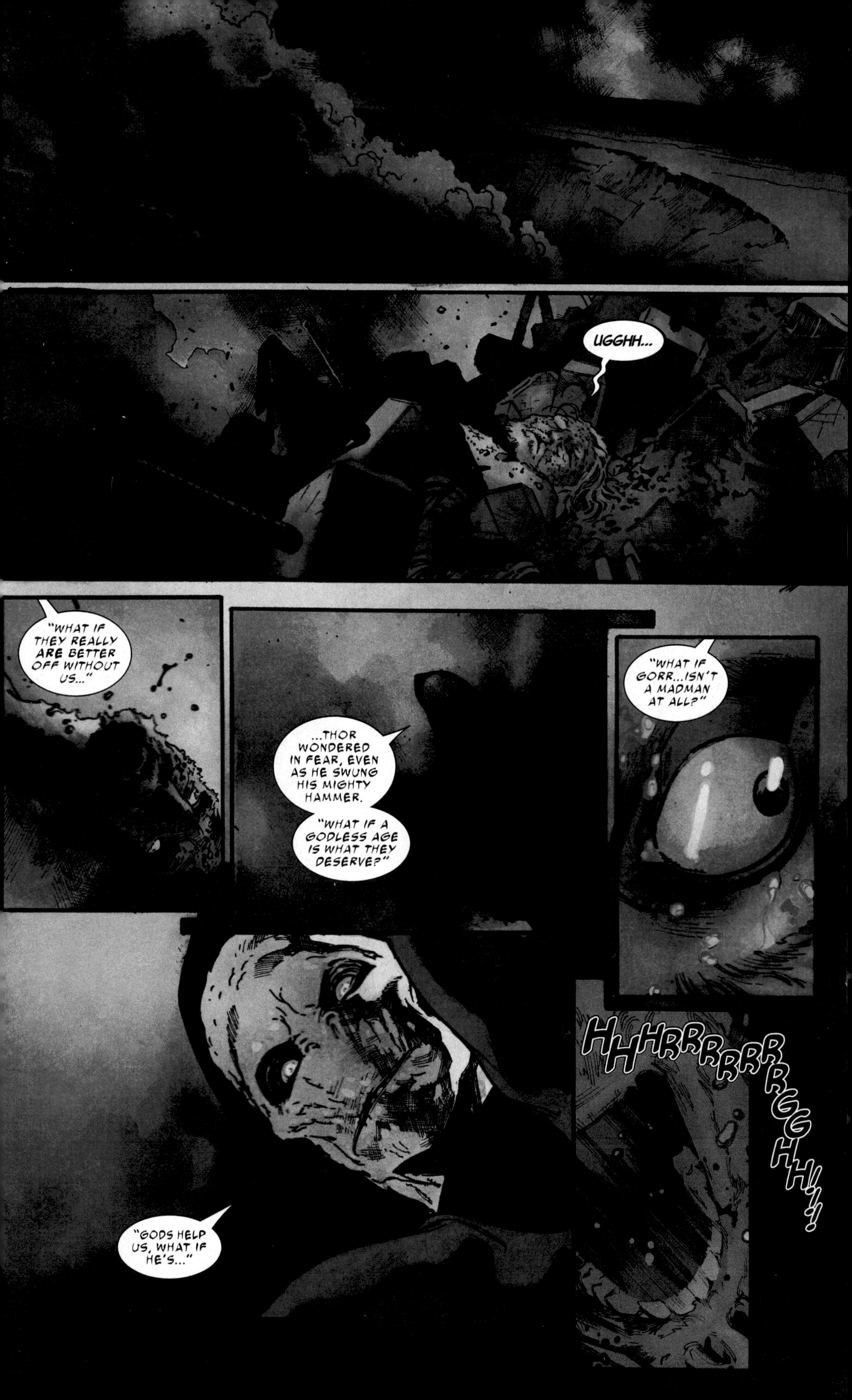
UGGHH...
"WHAT IF THEY REALLY ARE BETTER OFF WITHOUT US..."
...THOR WONDERED IN FEAR, EVEN AS HE SWUNG HIS MIGHTY HAMMER.
"WHAT IF A GODLESS AGE IS WHAT THEY DESERVE?"
"WHAT IF GORR...ISN'T A MADMAN AT ALL?"
"GODS HELP US, WHAT IF HE'S..."
HHHRRRRRRRRGGHH!!!

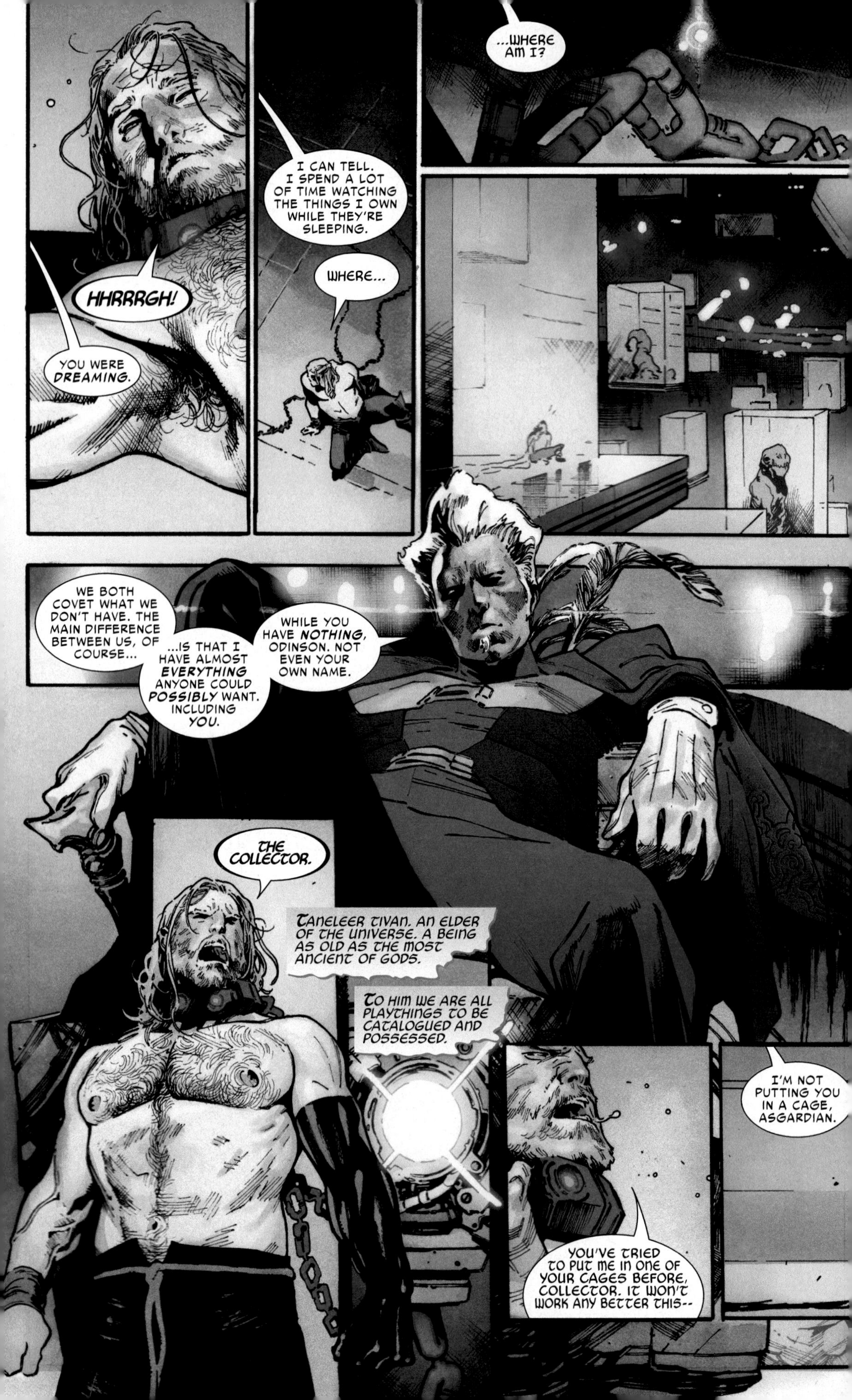

HHRRRGH!
YOU WERE DREAMING.
I CAN TELL. I SPEND A LOT OF TIME WATCHING THE THINGS I OWN WHILE THEY'RE SLEEPING.
WHERE...
...WHERE AM I?
WE BOTH COVET WHAT WE DON'T HAVE. THE MAIN DIFFERENCE BETWEEN US, OF COURSE...
...IS THAT I HAVE ALMOST EVERYTHING ANYONE COULD POSSIBLY WANT. INCLUDING YOU.
WHILE YOU HAVE NOTHING, ODINSON. NOT EVEN YOUR OWN NAME.
THE COLLECTOR.
TANELEER TIVAN. AN ELDER OF THE UNIVERSE. A BEING AS OLD AS THE MOST ANCIENT OF GODS.
TO HIM WE ARE ALL PLAYTHINGS TO BE CATALOGUED AND POSSESSED.
YOU'VE TRIED TO PUT ME IN ONE OF YOUR CAGES BEFORE, COLLECTOR. IT WON'T WORK ANY BETTER THIS--
I'M NOT PUTTING YOU IN A CAGE, ASGARDIAN.

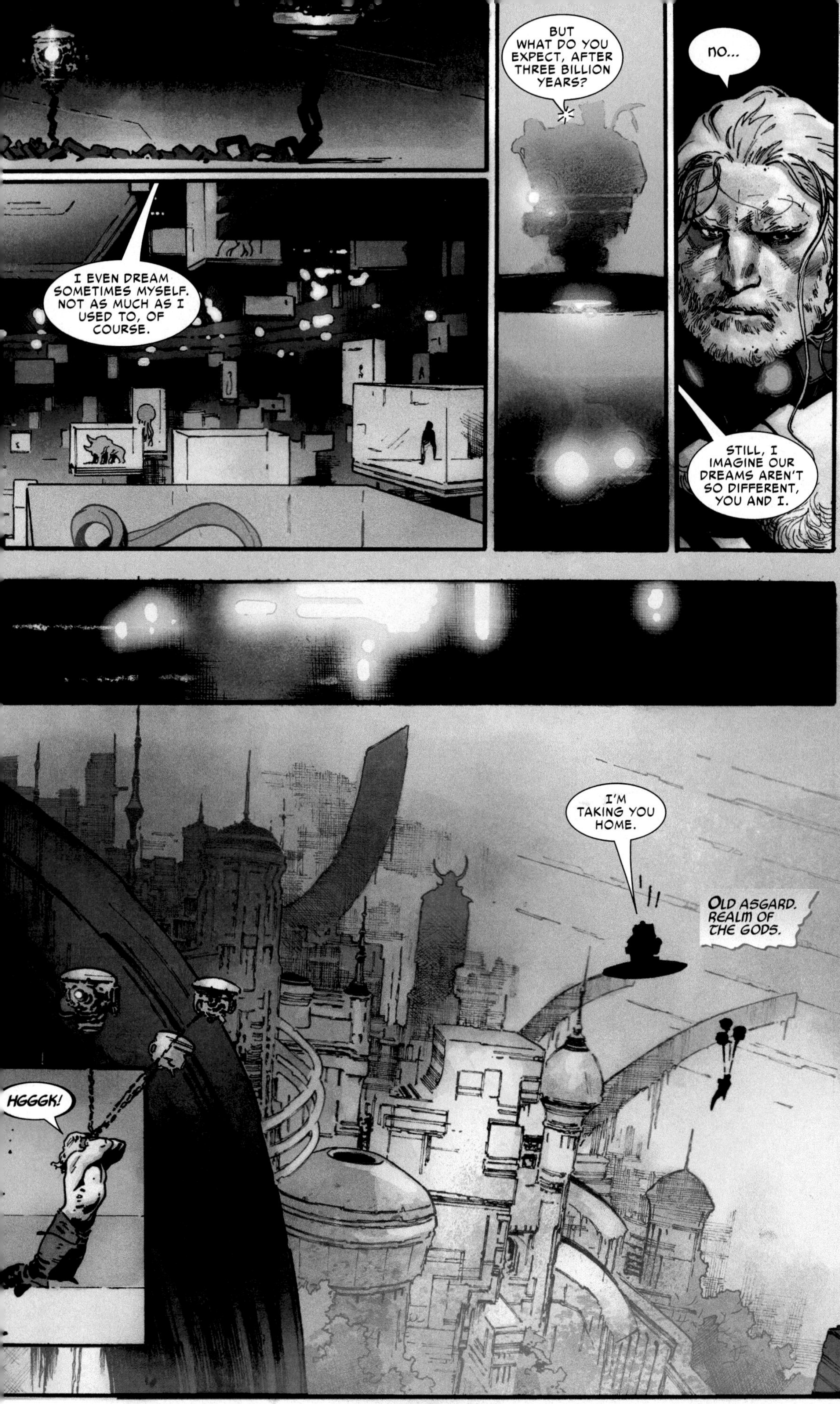
I EVEN DREAM SOMETIMES MYSELF. NOT AS MUCH AS I USED TO, OF COURSE.
BUT WHAT DO YOU EXPECT, AFTER THREE BILLION YEARS?
no...
STILL, I IMAGINE OUR DREAMS AREN'T SO DIFFERENT, YOU AND I.
I'M TAKING YOU HOME.
OLD ASGARD. REALM OF THE GODS.
HGGGK!

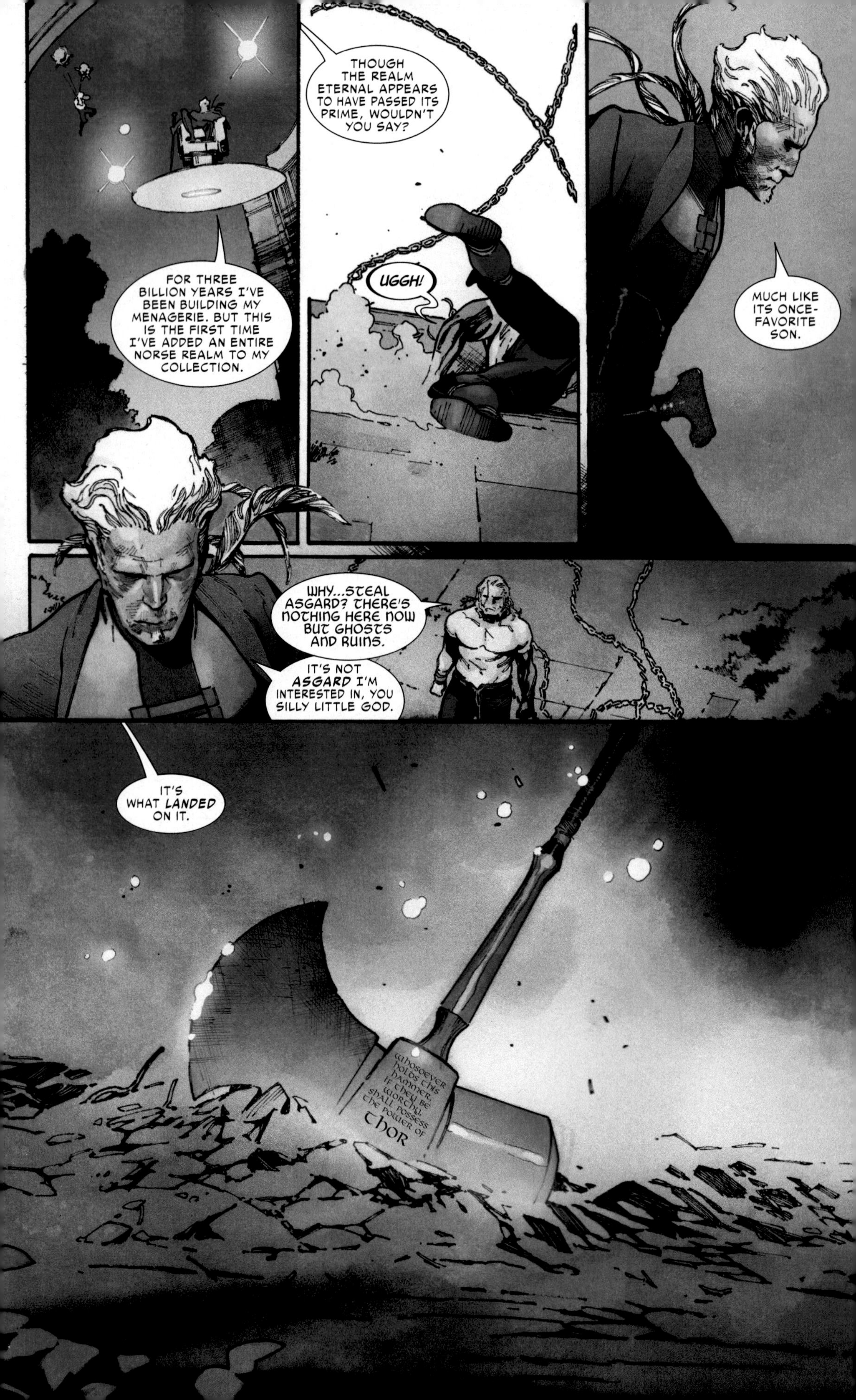

FOR THREE BILLION YEARS I'VE BEEN BUILDING MY MENAGERIE. BUT THIS IS THE FIRST TIME I'VE ADDED AN ENTIRE NORSE REALM TO MY COLLECTION.
THOUGH THE REALM ETERNAL APPEARS TO HAVE PASSED ITS PRIME, WOULDN'T YOU SAY?
UGGH!
MUCH LIKE ITS ONCE-FAVORITE SON.
WHY...STEAL ASGARD? THERE'S NOTHING HERE NOW BUT GHOSTS AND RUINS.
IT'S NOT ASGARD I'M INTERESTED IN, YOU SILLY LITTLE GOD.
IT'S WHAT LANDED ON IT.
WHOSOEVER HOLDS THIS HAMMER, IF THEY BE WORTHY, SHALL POSSESS THE POWER OF THOR

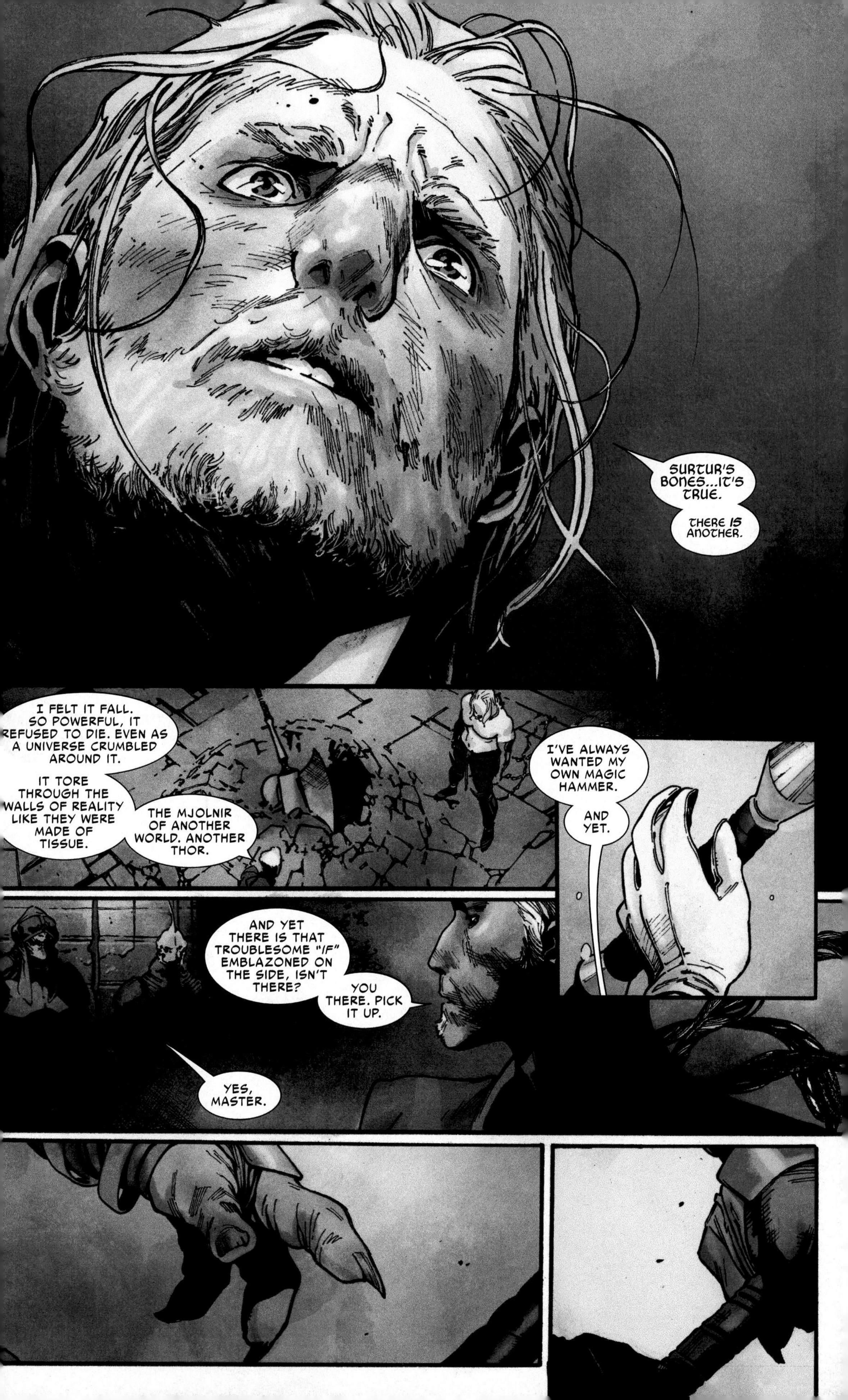
SURTUR'S BONES...IT'S TRUE.
THERE IS ANOTHER.
I FELT IT FALL. SO POWERFUL, IT REFUSED TO DIE. EVEN AS A UNIVERSE CRUMBLED AROUND IT.
IT TORE THROUGH THE WALLS OF REALITY LIKE THEY WERE MADE OF TISSUE.
THE MJOLNIR OF ANOTHER WORLD. ANOTHER THOR.
I'VE ALWAYS WANTED MY OWN MAGIC HAMMER.
AND YET.
AND YET THERE IS THAT TROUBLESOME "IF" EMBLAZONED ON THE SIDE, ISN'T THERE?
YOU THERE. PICK IT UP.
YES, MASTER.

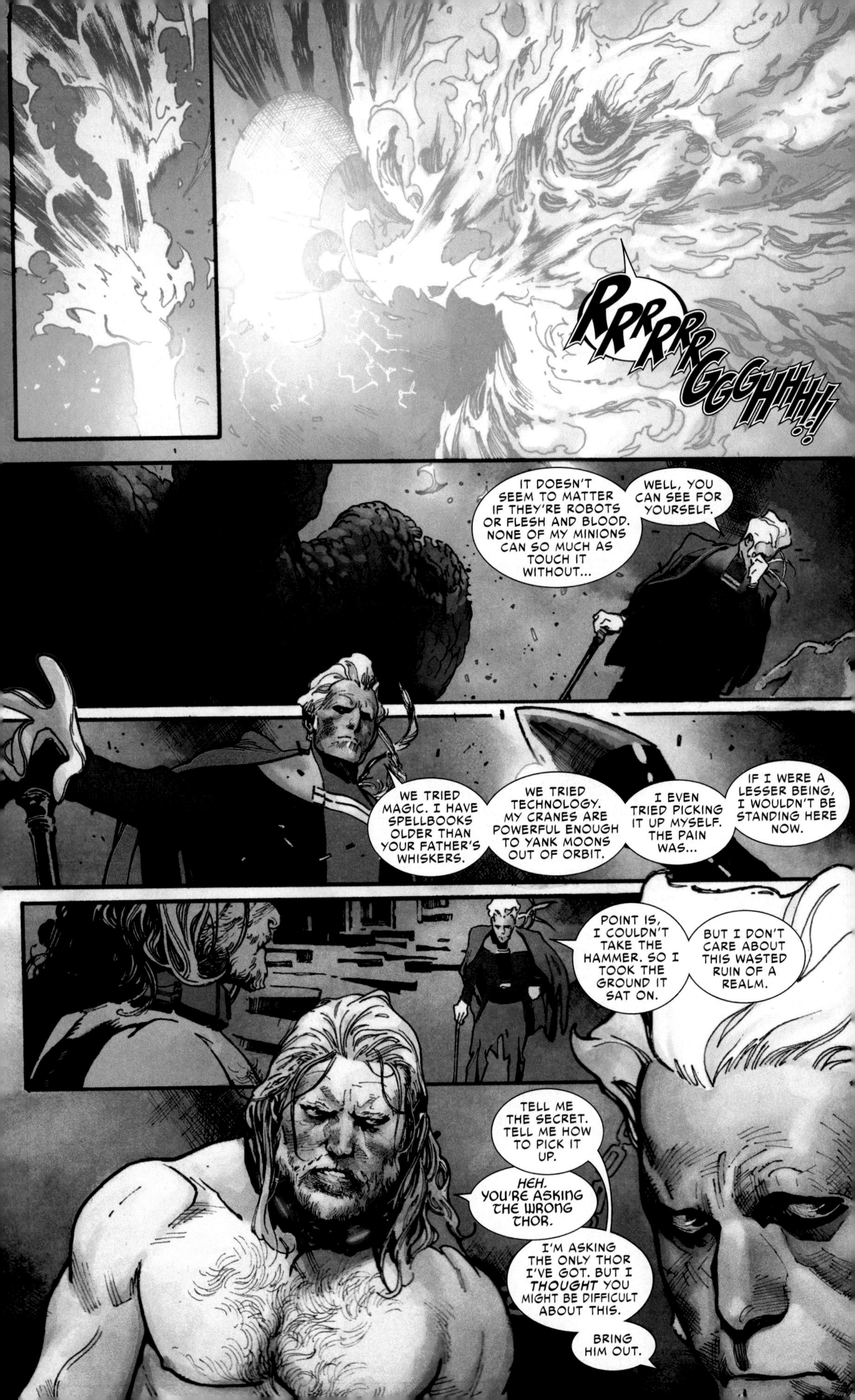
RRRRRGGGHHH!!?!
IT DOESN'T SEEM TO MATTER IF THEY'RE ROBOTS OR FLESH AND BLOOD. NONE OF MY MINIONS CAN SO MUCH AS TOUCH IT WITHOUT...
WELL, YOU CAN SEE FOR YOURSELF.
WE TRIED MAGIC. I HAVE SPELLBOOKS OLDER THAN YOUR FATHER'S WHISKERS.
WE TRIED TECHNOLOGY. MY CRANES ARE POWERFUL ENOUGH TO YANK MOONS OUT OF ORBIT.
I EVEN TRIED PICKING IT UP MYSELF. THE PAIN WAS...
IF I WERE A LESSER BEING, I WOULDN'T BE STANDING HERE NOW.
POINT IS, I COULDN'T TAKE THE HAMMER. SO I TOOK THE GROUND IT SAT ON.
BUT I DON'T CARE ABOUT THIS WASTED RUIN OF A REALM.
TELL ME THE SECRET. TELL ME HOW TO PICK IT UP.
HEH. YOU'RE ASKING THE WRONG THOR.
I'M ASKING THE ONLY THOR I'VE GOT. BUT I *THOUGHT* YOU MIGHT BE DIFFICULT ABOUT THIS.
BRING HIM OUT.

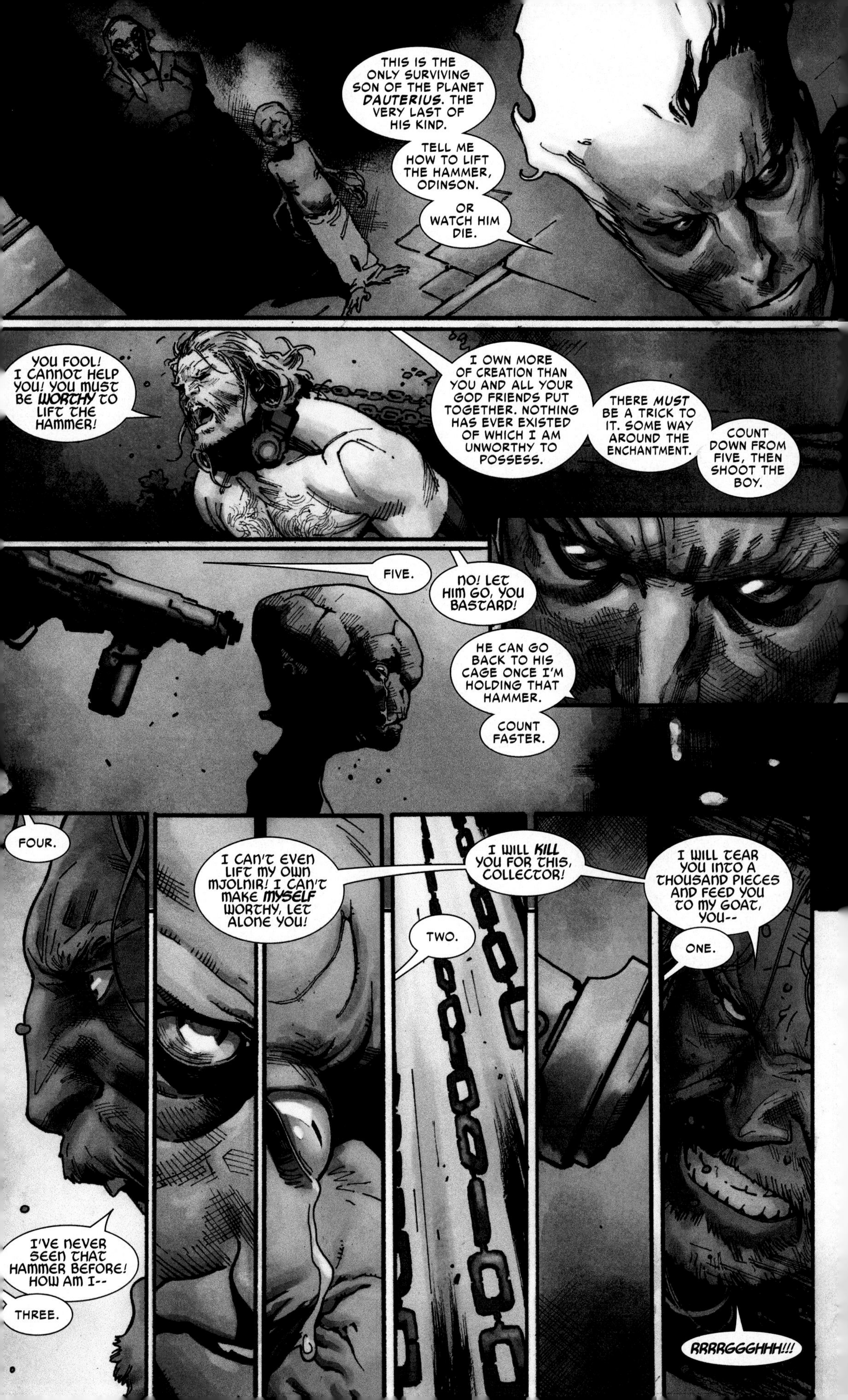
THIS IS THE ONLY SURVIVING SON OF THE PLANET DAUTERIUS. THE VERY LAST OF HIS KIND.
TELL ME HOW TO LIFT THE HAMMER, ODINSON.
OR WATCH HIM DIE.
YOU FOOL! I CANNOT HELP YOU! YOU MUST BE WORTHY TO LIFT THE HAMMER!
I OWN MORE OF CREATION THAN YOU AND ALL YOUR GOD FRIENDS PUT TOGETHER. NOTHING HAS EVER EXISTED OF WHICH I AM UNWORTHY TO POSSESS.
THERE MUST BE A TRICK TO IT. SOME WAY AROUND THE ENCHANTMENT.
COUNT DOWN FROM FIVE, THEN SHOOT THE BOY.
FIVE.
NO! LET HIM GO, YOU BASTARD!
HE CAN GO BACK TO HIS CAGE ONCE I'M HOLDING THAT HAMMER.
COUNT FASTER.
FOUR.
I'VE NEVER SEEN THAT HAMMER BEFORE! HOW AM I--
THREE.
I CAN'T EVEN LIFT MY OWN MJOLNIR! I CAN'T MAKE MYSELF WORTHY, LET ALONE YOU!
TWO.
I WILL KILL YOU FOR THIS, COLLECTOR!
I WILL TEAR YOU INTO A THOUSAND PIECES AND FEED YOU TO MY GOAT, YOU--
ONE.
RRRRGGGHHH!!!

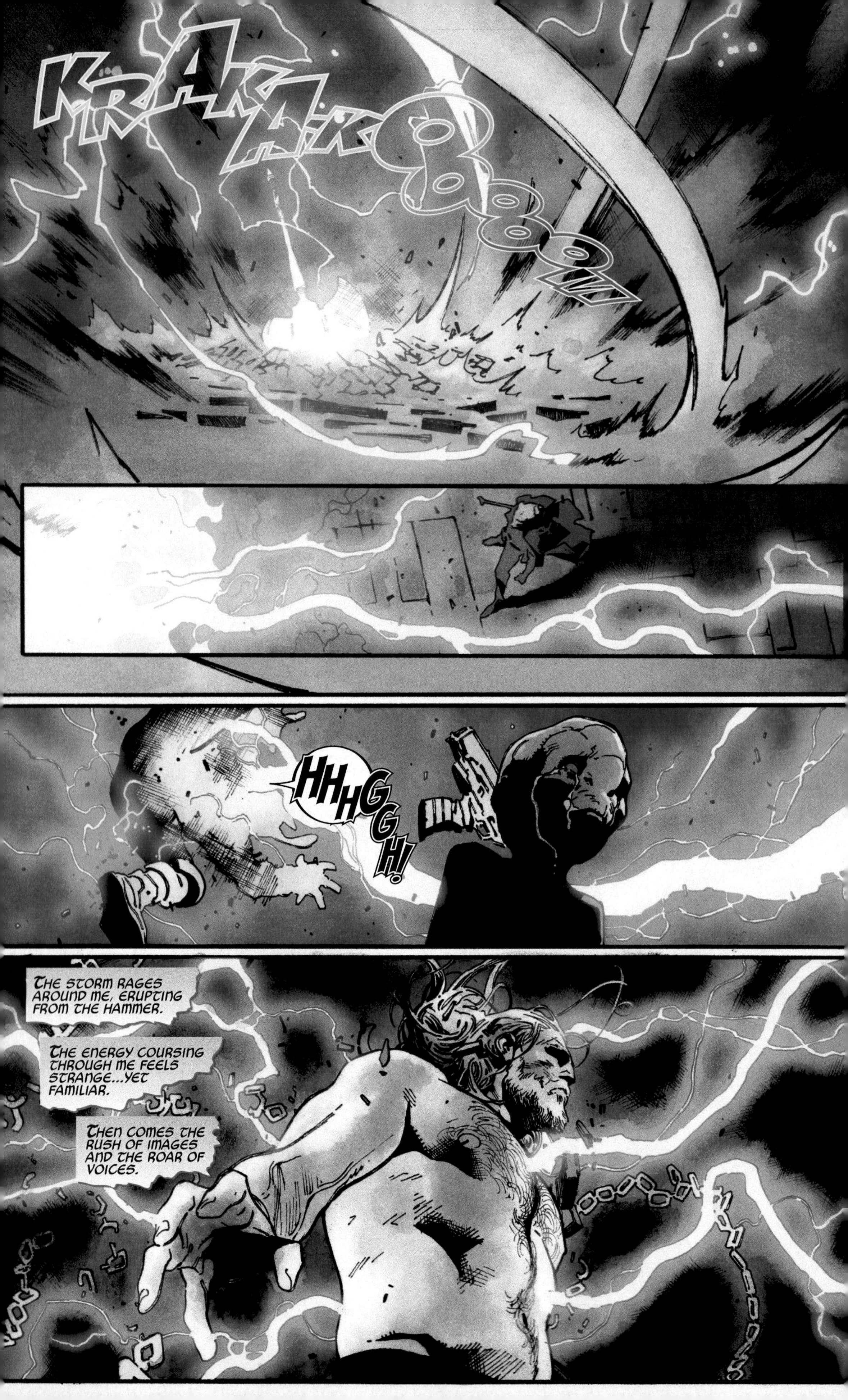
KRAKA-KOOOOOM
HHHGGH!
THE STORM RAGES AROUND ME, ERUPTING FROM THE HAMMER.
THE ENERGY COURSING THROUGH ME FEELS STRANGE...YET FAMILIAR.
THEN COMES THE RUSH OF IMAGES AND THE ROAR OF VOICES.

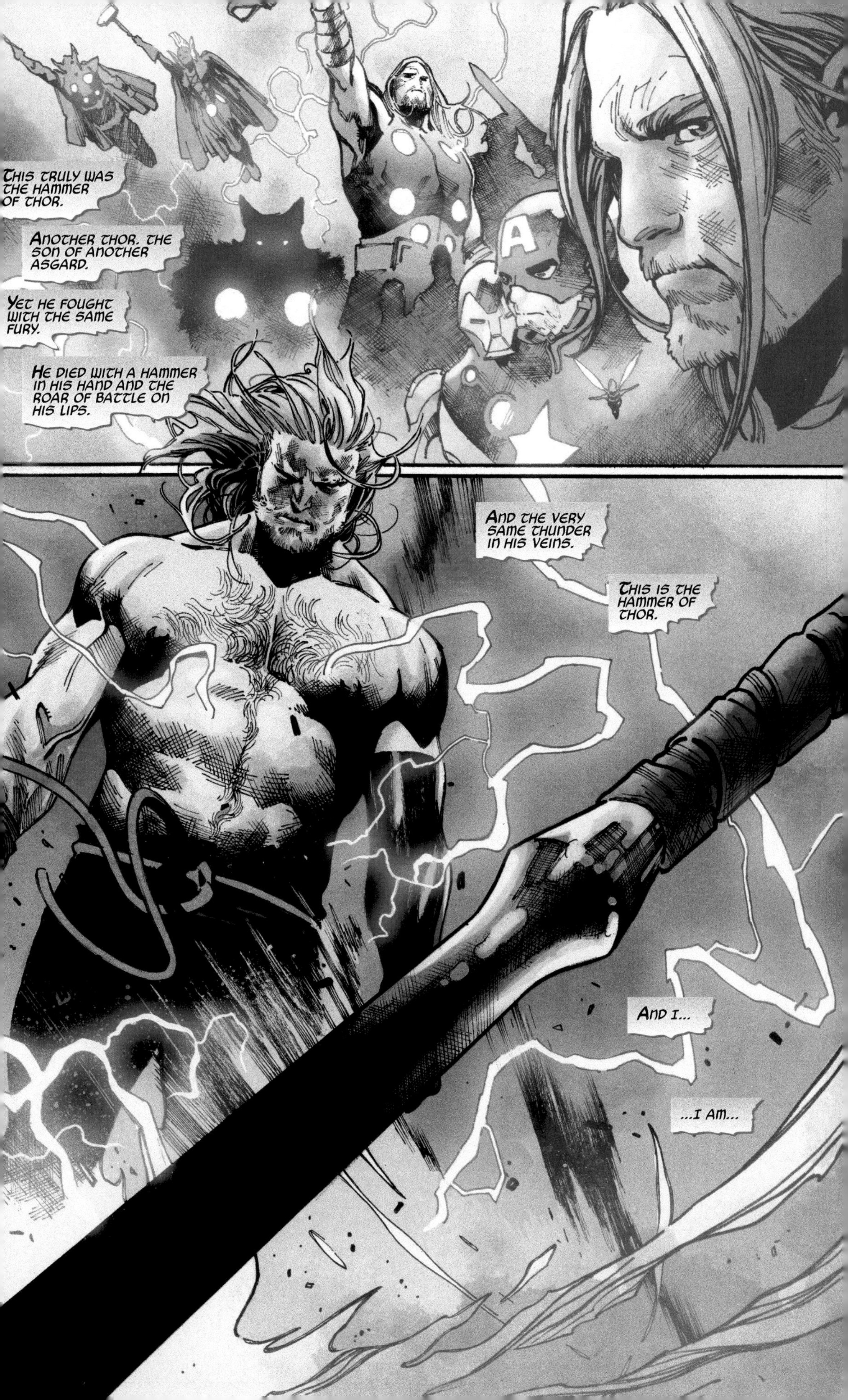
THIS TRULY WAS THE HAMMER OF THOR.
ANOTHER THOR. THE SON OF ANOTHER ASGARD.
YET HE FOUGHT WITH THE SAME FURY.
HE DIED WITH A HAMMER IN HIS HAND AND THE ROAR OF BATTLE ON HIS LIPS.
AND THE VERY SAME THUNDER IN HIS VEINS.
THIS IS THE HAMMER OF THOR.
AND I...
...I AM...

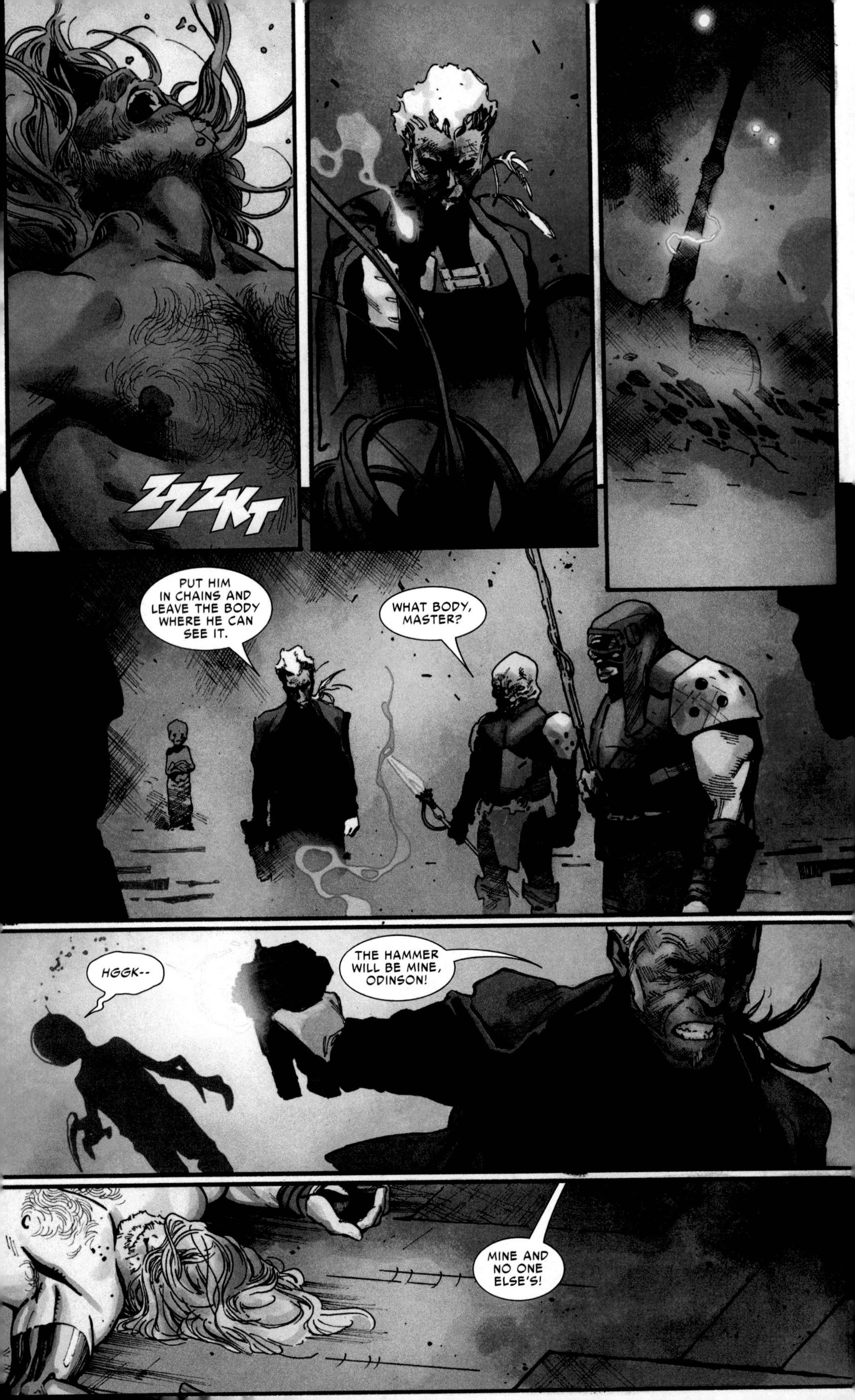
ZZZKT
PUT HIM IN CHAINS AND LEAVE THE BODY WHERE HE CAN SEE IT.
WHAT BODY, MASTER?
HGGK--
THE HAMMER WILL BE MINE, ODINSON!
MINE AND NO ONE ELSE'S!

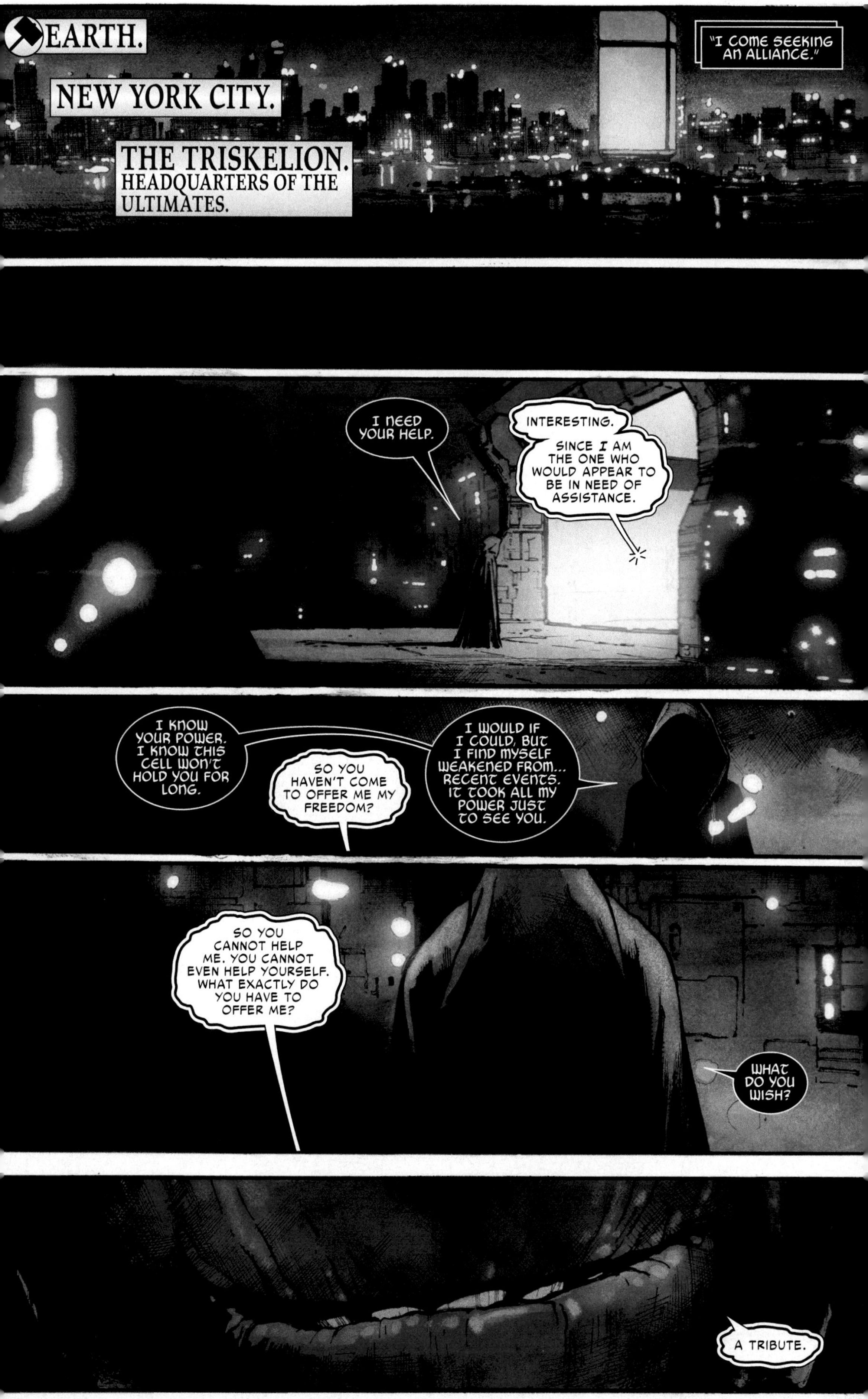
EARTH.
NEW YORK CITY.
THE TRISKELION. HEADQUARTERS OF THE ULTIMATES.
"I COME SEEKING AN ALLIANCE."
I NEED YOUR HELP.
INTERESTING.
SINCE I AM THE ONE WHO WOULD APPEAR TO BE IN NEED OF ASSISTANCE.
I KNOW YOUR POWER. I KNOW THIS CELL WON'T HOLD YOU FOR LONG.
SO YOU HAVEN'T COME TO OFFER ME MY FREEDOM?
I WOULD IF I COULD, BUT I FIND MYSELF WEAKENED FROM... RECENT EVENTS. IT TOOK ALL MY POWER JUST TO SEE YOU.
SO YOU CANNOT HELP ME. YOU CANNOT EVEN HELP YOURSELF. WHAT EXACTLY DO YOU HAVE TO OFFER ME?
WHAT DO YOU WISH?
A TRIBUTE.

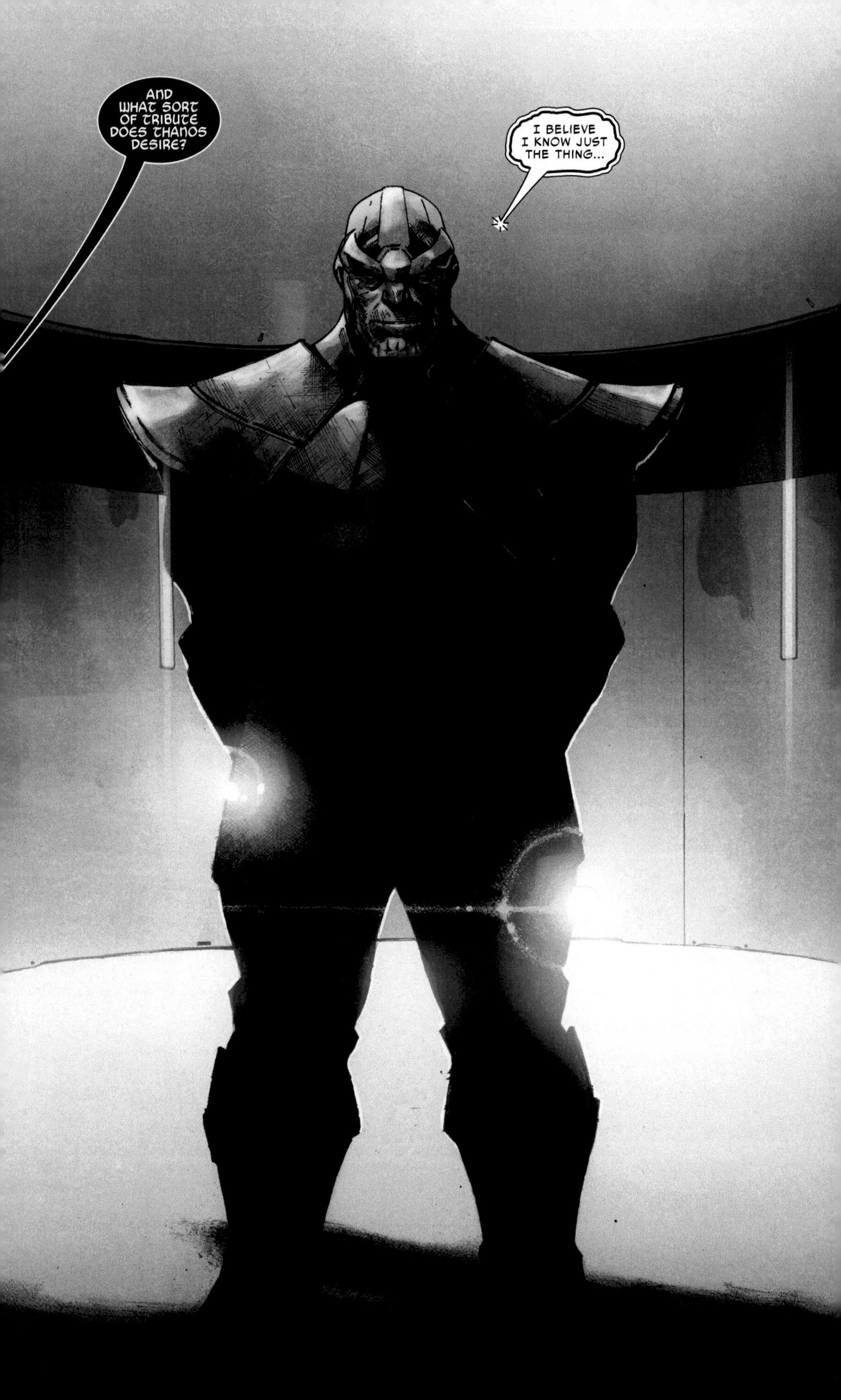
AND WHAT SORT OF TRIBUTE DOES THANOS DESIRE?
I BELIEVE I KNOW JUST THE THING...

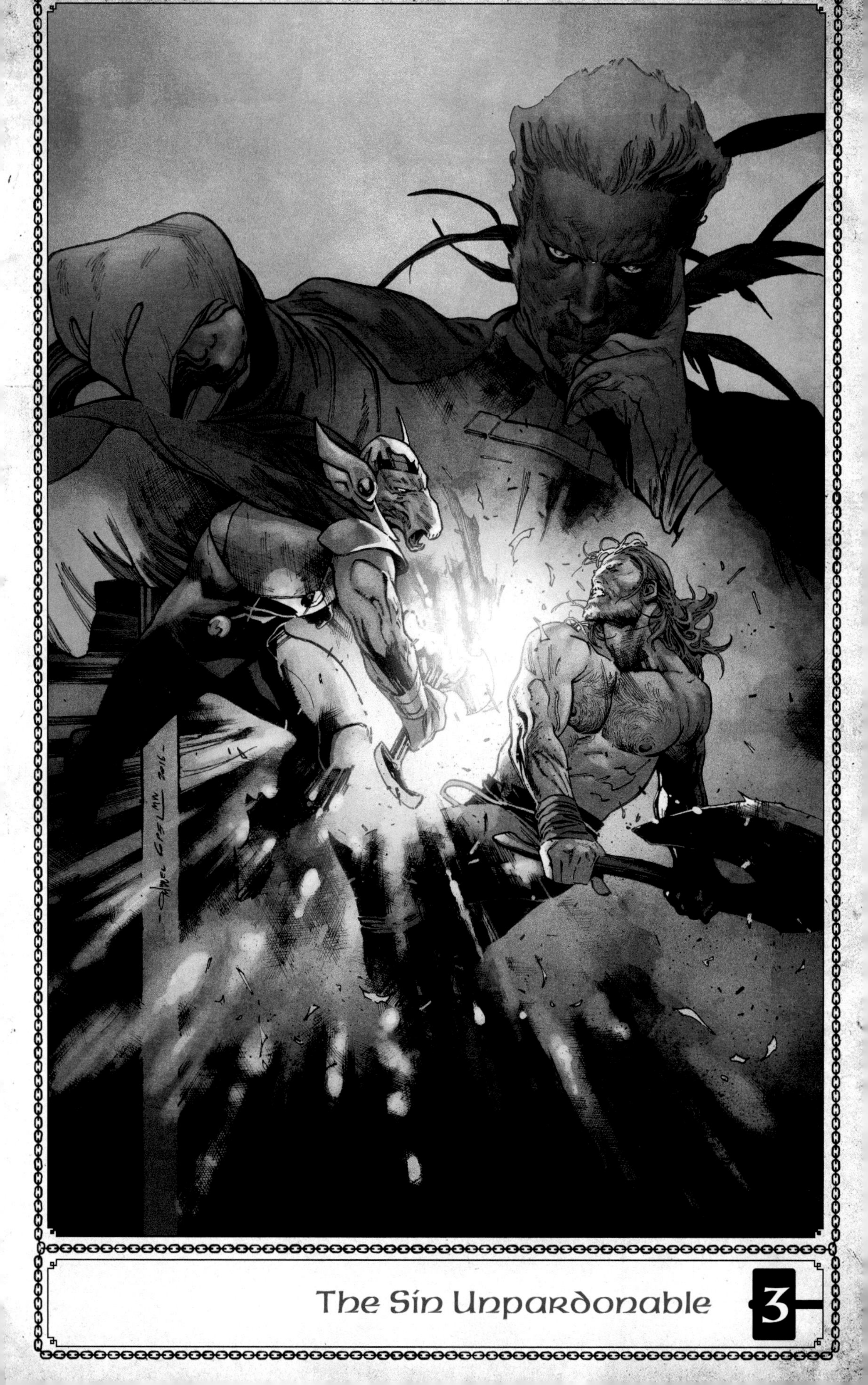

The Sin Unpardonable 3

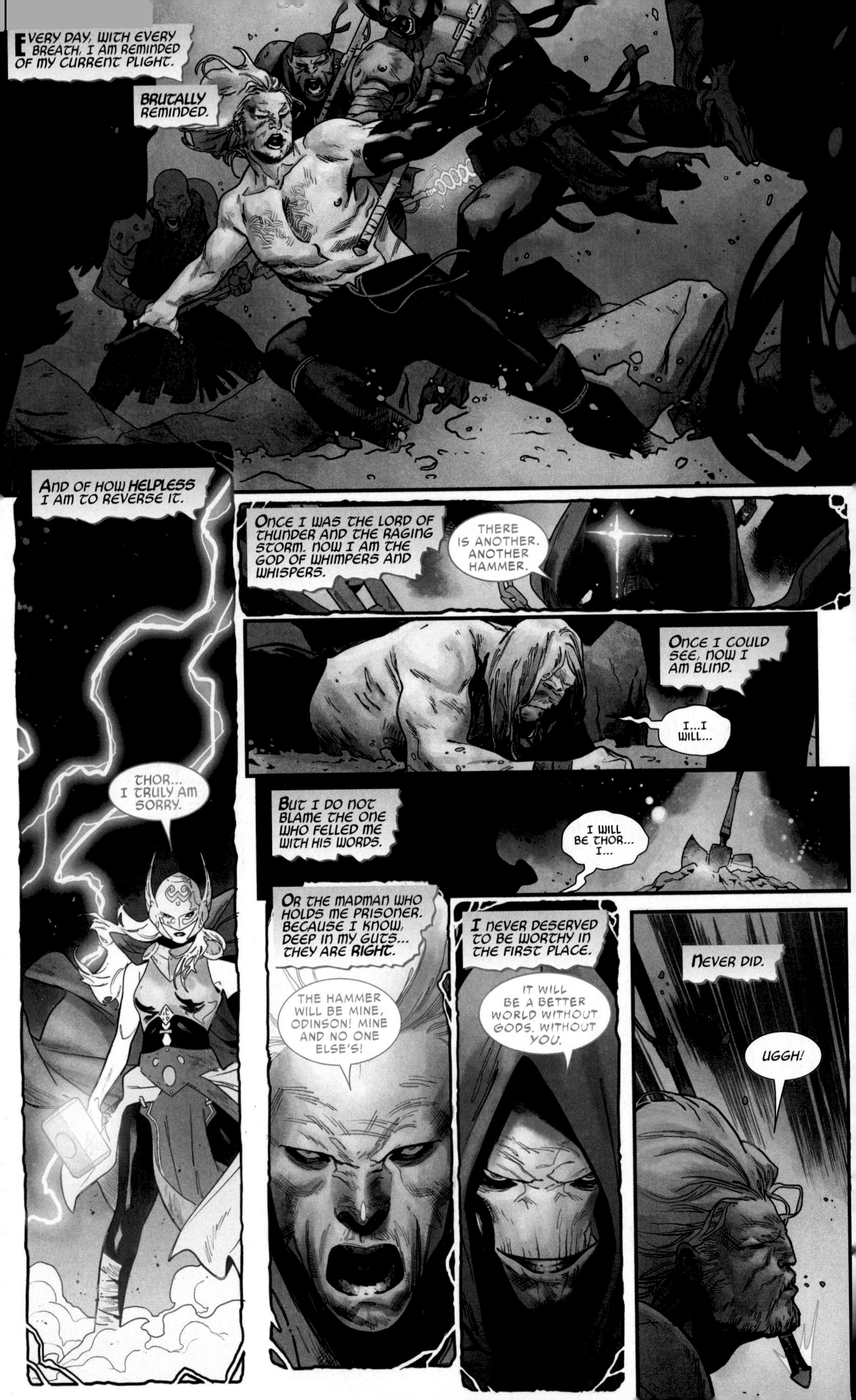
EVERY DAY, WITH EVERY BREATH, I AM REMINDED OF MY CURRENT PLIGHT.
BRUTALLY REMINDED.
AND OF HOW HELPLESS I AM TO REVERSE IT.
ONCE I WAS THE LORD OF THUNDER AND THE RAGING STORM. NOW I AM THE GOD OF WHIMPERS AND WHISPERS.
THERE IS ANOTHER. ANOTHER HAMMER.
ONCE I COULD SEE, NOW I AM BLIND.
I...I WILL...
THOR... I TRULY AM SORRY.
BUT I DO NOT BLAME THE ONE WHO FELLED ME WITH HIS WORDS.
I WILL BE THOR... I...
OR THE MADMAN WHO HOLDS ME PRISONER. BECAUSE I KNOW, DEEP IN MY GUTS... THEY ARE RIGHT.
THE HAMMER WILL BE MINE, ODINSON! MINE AND NO ONE ELSE'S!
I NEVER DESERVED TO BE WORTHY IN THE FIRST PLACE.
IT WILL BE A BETTER WORLD WITHOUT GODS. WITHOUT YOU.
NEVER DID.
UGGH!

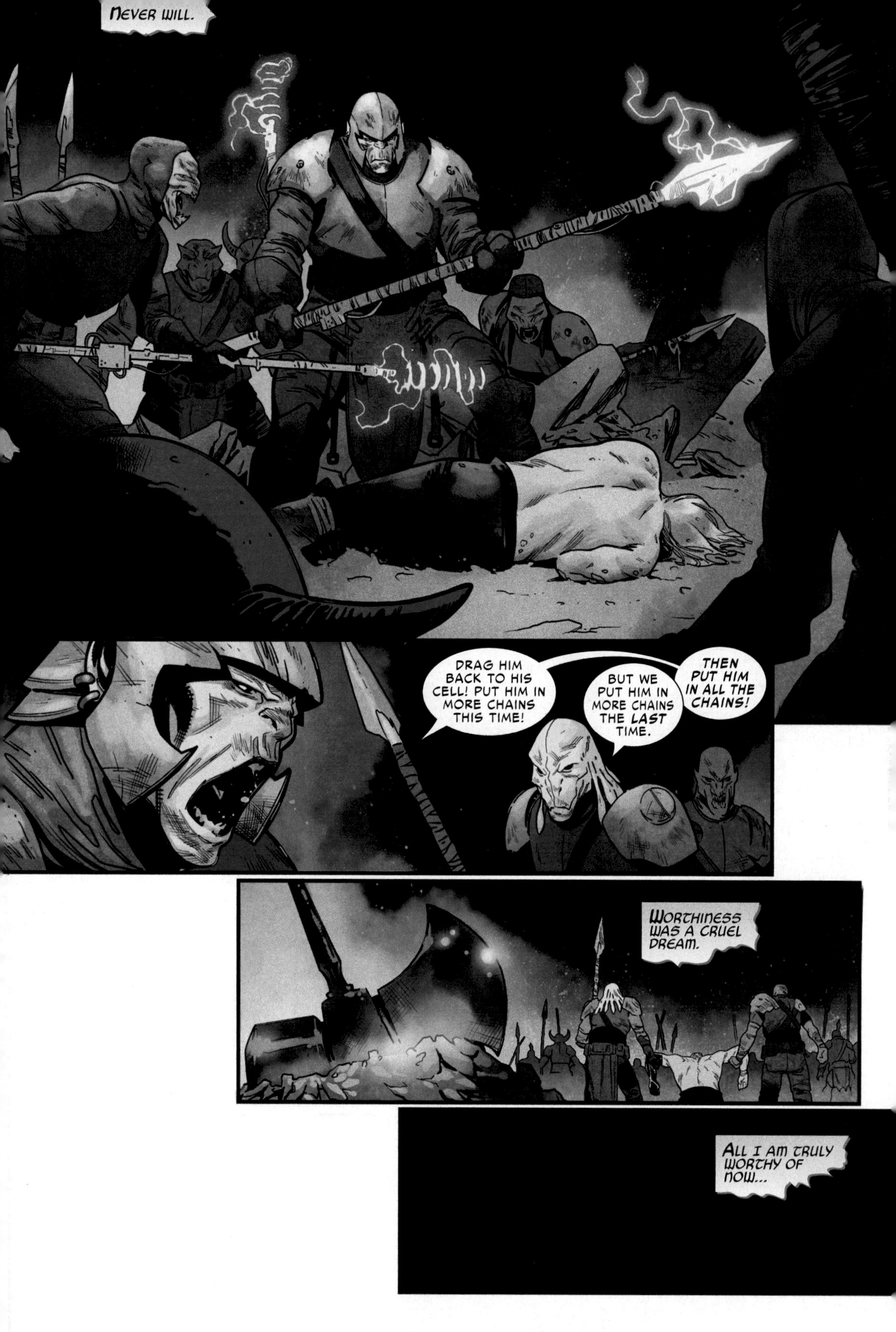
NEVER WILL.
DRAG HIM BACK TO HIS CELL! PUT HIM IN MORE CHAINS THIS TIME!
BUT WE PUT HIM IN MORE CHAINS THE LAST TIME.
THEN PUT HIM IN ALL THE CHAINS!
WORTHINESS WAS A CRUEL DREAM.
ALL I AM TRULY WORTHY OF NOW...

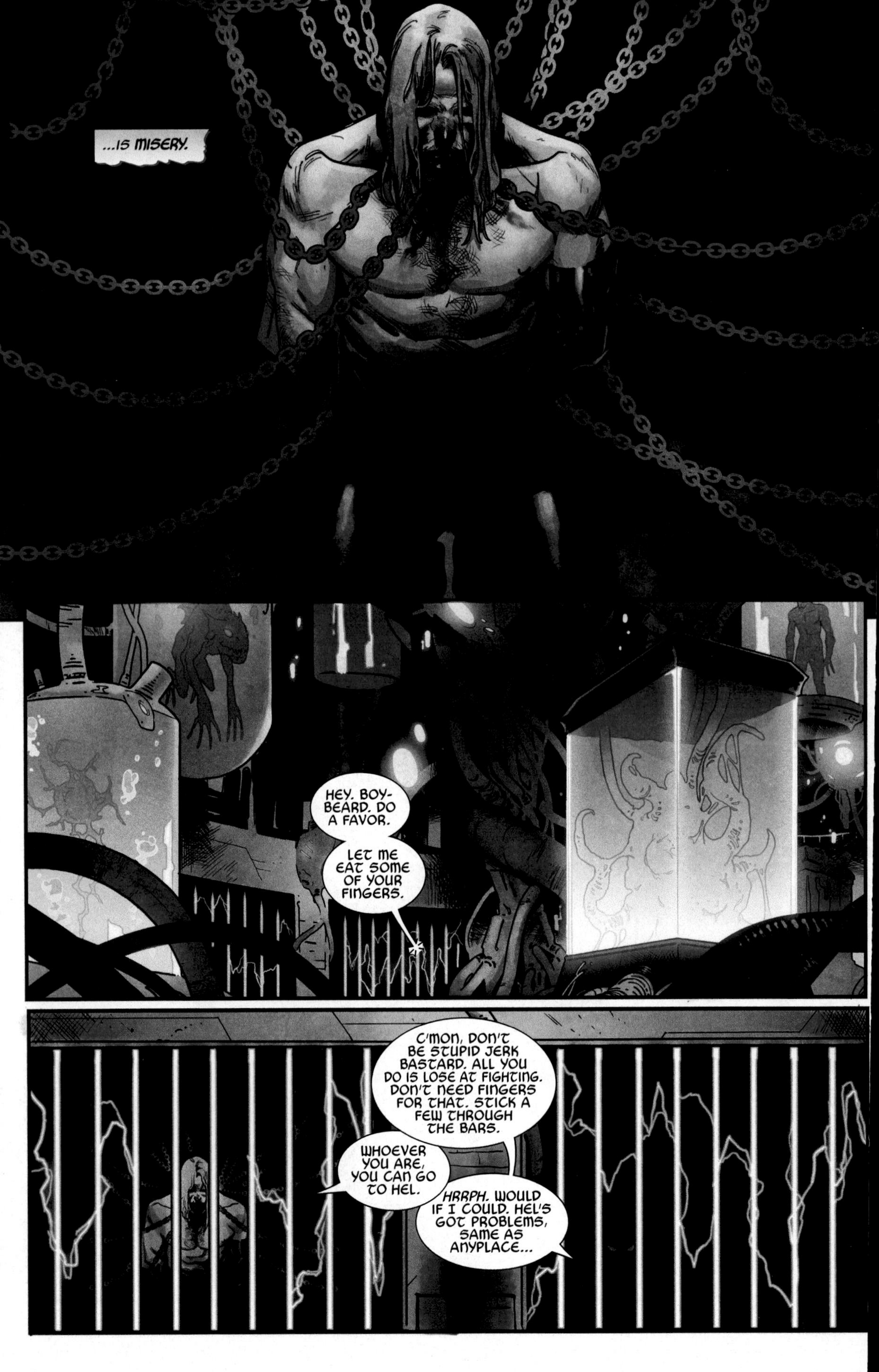

...IS MISERY.
HEY. BOY-BEARD. DO A FAVOR.
LET ME EAT SOME OF YOUR FINGERS.
C'MON, DON'T BE STUPID JERK BASTARD. ALL YOU DO IS LOSE AT FIGHTING. DON'T NEED FINGERS FOR THAT. STICK A FEW THROUGH THE BARS.
WHOEVER YOU ARE, YOU CAN GO TO HEL.
HRRPH. WOULD IF I COULD. HEL'S GOT PROBLEMS, SAME AS ANYPLACE...

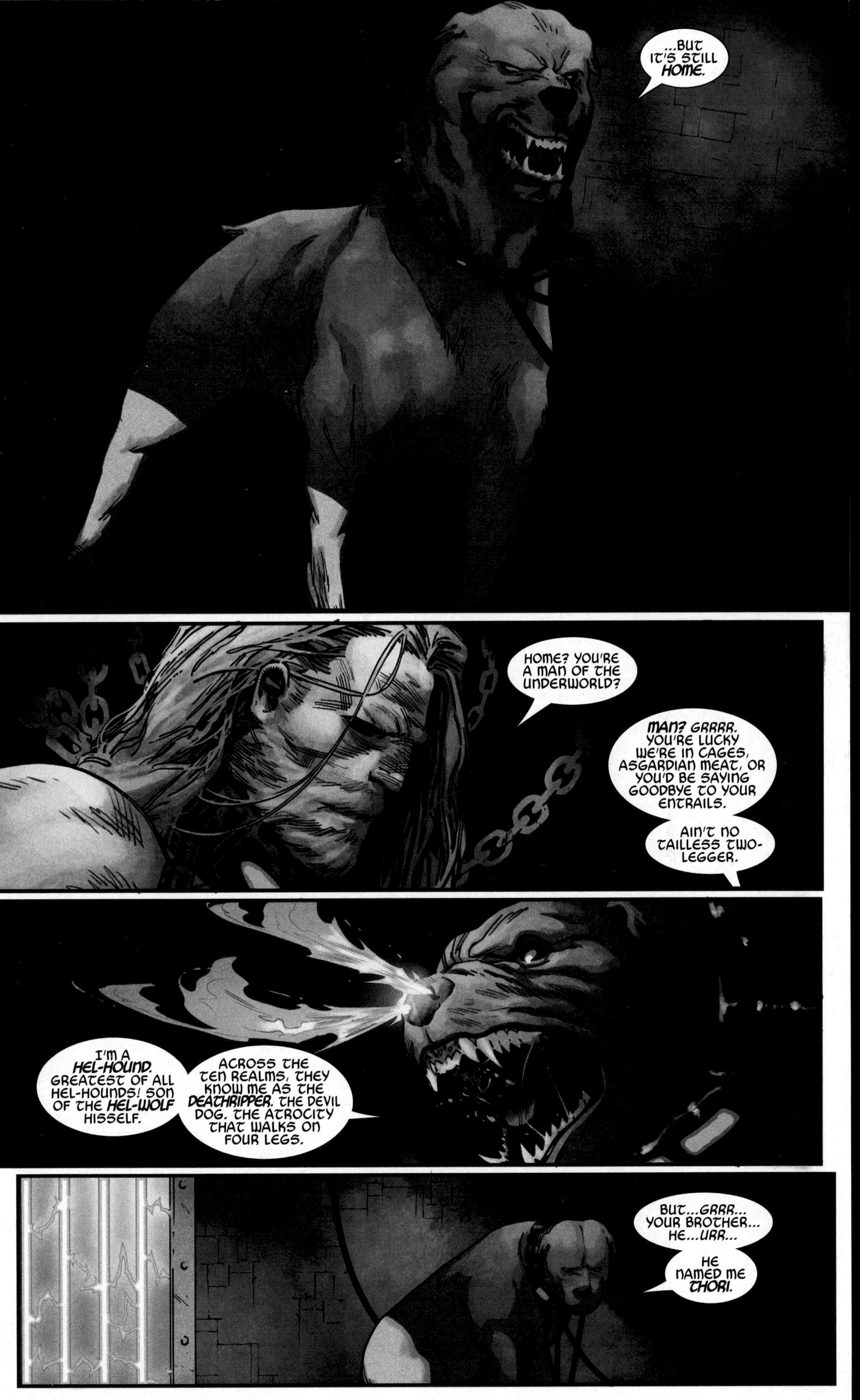
...BUT IT'S STILL HOME.
HOME? YOU'RE A MAN OF THE UNDERWORLD?
MAN? GRRRR. YOU'RE LUCKY WE'RE IN CAGES, ASGARDIAN MEAT, OR YOU'D BE SAYING GOODBYE TO YOUR ENTRAILS.
AIN'T NO TAILLESS TWO-LEGGER.
I'M A HEL-HOUND. GREATEST OF ALL HEL-HOUNDS! SON OF THE HEL-WOLF HISSELF.
ACROSS THE TEN REALMS, THEY KNOW ME AS THE DEATHRIPPER. THE DEVIL DOG. THE ATROCITY THAT WALKS ON FOUR LEGS.
BUT...GRRR... YOUR BROTHER... HE...URR...
HE NAMED ME THORI.

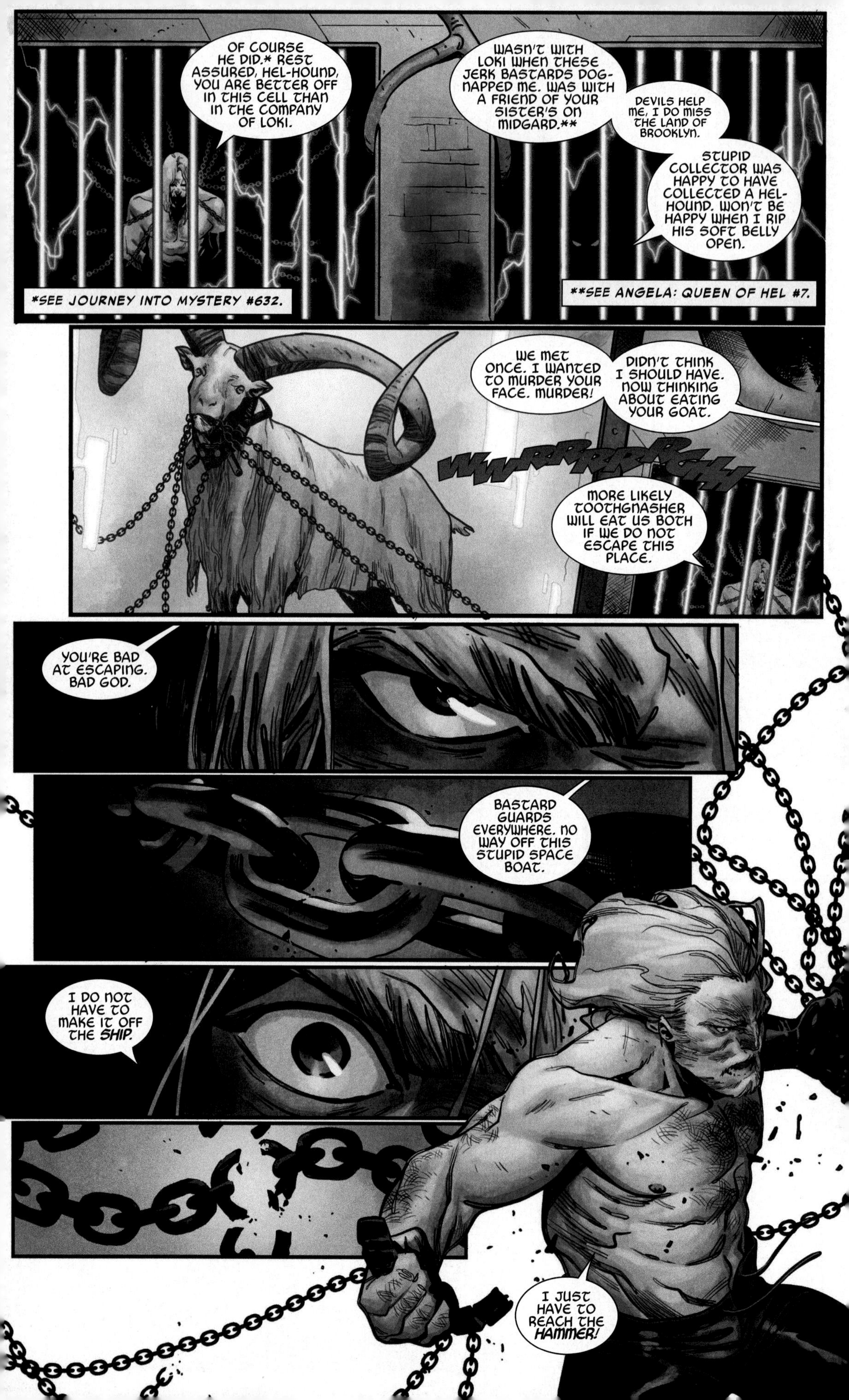
OF COURSE HE DID.* REST ASSURED, HEL-HOUND, YOU ARE BETTER OFF IN THIS CELL THAN IN THE COMPANY OF LOKI.
WASN'T WITH LOKI WHEN THESE JERK BASTARDS DOG-NAPPED ME. WAS WITH A FRIEND OF YOUR SISTER'S ON MIDGARD.**
DEVILS HELP ME, I DO MISS THE LAND OF BROOKLYN.
STUPID COLLECTOR WAS HAPPY TO HAVE COLLECTED A HEL-HOUND. WON'T BE HAPPY WHEN I RIP HIS SOFT BELLY OPEN.
*SEE JOURNEY INTO MYSTERY #632.
**SEE ANGELA: QUEEN OF HEL #7.
WE MET ONCE. I WANTED TO MURDER YOUR FACE. MURDER!
DIDN'T THINK I SHOULD HAVE. NOW THINKING ABOUT EATING YOUR GOAT.
WWRRRRRGH
MORE LIKELY TOOTHGNASHER WILL EAT US BOTH IF WE DO NOT ESCAPE THIS PLACE.
YOU'RE BAD AT ESCAPING. BAD GOD.
BASTARD GUARDS EVERYWHERE. NO WAY OFF THIS STUPID SPACE BOAT.
I DO NOT HAVE TO MAKE IT OFF THE SHIP.
I JUST HAVE TO REACH THE HAMMER!

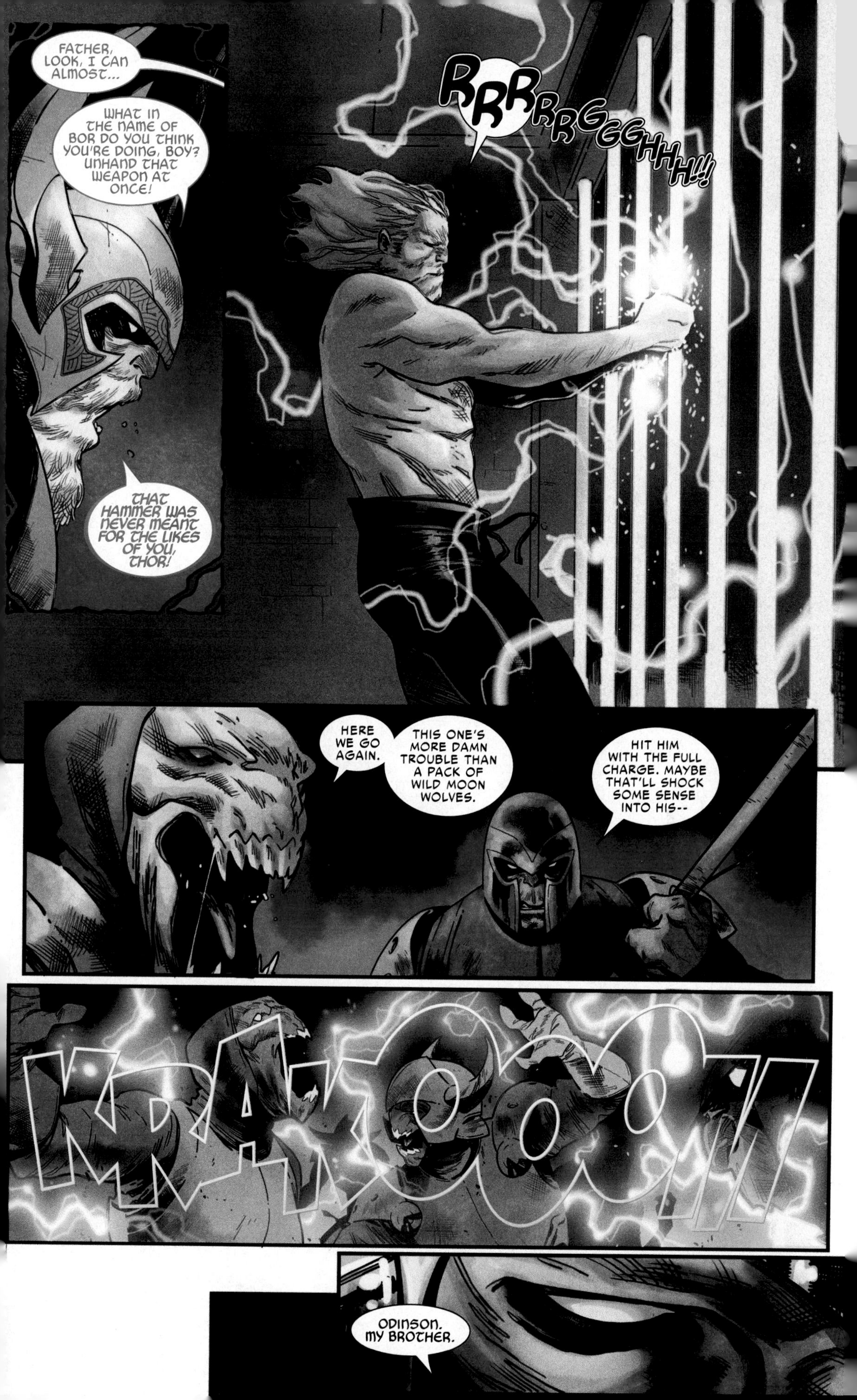
FATHER, LOOK, I CAN ALMOST...
WHAT IN THE NAME OF BOR DO YOU THINK YOU'RE DOING, BOY? UNHAND THAT WEAPON AT ONCE!
THAT HAMMER WAS NEVER MEANT FOR THE LIKES OF YOU, THOR!
RRRRRRGGGHHHH!!
HERE WE GO AGAIN.
THIS ONE'S MORE DAMN TROUBLE THAN A PACK OF WILD MOON WOLVES.
HIT HIM WITH THE FULL CHARGE. MAYBE THAT'LL SHOCK SOME SENSE INTO HIS--
KRAKOOOM!
ODINSON. MY BROTHER.

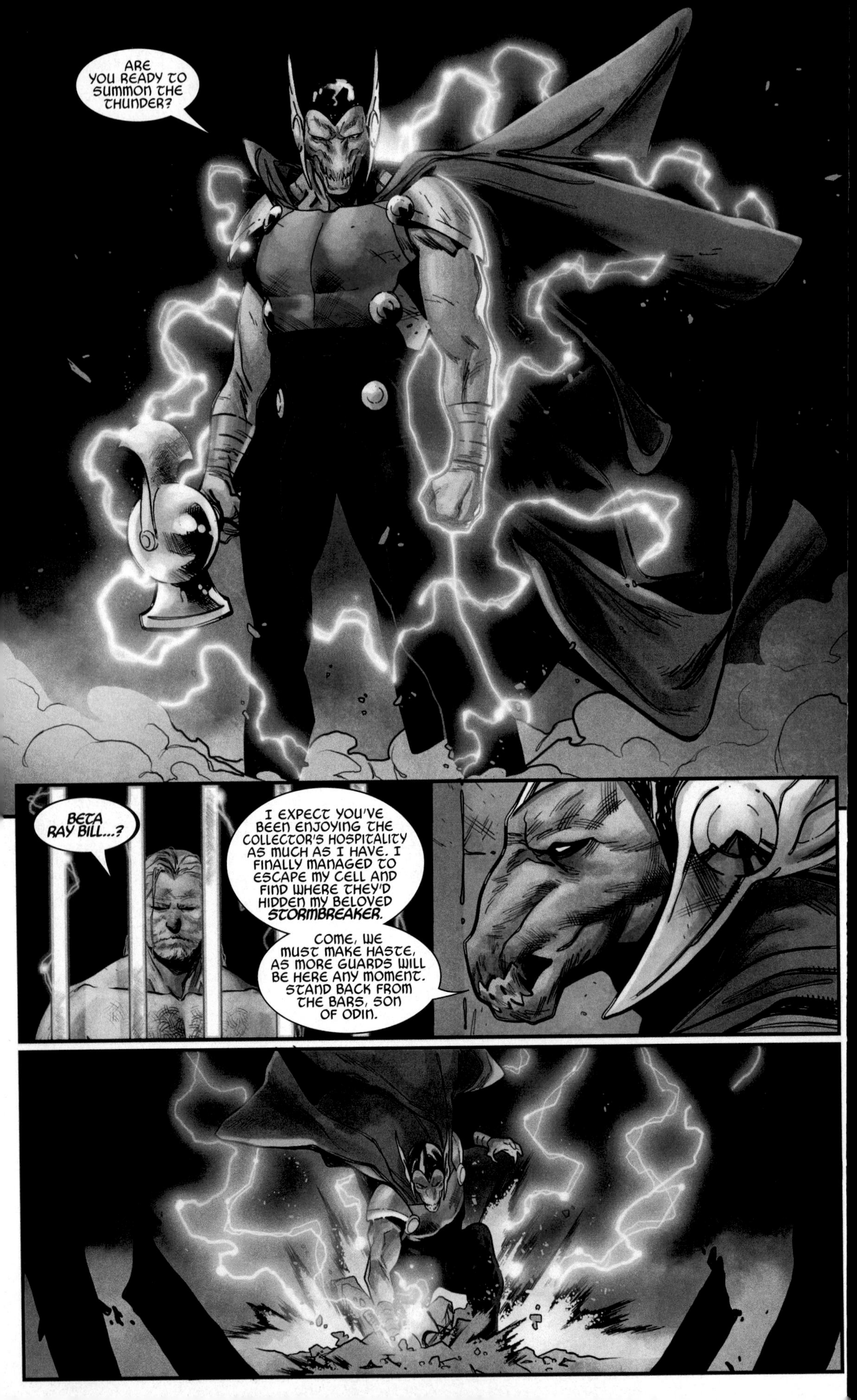
ARE YOU READY TO SUMMON THE THUNDER?
BETA RAY BILL...?
I EXPECT YOU'VE BEEN ENJOYING THE COLLECTOR'S HOSPITALITY AS MUCH AS I HAVE. I FINALLY MANAGED TO ESCAPE MY CELL AND FIND WHERE THEY'D HIDDEN MY BELOVED STORMBREAKER.
COME, WE MUST MAKE HASTE, AS MORE GUARDS WILL BE HERE ANY MOMENT. STAND BACK FROM THE BARS, SON OF ODIN.

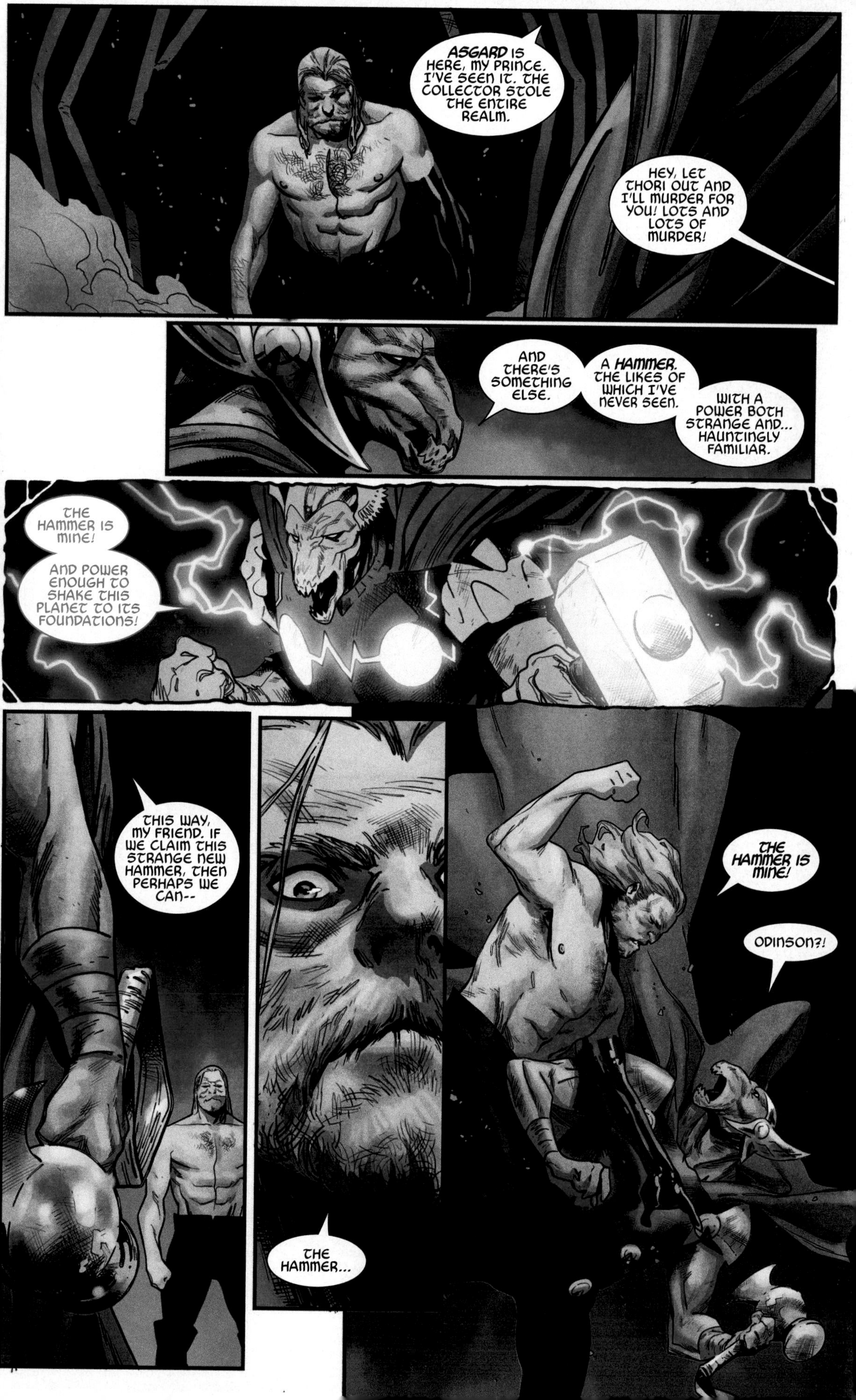
ASGARD IS HERE, MY PRINCE. I'VE SEEN IT. THE COLLECTOR STOLE THE ENTIRE REALM.
HEY, LET THORI OUT AND I'LL MURDER FOR YOU! LOTS AND LOTS OF MURDER!
AND THERE'S SOMETHING ELSE.
A HAMMER. THE LIKES OF WHICH I'VE NEVER SEEN.
WITH A POWER BOTH STRANGE AND... HAUNTINGLY FAMILIAR.
THE HAMMER IS MINE!
AND POWER ENOUGH TO SHAKE THIS PLANET TO ITS FOUNDATIONS!
THIS WAY, MY FRIEND. IF WE CLAIM THIS STRANGE NEW HAMMER, THEN PERHAPS WE CAN--
THE HAMMER...
THE HAMMER IS MINE!
ODINSON?!

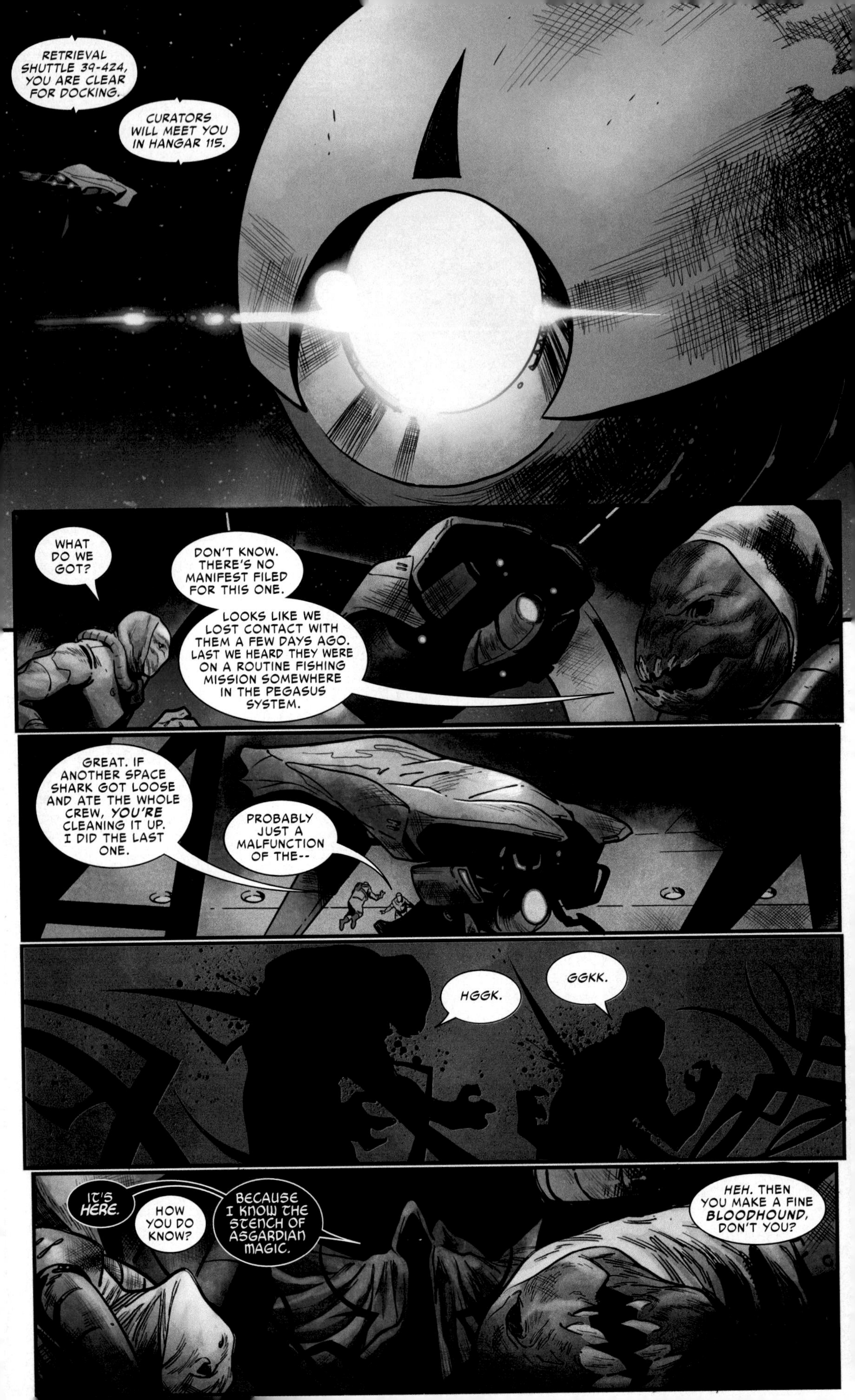
RETRIEVAL SHUTTLE 39-424, YOU ARE CLEAR FOR DOCKING.
CURATORS WILL MEET YOU IN HANGAR 115.
WHAT DO WE GOT?
DON'T KNOW. THERE'S NO MANIFEST FILED FOR THIS ONE.
LOOKS LIKE WE LOST CONTACT WITH THEM A FEW DAYS AGO. LAST WE HEARD THEY WERE ON A ROUTINE FISHING MISSION SOMEWHERE IN THE PEGASUS SYSTEM.
GREAT. IF ANOTHER SPACE SHARK GOT LOOSE AND ATE THE WHOLE CREW, *YOU'RE* CLEANING IT UP. I DID THE LAST ONE.
PROBABLY JUST A MALFUNCTION OF THE--
HGGK.
GGKK.
IT'S *HERE*.
HOW YOU DO KNOW?
BECAUSE I KNOW THE STENCH OF ASGARDIAN MAGIC.
HEH. THEN YOU MAKE A FINE *BLOODHOUND*, DON'T YOU?

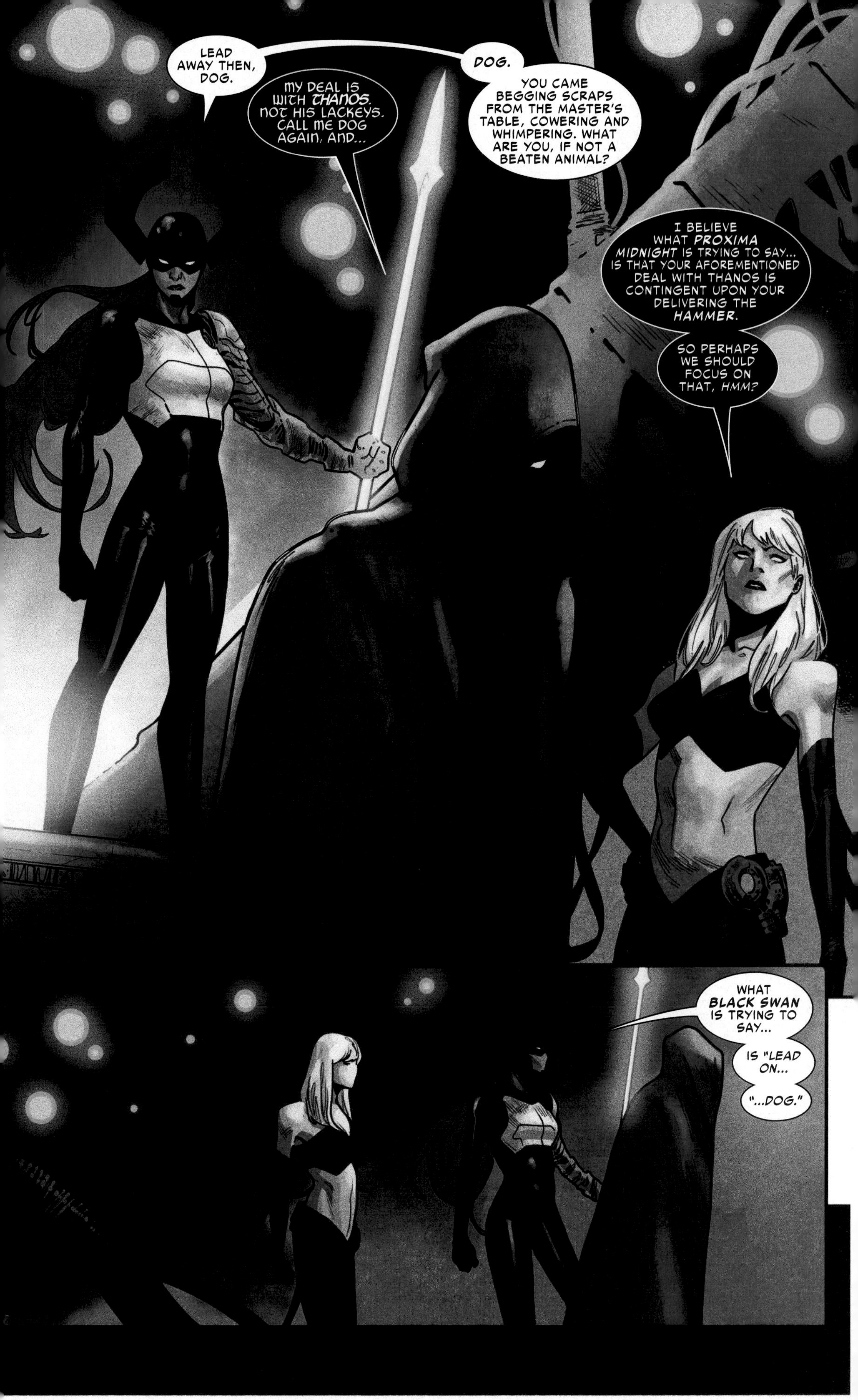
LEAD AWAY THEN, DOG.
DOG.
MY DEAL IS WITH *THANOS*. NOT HIS LACKEYS. CALL ME DOG AGAIN, AND...
YOU CAME BEGGING SCRAPS FROM THE MASTER'S TABLE, COWERING AND WHIMPERING. WHAT ARE YOU, IF NOT A BEATEN ANIMAL?
I BELIEVE WHAT *PROXIMA MIDNIGHT* IS TRYING TO SAY... IS THAT YOUR AFOREMENTIONED DEAL WITH THANOS IS CONTINGENT UPON YOUR DELIVERING THE *HAMMER*.
SO PERHAPS WE SHOULD FOCUS ON THAT, *HMM?*
WHAT *BLACK SWAN* IS TRYING TO SAY...
IS "LEAD ON...
"...DOG."

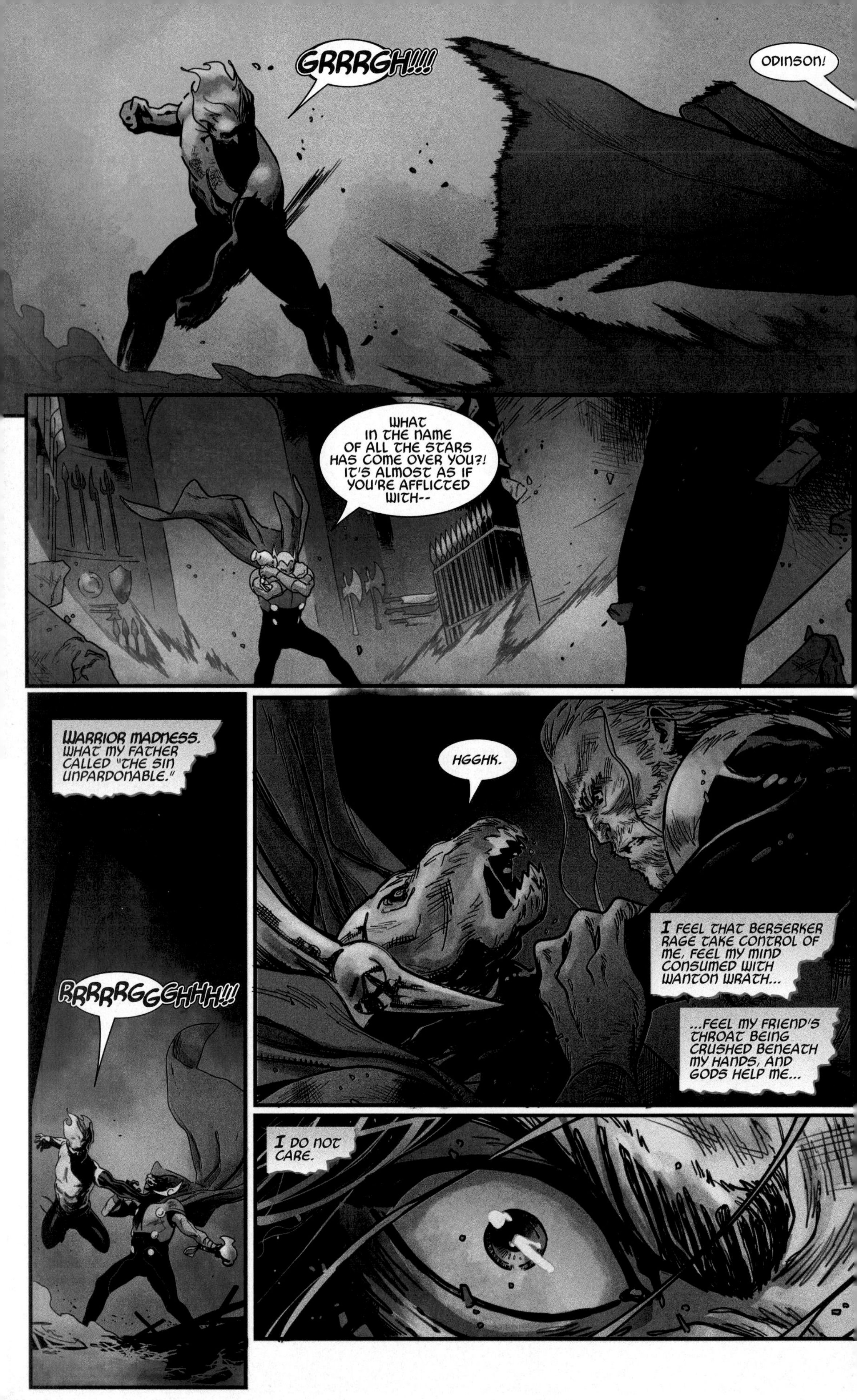
GRRRGH!!!
ODINSON!
WHAT IN THE NAME OF ALL THE STARS HAS COME OVER YOU?! IT'S ALMOST AS IF YOU'RE AFFLICTED WITH--
WARRIOR MADNESS. WHAT MY FATHER CALLED "THE SIN UNPARDONABLE."
RRRRRGGGHHH!!!
HGGHK.
I FEEL THAT BERSERKER RAGE TAKE CONTROL OF ME, FEEL MY MIND CONSUMED WITH WANTON WRATH...
...FEEL MY FRIEND'S THROAT BEING CRUSHED BENEATH MY HANDS, AND GODS HELP ME...
I DO NOT CARE.

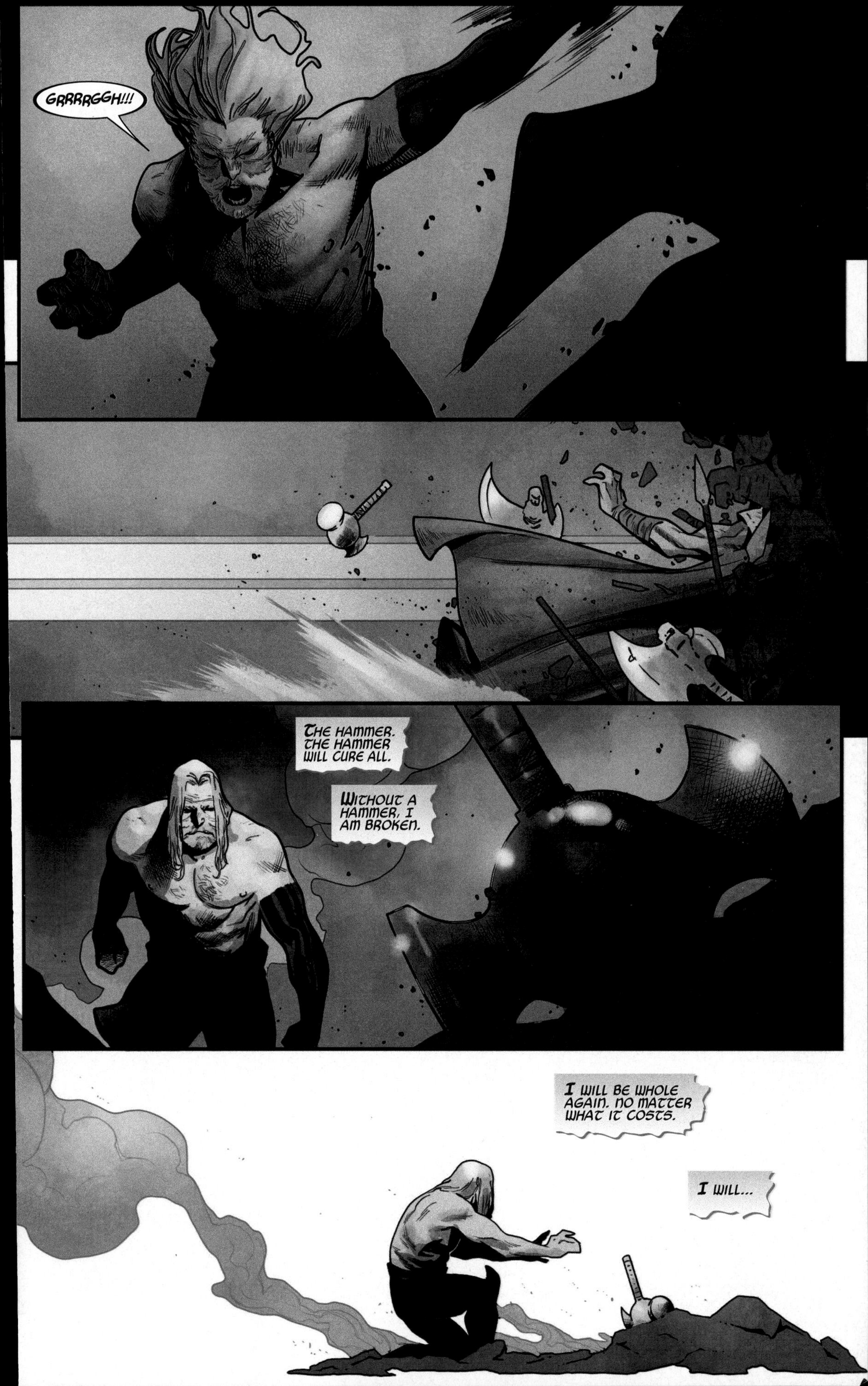
GRRRRGGH!!!
THE HAMMER. THE HAMMER WILL CURE ALL.
WITHOUT A HAMMER, I AM BROKEN.
I WILL BE WHOLE AGAIN. NO MATTER WHAT IT COSTS.
I WILL...

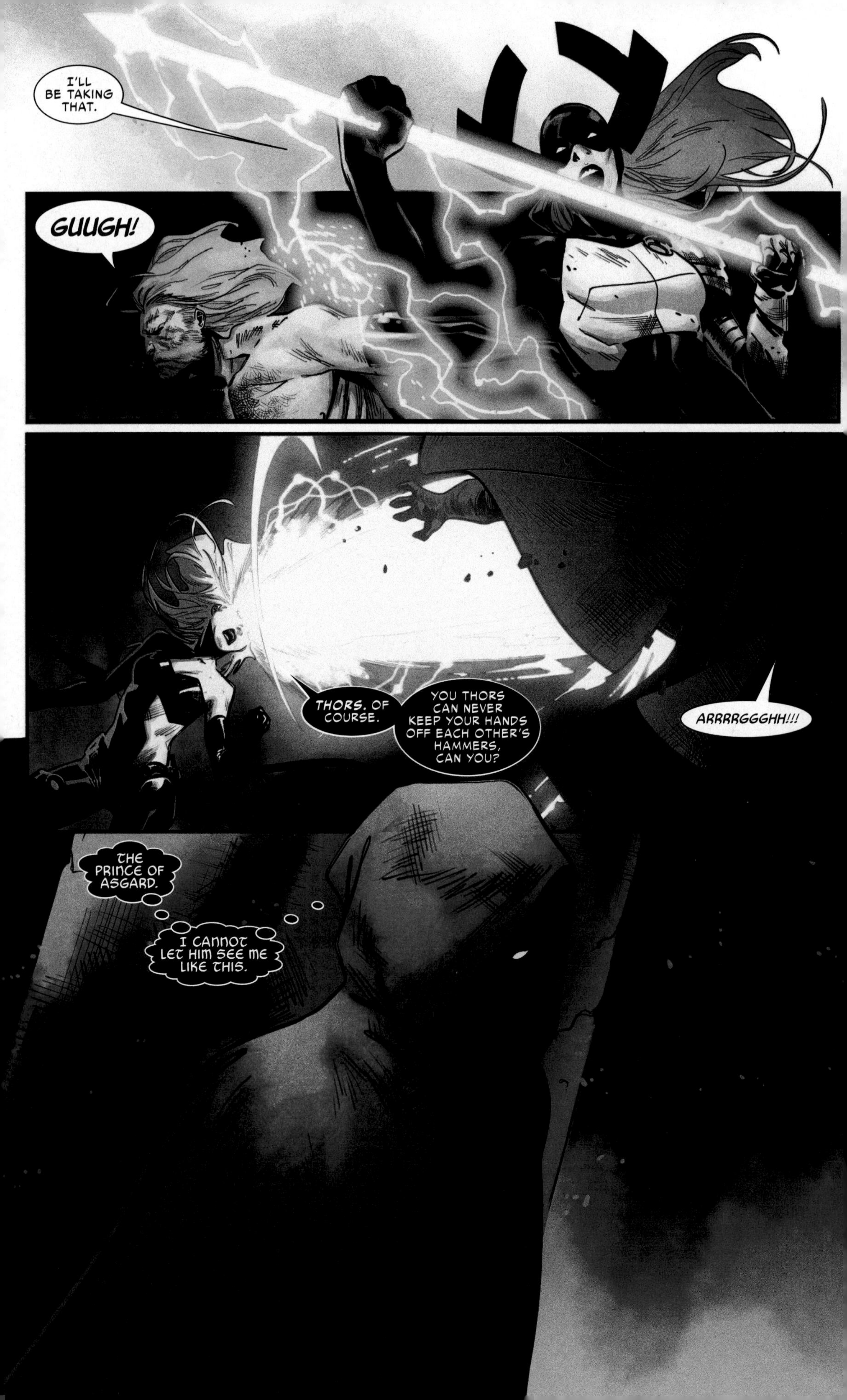
I'LL BE TAKING THAT.
GUUGH!
THORS. OF COURSE.
YOU THORS CAN NEVER KEEP YOUR HANDS OFF EACH OTHER'S HAMMERS, CAN YOU?
ARRRRGGGHH!!!
THE PRINCE OF ASGARD.
I CANNOT LET HIM SEE ME LIKE THIS.

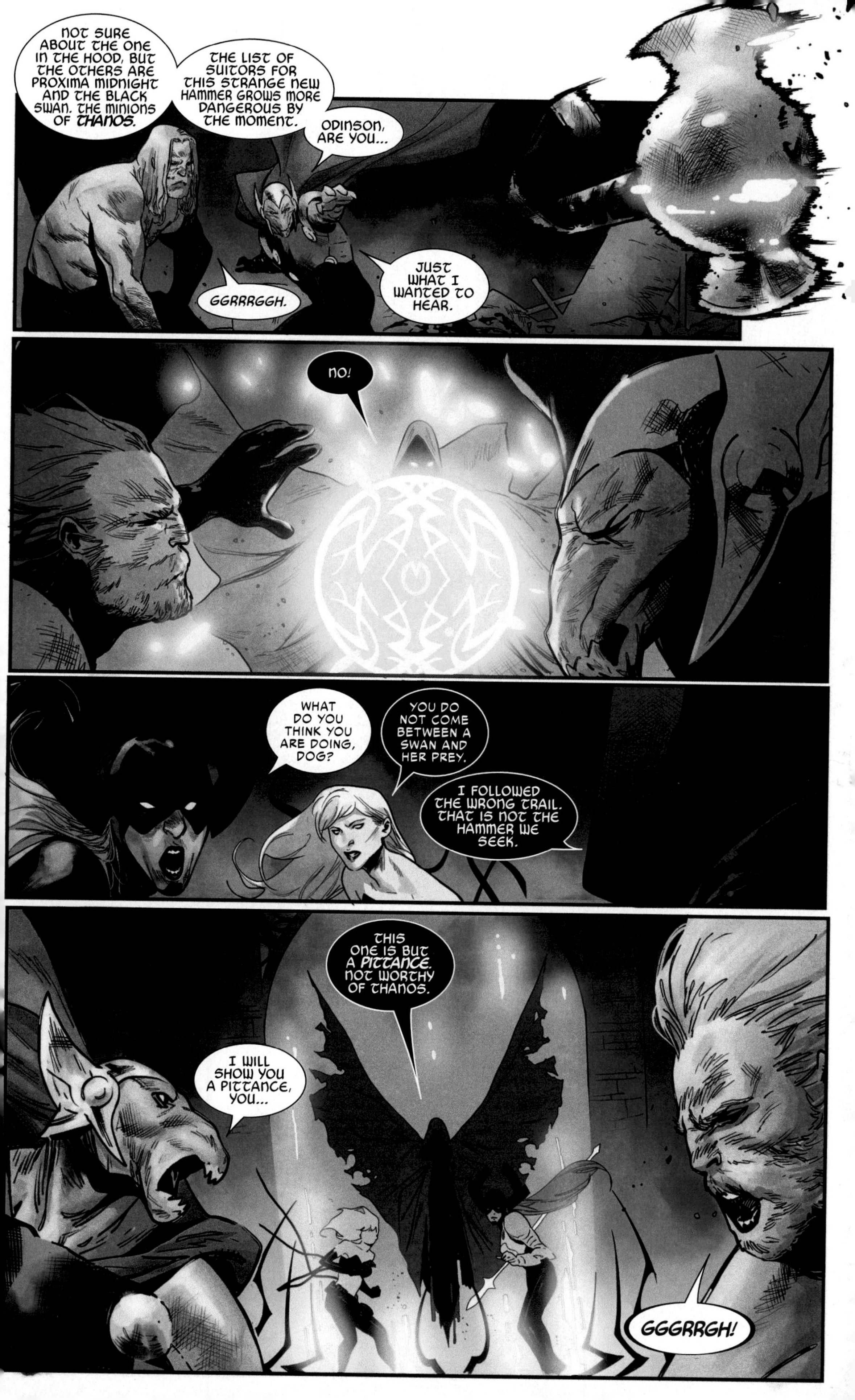
NOT SURE ABOUT THE ONE IN THE HOOD, BUT THE OTHERS ARE PROXIMA MIDNIGHT AND THE BLACK SWAN. THE MINIONS OF THANOS.
THE LIST OF SUITORS FOR THIS STRANGE NEW HAMMER GROWS MORE DANGEROUS BY THE MOMENT.
ODINSON, ARE YOU...
GGRRRGGH.
JUST WHAT I WANTED TO HEAR.
NO!
WHAT DO YOU THINK YOU ARE DOING, DOG?
YOU DO NOT COME BETWEEN A SWAN AND HER PREY.
I FOLLOWED THE WRONG TRAIL. THAT IS NOT THE HAMMER WE SEEK.
THIS ONE IS BUT A PITTANCE. NOT WORTHY OF THANOS.
I WILL SHOW YOU A PITTANCE, YOU...
GGGRRGH!

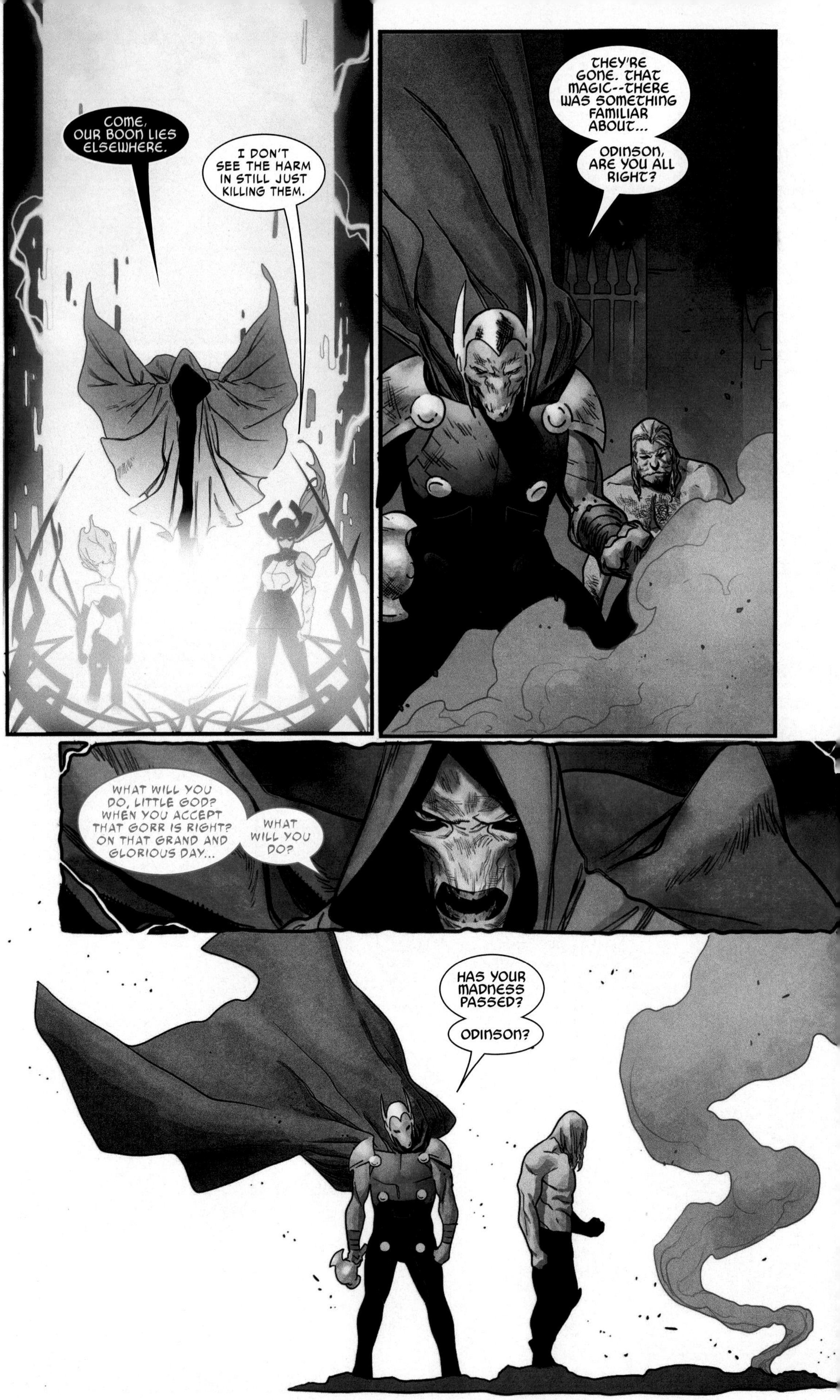
COME, OUR BOON LIES ELSEWHERE.
I DON'T SEE THE HARM IN STILL JUST KILLING THEM.
THEY'RE GONE. THAT MAGIC--THERE WAS SOMETHING FAMILIAR ABOUT...
ODINSON, ARE YOU ALL RIGHT?
WHAT WILL YOU DO, LITTLE GOD? WHEN YOU ACCEPT THAT GORR IS RIGHT? ON THAT GRAND AND GLORIOUS DAY...
WHAT WILL YOU DO?
HAS YOUR MADNESS PASSED?
ODINSON?

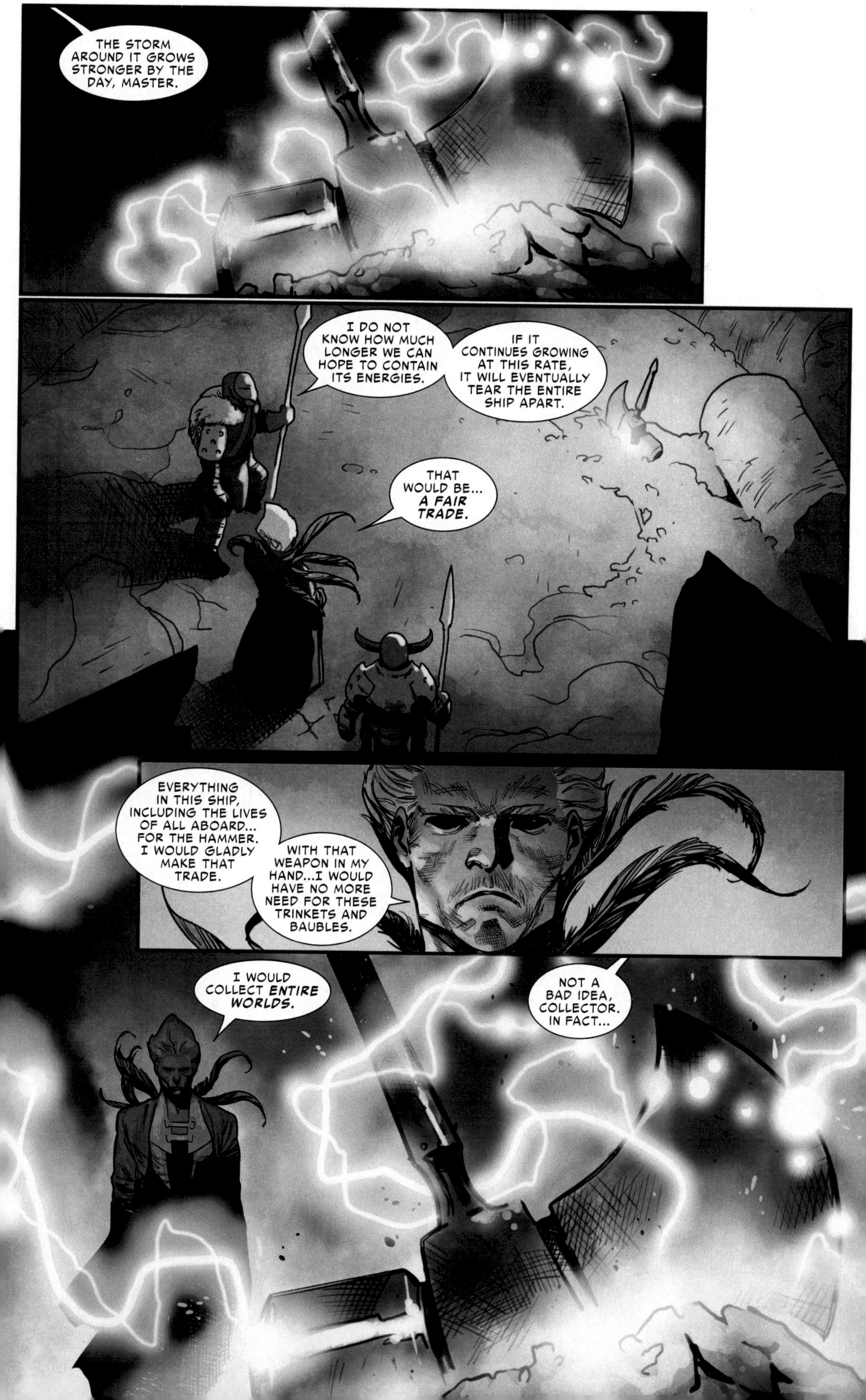
THE STORM AROUND IT GROWS STRONGER BY THE DAY, MASTER.
I DO NOT KNOW HOW MUCH LONGER WE CAN HOPE TO CONTAIN ITS ENERGIES.
IF IT CONTINUES GROWING AT THIS RATE, IT WILL EVENTUALLY TEAR THE ENTIRE SHIP APART.
THAT WOULD BE... ***A FAIR TRADE.***
EVERYTHING IN THIS SHIP, INCLUDING THE LIVES OF ALL ABOARD... FOR THE HAMMER. I WOULD GLADLY MAKE THAT TRADE.
WITH THAT WEAPON IN MY HAND...I WOULD HAVE NO MORE NEED FOR THESE TRINKETS AND BAUBLES.
I WOULD COLLECT ***ENTIRE WORLDS.***
NOT A BAD IDEA, COLLECTOR. IN FACT...

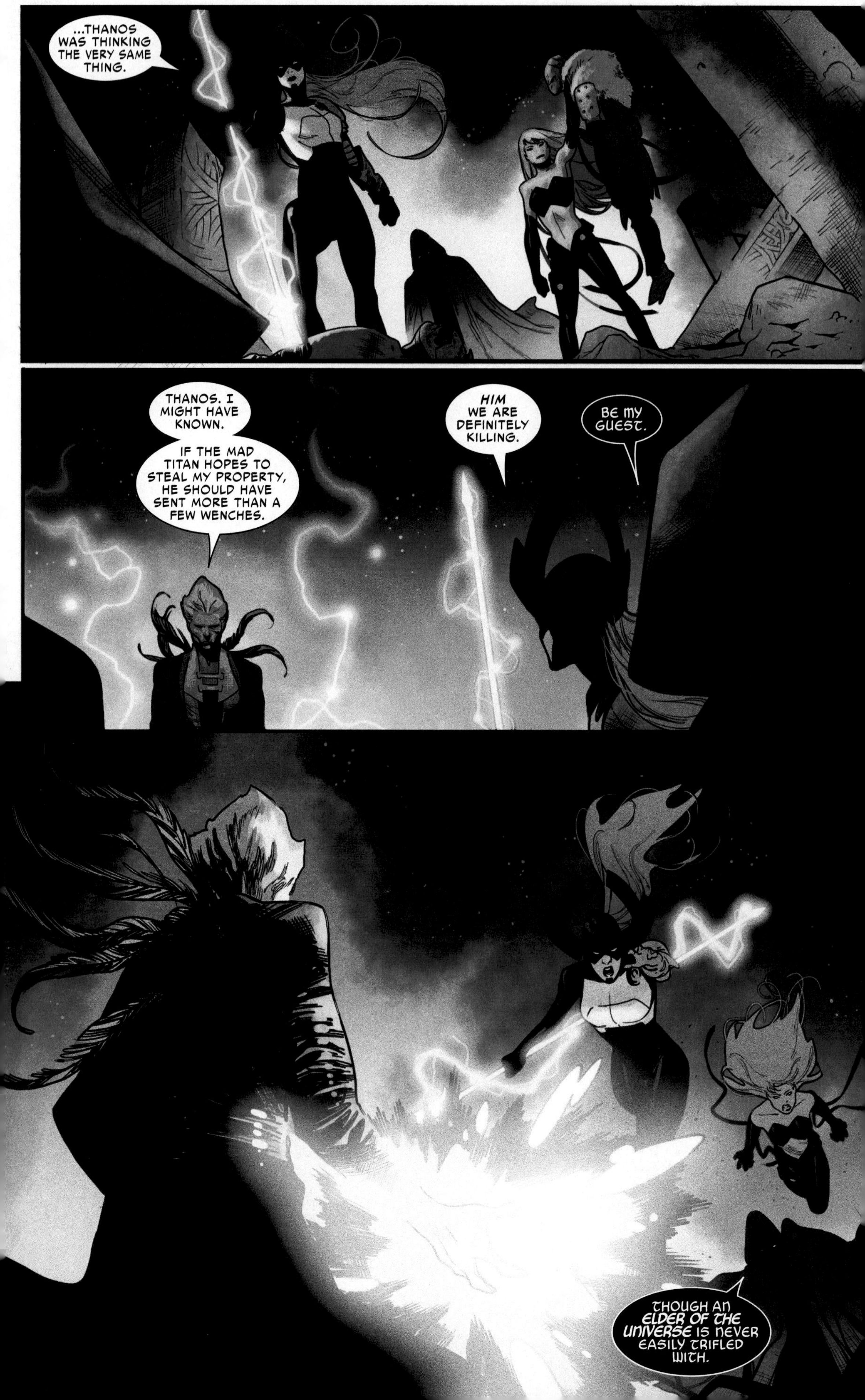
...THANOS WAS THINKING THE VERY SAME THING.
THANOS. I MIGHT HAVE KNOWN.
IF THE MAD TITAN HOPES TO STEAL MY PROPERTY, HE SHOULD HAVE SENT MORE THAN A FEW WENCHES.
HIM WE ARE DEFINITELY KILLING.
BE MY GUEST.
THOUGH AN *ELDER OF THE UNIVERSE* IS NEVER EASILY TRIFLED WITH.

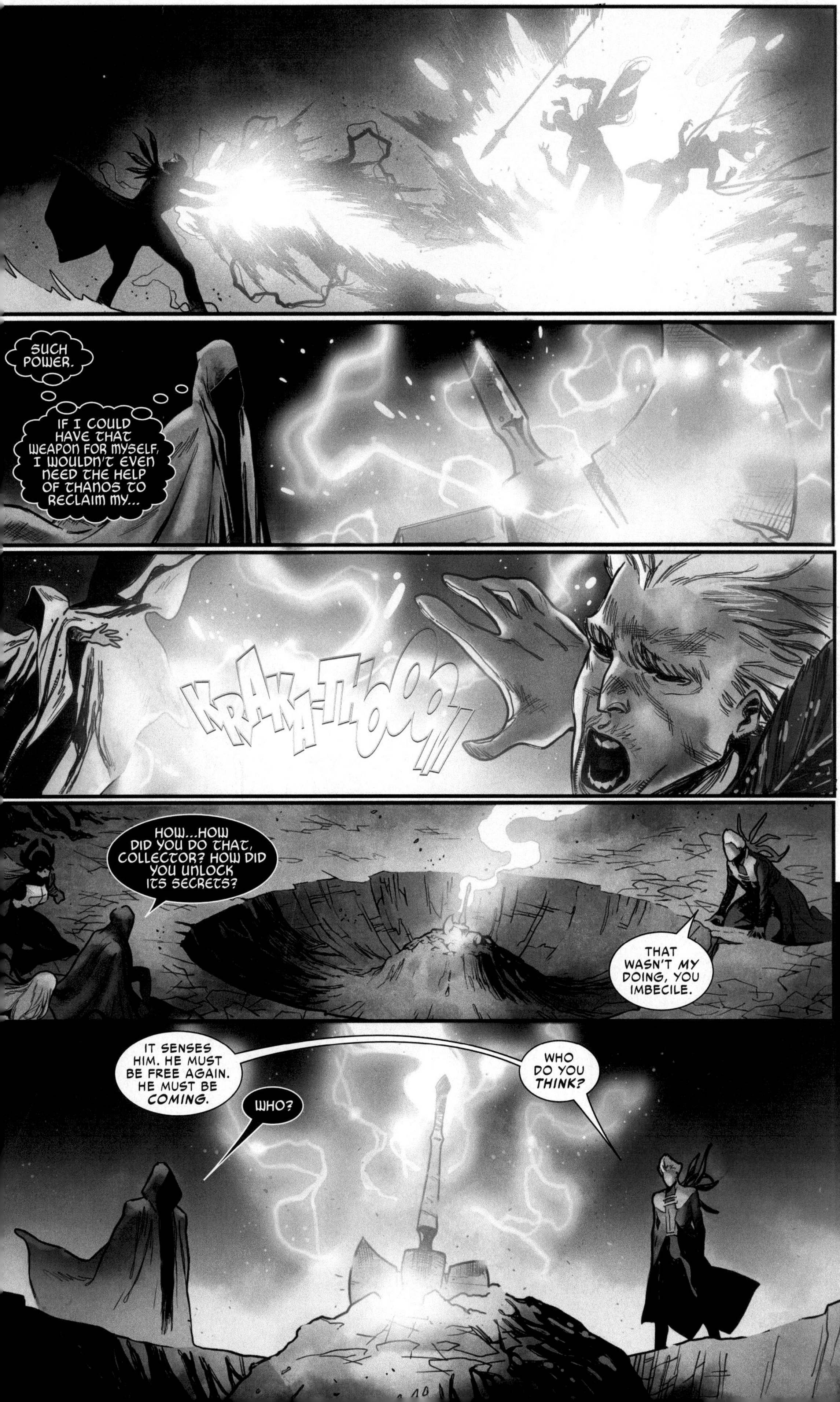
SUCH POWER.
IF I COULD HAVE THAT WEAPON FOR MYSELF, I WOULDN'T EVEN NEED THE HELP OF THANOS TO RECLAIM MY...
KRAKA-THOOOOM
HOW...HOW DID YOU DO THAT, COLLECTOR? HOW DID YOU UNLOCK ITS SECRETS?
THAT WASN'T MY DOING, YOU IMBECILE.
IT SENSES HIM. HE MUST BE FREE AGAIN. HE MUST BE COMING.
WHO?
WHO DO YOU THINK?

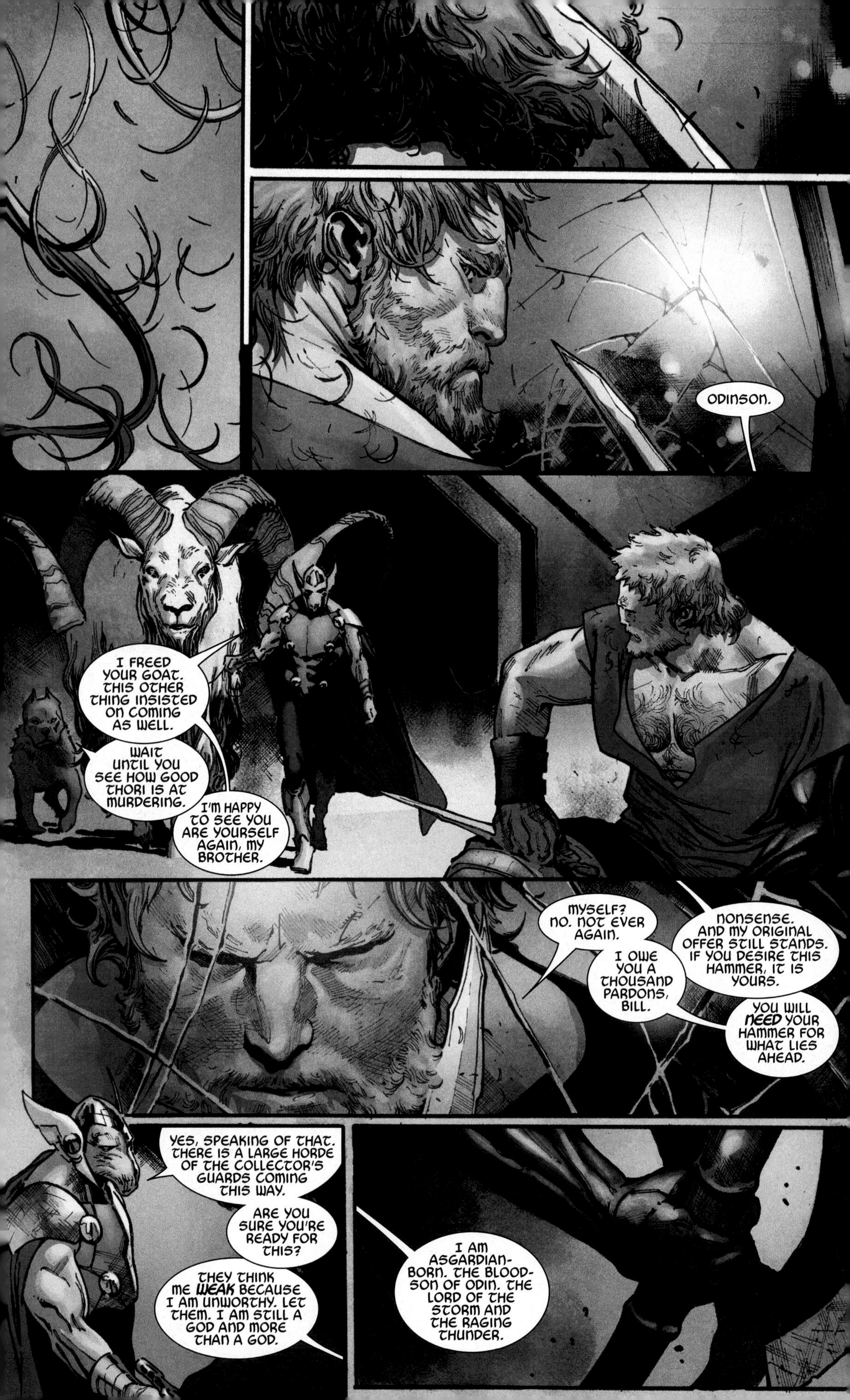
ODINSON.
I FREED YOUR GOAT. THIS OTHER THING INSISTED ON COMING AS WELL.
WAIT UNTIL YOU SEE HOW GOOD THORI IS AT MURDERING.
I'M HAPPY TO SEE YOU ARE YOURSELF AGAIN, MY BROTHER.
MYSELF? NO. NOT EVER AGAIN.
I OWE YOU A THOUSAND PARDONS, BILL.
NONSENSE. AND MY ORIGINAL OFFER STILL STANDS. IF YOU DESIRE THIS HAMMER, IT IS YOURS.
YOU WILL NEED YOUR HAMMER FOR WHAT LIES AHEAD.
YES, SPEAKING OF THAT. THERE IS A LARGE HORDE OF THE COLLECTOR'S GUARDS COMING THIS WAY.
ARE YOU SURE YOU'RE READY FOR THIS?
THEY THINK ME WEAK BECAUSE I AM UNWORTHY. LET THEM. I AM STILL A GOD AND MORE THAN A GOD.
I AM ASGARDIAN-BORN. THE BLOOD-SON OF ODIN. THE LORD OF THE STORM AND THE RAGING THUNDER.

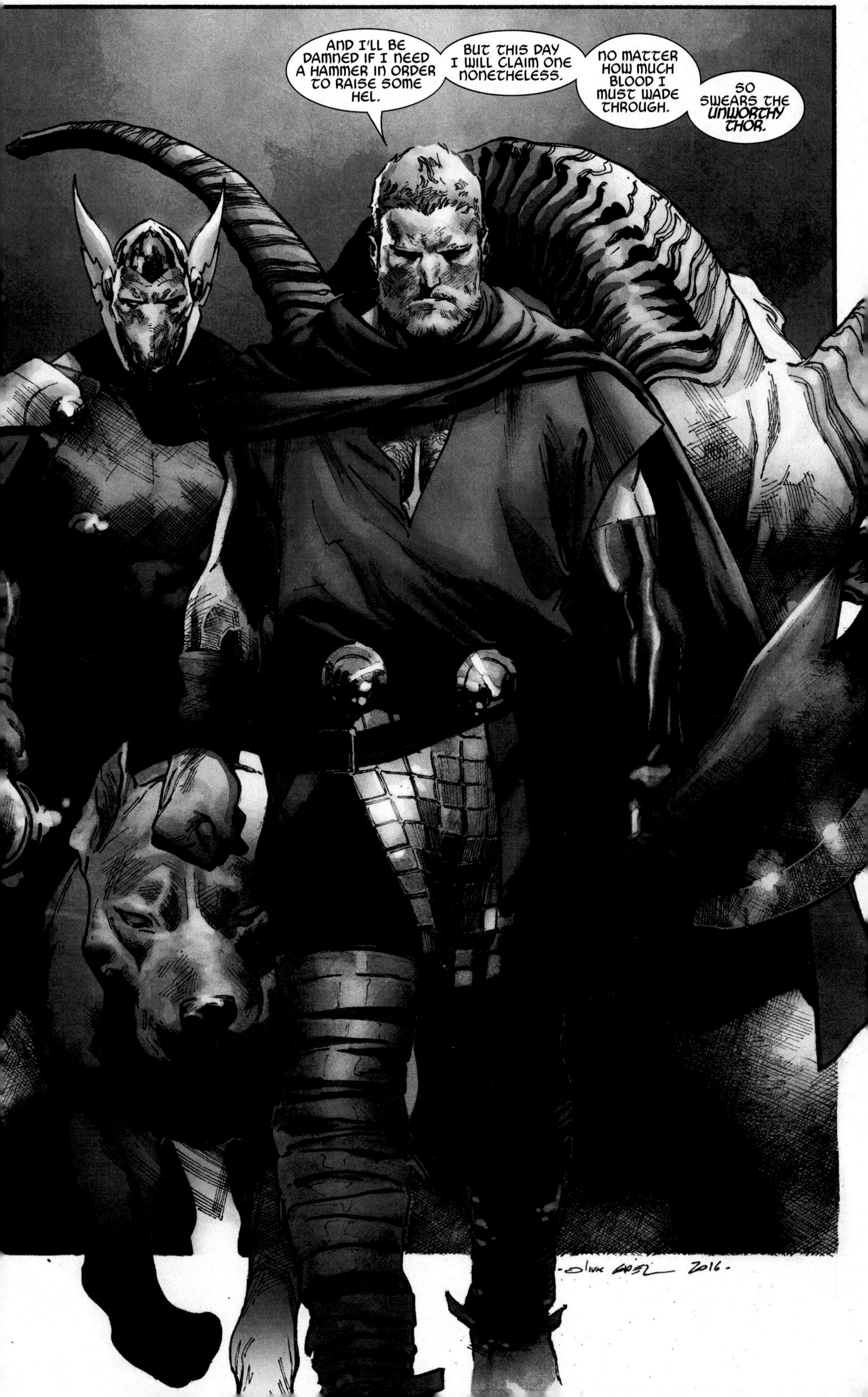
AND I'LL BE DAMNED IF I NEED A HAMMER IN ORDER TO RAISE SOME HEL.
BUT THIS DAY I WILL CLAIM ONE NONETHELESS.
NO MATTER HOW MUCH BLOOD I MUST WADE THROUGH.
SO SWEARS THE *UNWORTHY THOR*.

UNWORTHY THOR #1 VARIANT
BY **BRYAN HITCH** &
NATHAN FAIRBAIRN

UNWORTHY THOR #1
DIVIDED WE STAND VARIANT
BY **PASQUAL FERRY** &
FRANK D'ARMATA

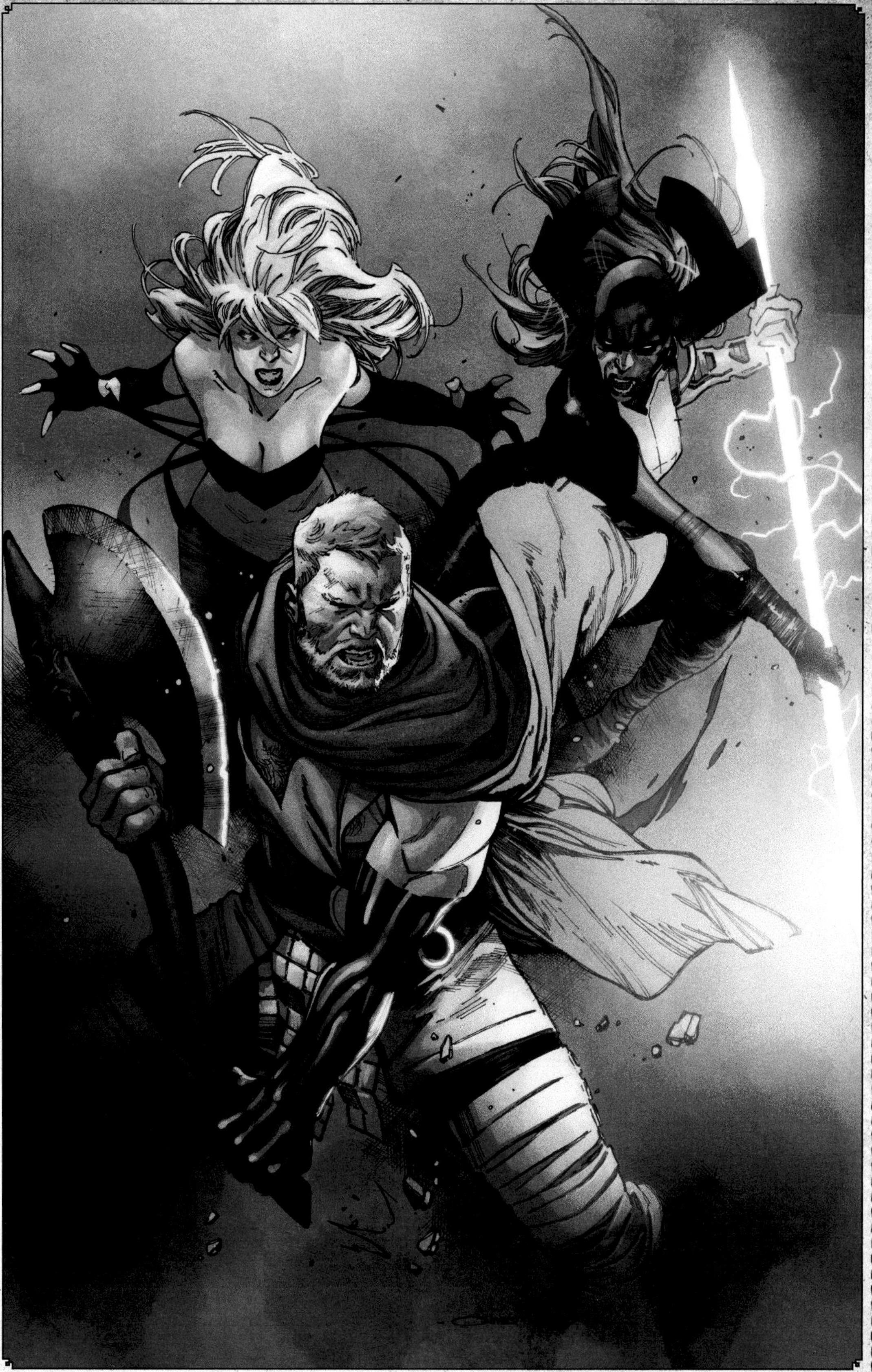

War of the Unworthy 4

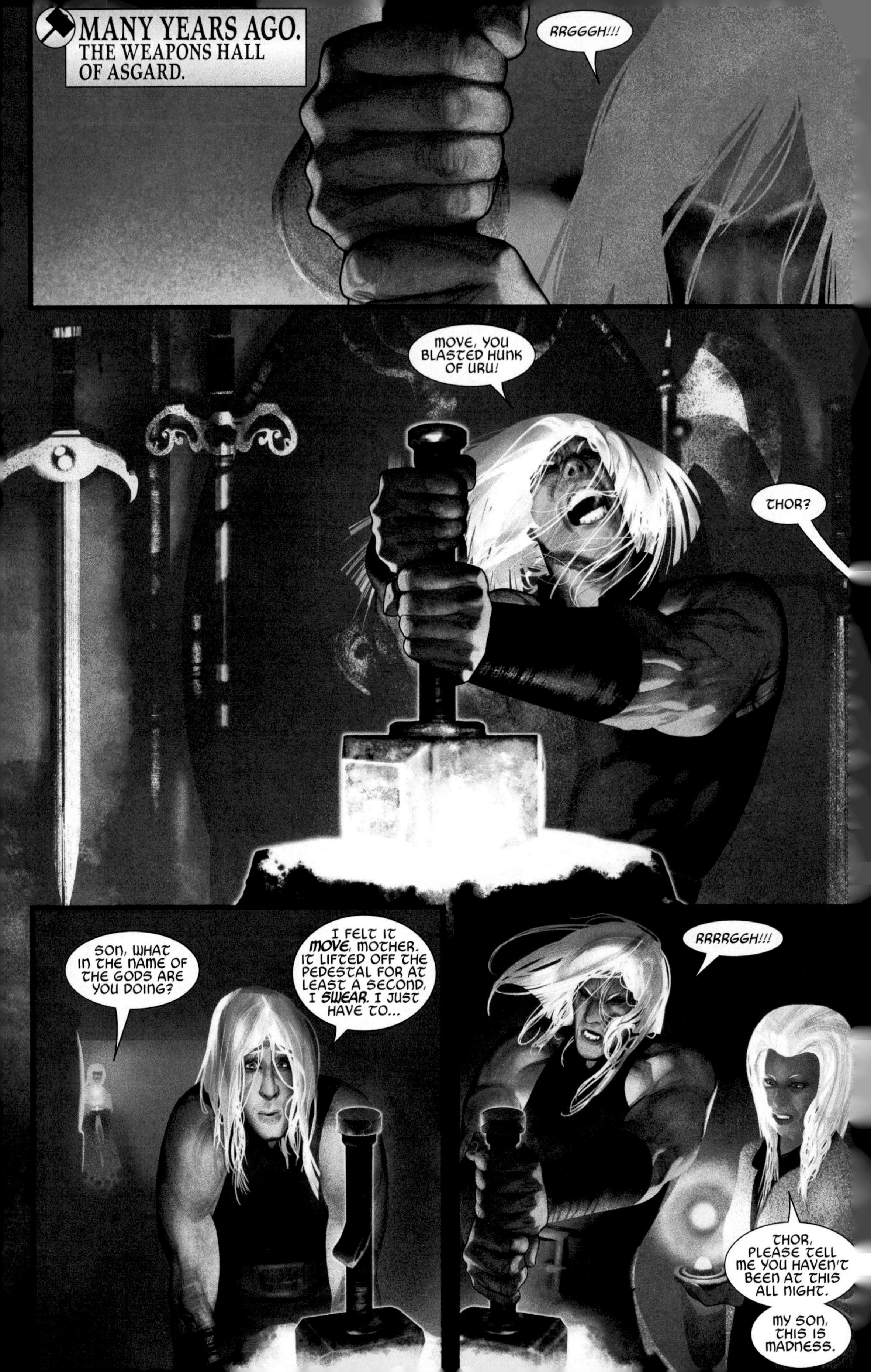
MANY YEARS AGO. THE WEAPONS HALL OF ASGARD.
RRGGGH!!!
MOVE, YOU BLASTED HUNK OF URU!
THOR?
SON, WHAT IN THE NAME OF THE GODS ARE YOU DOING?
I FELT IT MOVE, MOTHER. IT LIFTED OFF THE PEDESTAL FOR AT LEAST A SECOND, I SWEAR. I JUST HAVE TO...
RRRRGGH!!!
THOR, PLEASE TELL ME YOU HAVEN'T BEEN AT THIS ALL NIGHT.
MY SON, THIS IS MADNESS.

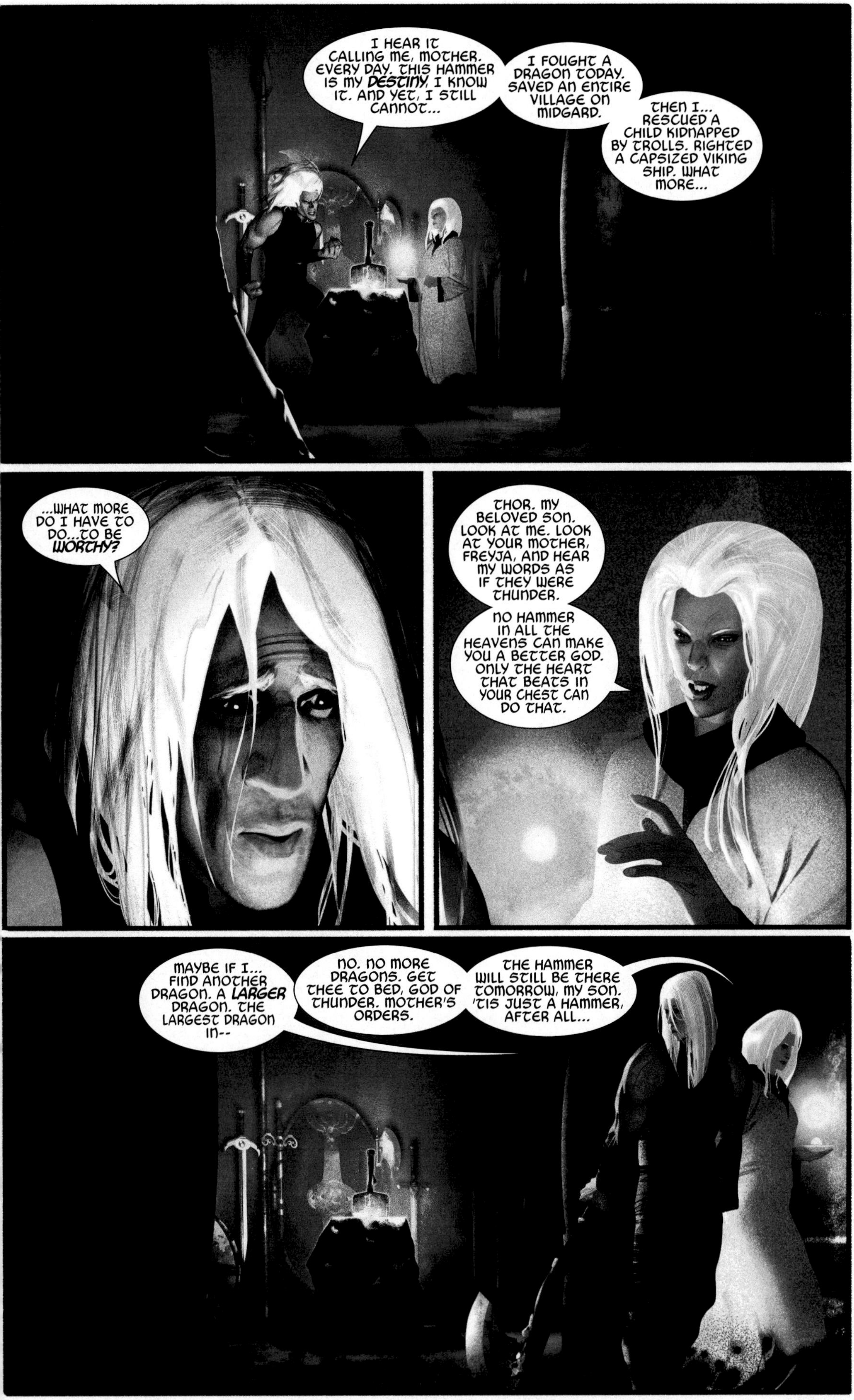
I HEAR IT CALLING ME, MOTHER. EVERY DAY. THIS HAMMER IS MY *DESTINY*, I KNOW IT. AND YET, I STILL CANNOT...
I FOUGHT A DRAGON TODAY. SAVED AN ENTIRE VILLAGE ON MIDGARD.
THEN I... RESCUED A CHILD KIDNAPPED BY TROLLS. RIGHTED A CAPSIZED VIKING SHIP. WHAT MORE...
...WHAT MORE DO I HAVE TO DO...TO BE *WORTHY?*
THOR. MY BELOVED SON. LOOK AT ME. LOOK AT YOUR MOTHER, FREYJA, AND HEAR MY WORDS AS IF THEY WERE THUNDER.
NO HAMMER IN ALL THE HEAVENS CAN MAKE YOU A BETTER GOD. ONLY THE HEART THAT BEATS IN YOUR CHEST CAN DO THAT.
MAYBE IF I... FIND ANOTHER DRAGON. A *LARGER* DRAGON. THE LARGEST DRAGON IN--
NO. NO MORE DRAGONS. GET THEE TO BED, GOD OF THUNDER. MOTHER'S ORDERS.
THE HAMMER WILL STILL BE THERE TOMORROW, MY SON. 'TIS JUST A HAMMER, AFTER ALL...

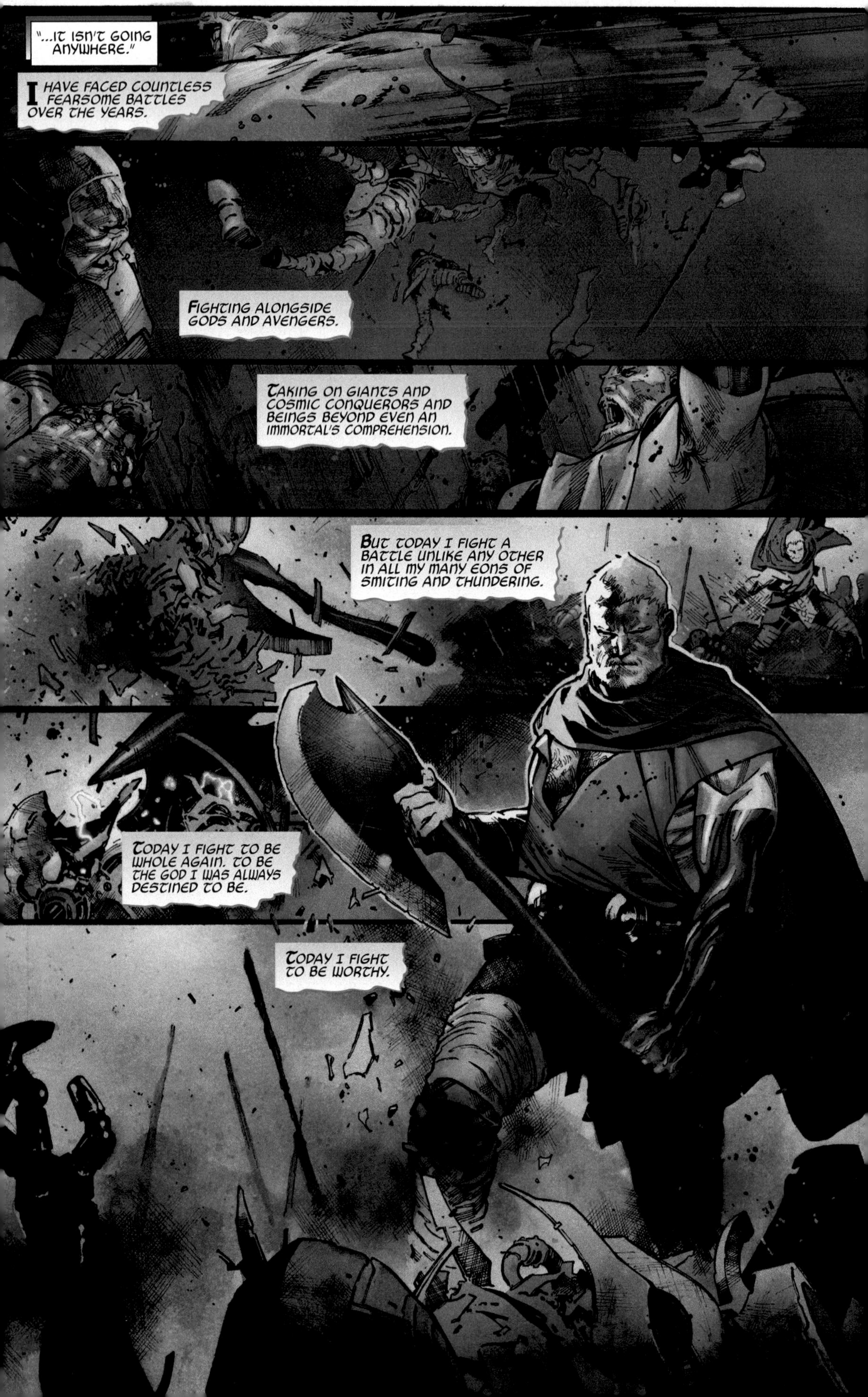
"...IT ISN'T GOING ANYWHERE."
I HAVE FACED COUNTLESS FEARSOME BATTLES OVER THE YEARS.
FIGHTING ALONGSIDE GODS AND AVENGERS.
TAKING ON GIANTS AND COSMIC CONQUERORS AND BEINGS BEYOND EVEN AN IMMORTAL'S COMPREHENSION.
BUT TODAY I FIGHT A BATTLE UNLIKE ANY OTHER IN ALL MY MANY EONS OF SMITING AND THUNDERING.
TODAY I FIGHT TO BE WHOLE AGAIN. TO BE THE GOD I WAS ALWAYS DESTINED TO BE.
TODAY I FIGHT TO BE WORTHY.

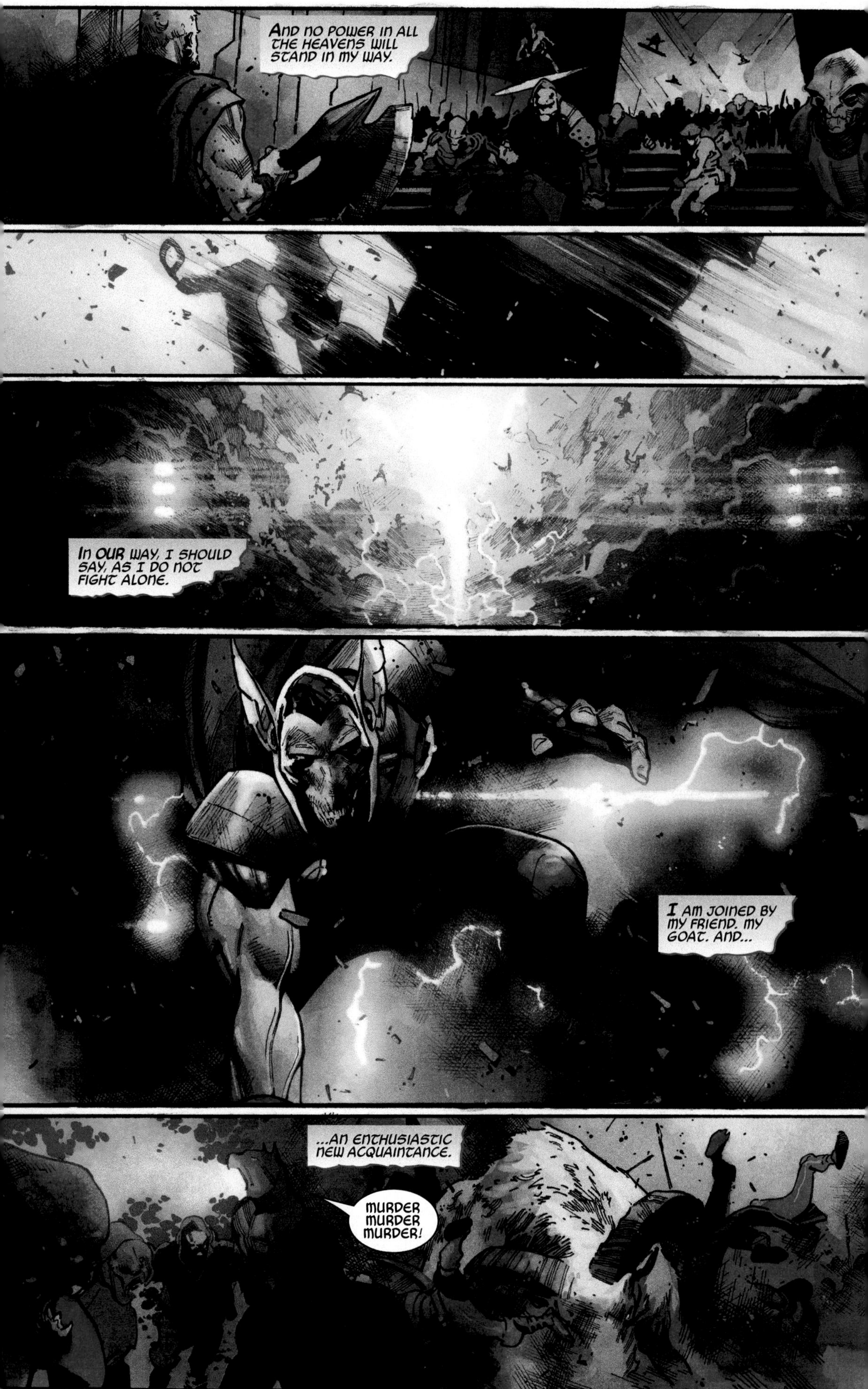

And no power in all the heavens will stand in my way.
In OUR way, I should say, as I do not fight alone.
I am joined by my friend. My goat. And...
...an enthusiastic new acquaintance.
Murder murder murder!

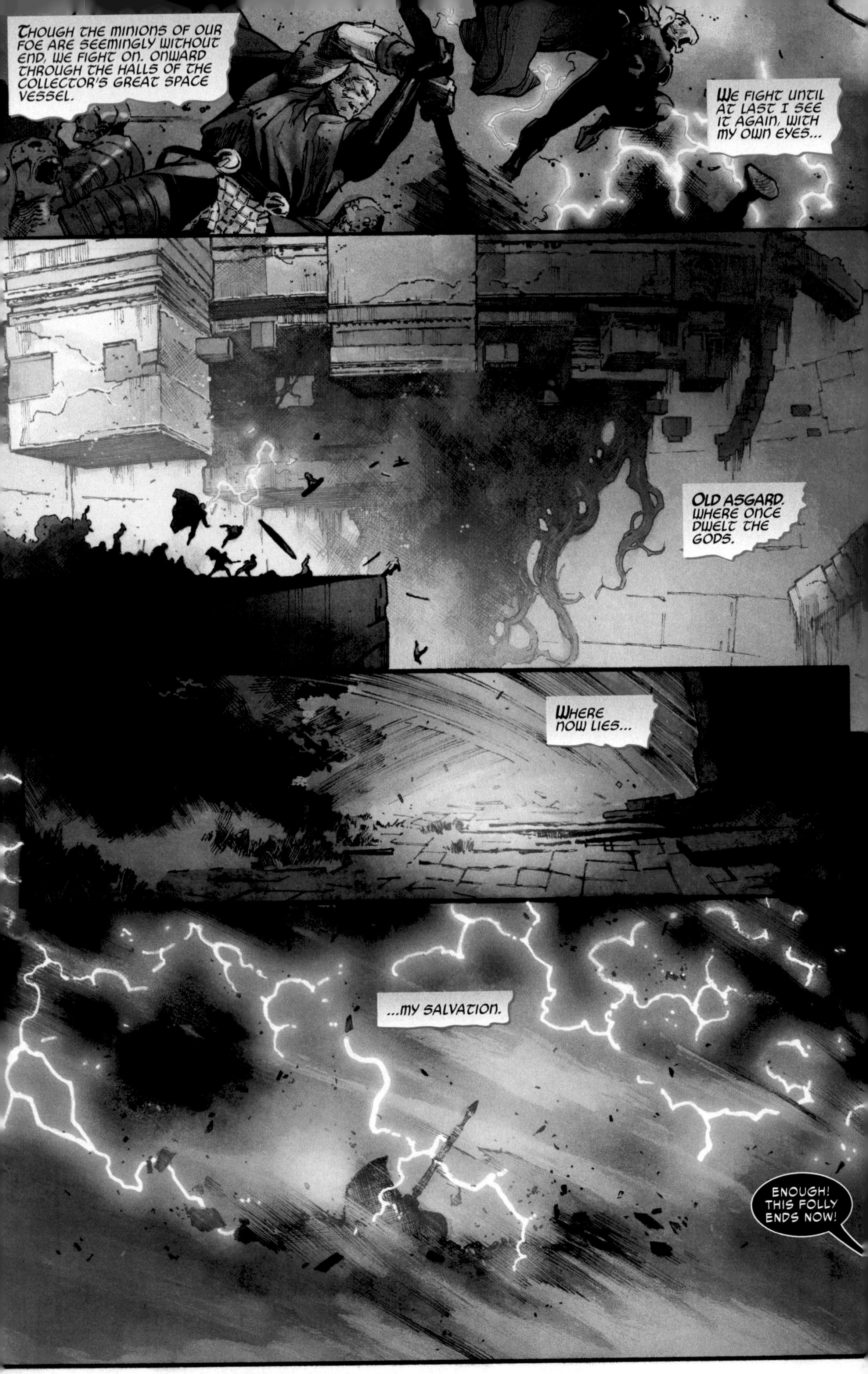
THOUGH THE MINIONS OF OUR FOE ARE SEEMINGLY WITHOUT END, WE FIGHT ON. ONWARD THROUGH THE HALLS OF THE COLLECTOR'S GREAT SPACE VESSEL.
WE FIGHT UNTIL AT LAST I SEE IT AGAIN, WITH MY OWN EYES...
OLD ASGARD. WHERE ONCE DWELT THE GODS.
WHERE NOW LIES...
...MY SALVATION.
ENOUGH! THIS FOLLY ENDS NOW!

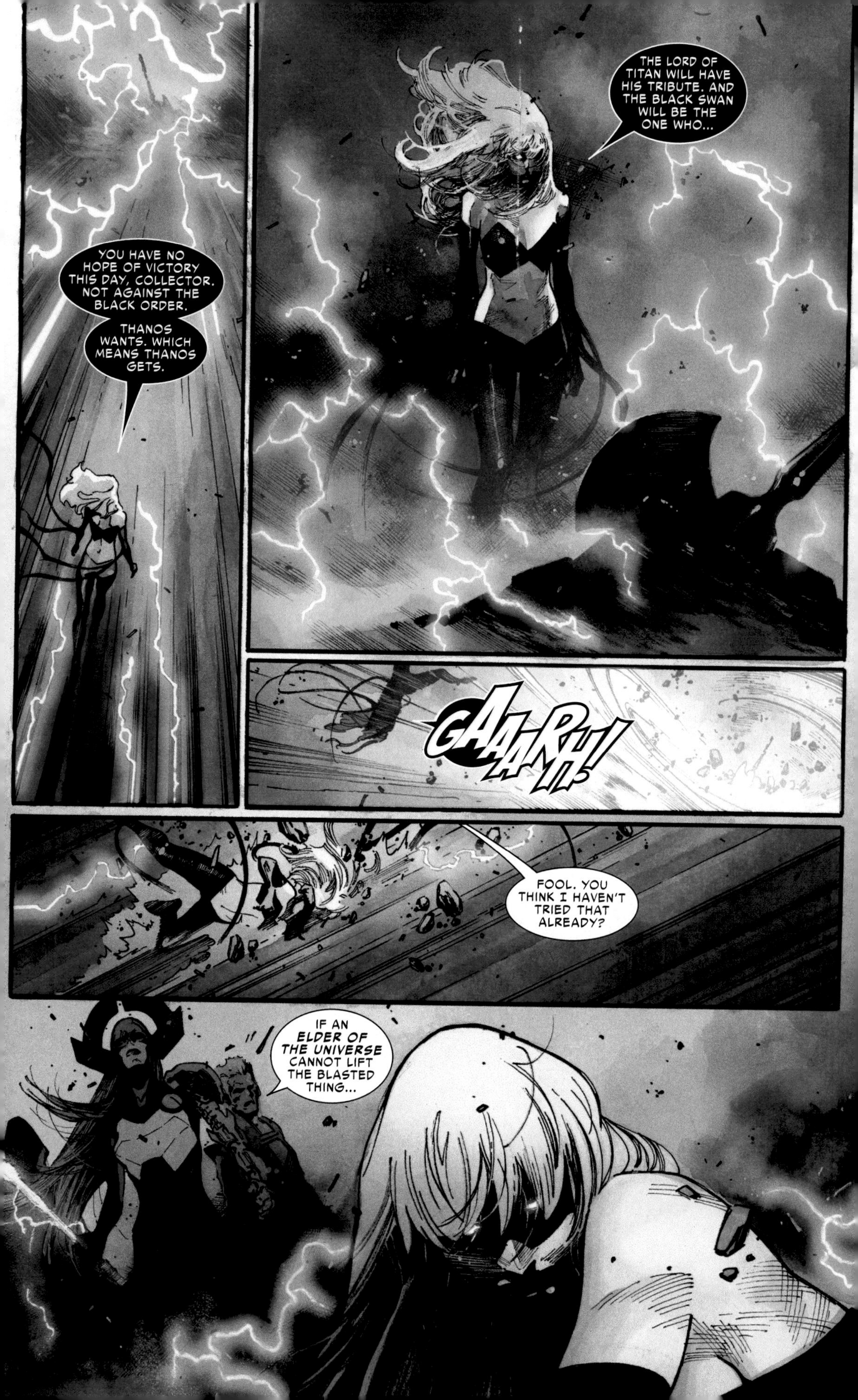
YOU HAVE NO HOPE OF VICTORY THIS DAY, COLLECTOR. NOT AGAINST THE BLACK ORDER.
THANOS WANTS. WHICH MEANS THANOS GETS.
THE LORD OF TITAN WILL HAVE HIS TRIBUTE. AND THE BLACK SWAN WILL BE THE ONE WHO...
GAAARHH!
FOOL. YOU THINK I HAVEN'T TRIED THAT ALREADY?
IF AN *ELDER OF THE UNIVERSE* CANNOT LIFT THE BLASTED THING...

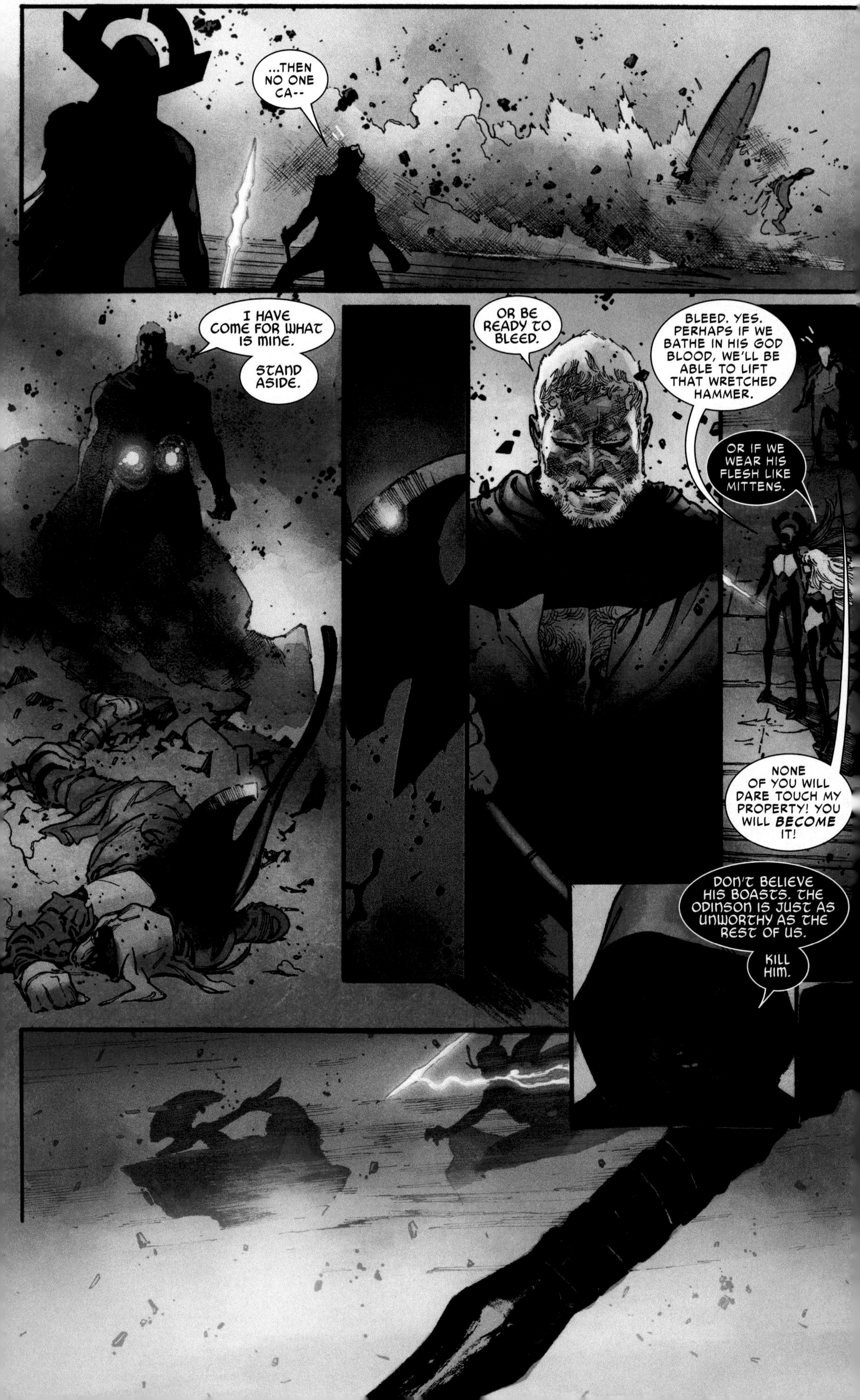
...THEN NO ONE CA--
I HAVE COME FOR WHAT IS MINE.
STAND ASIDE.
OR BE READY TO BLEED.
BLEED. YES. PERHAPS IF WE BATHE IN HIS GOD BLOOD, WE'LL BE ABLE TO LIFT THAT WRETCHED HAMMER.
OR IF WE WEAR HIS FLESH LIKE MITTENS.
NONE OF YOU WILL DARE TOUCH MY PROPERTY! YOU WILL BECOME IT!
DON'T BELIEVE HIS BOASTS. THE ODINSON IS JUST AS UNWORTHY AS THE REST OF US.
KILL HIM.

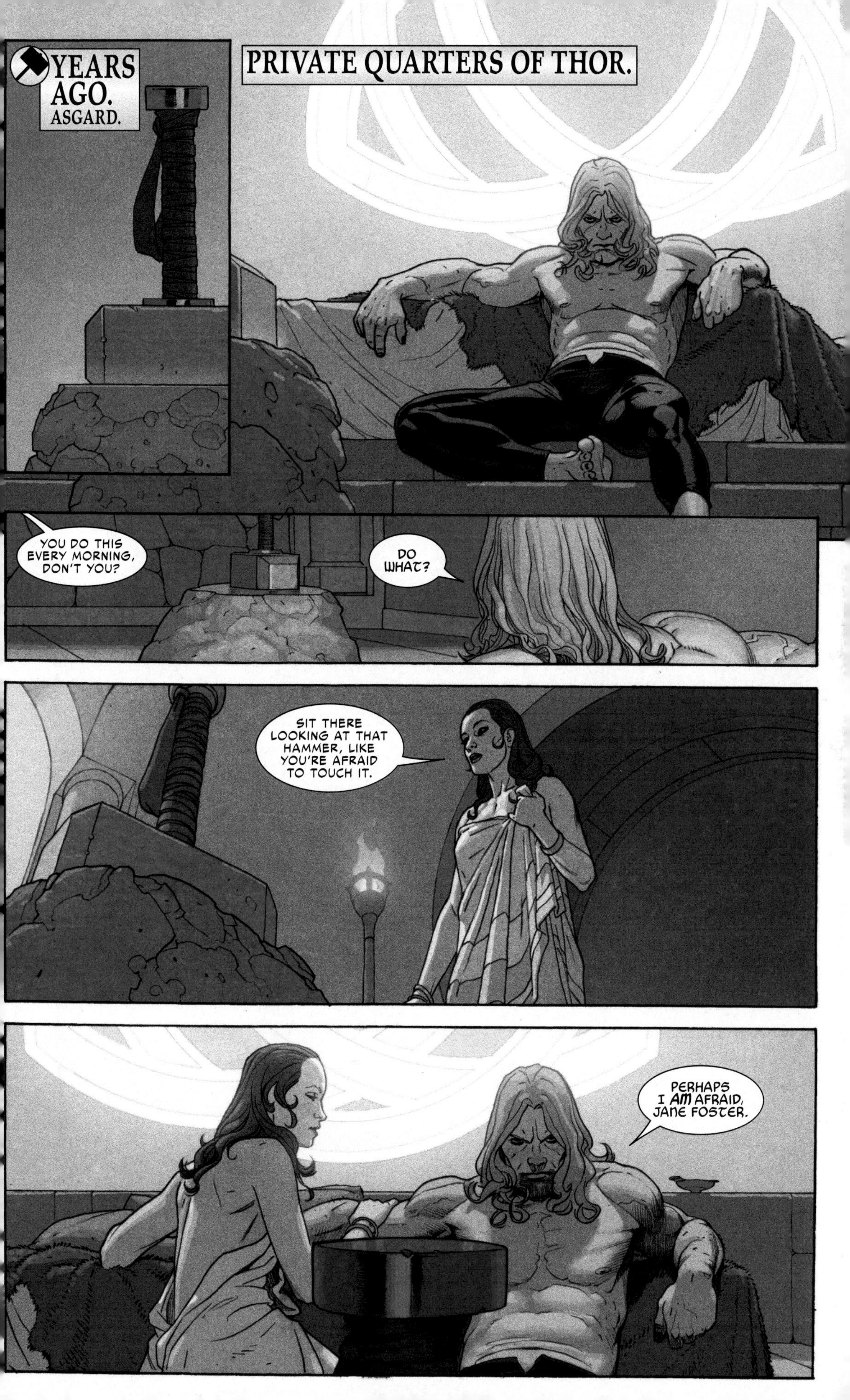
YEARS AGO. ASGARD.
PRIVATE QUARTERS OF THOR.
YOU DO THIS EVERY MORNING, DON'T YOU?
DO WHAT?
SIT THERE LOOKING AT THAT HAMMER, LIKE YOU'RE AFRAID TO TOUCH IT.
PERHAPS I AM AFRAID, JANE FOSTER.

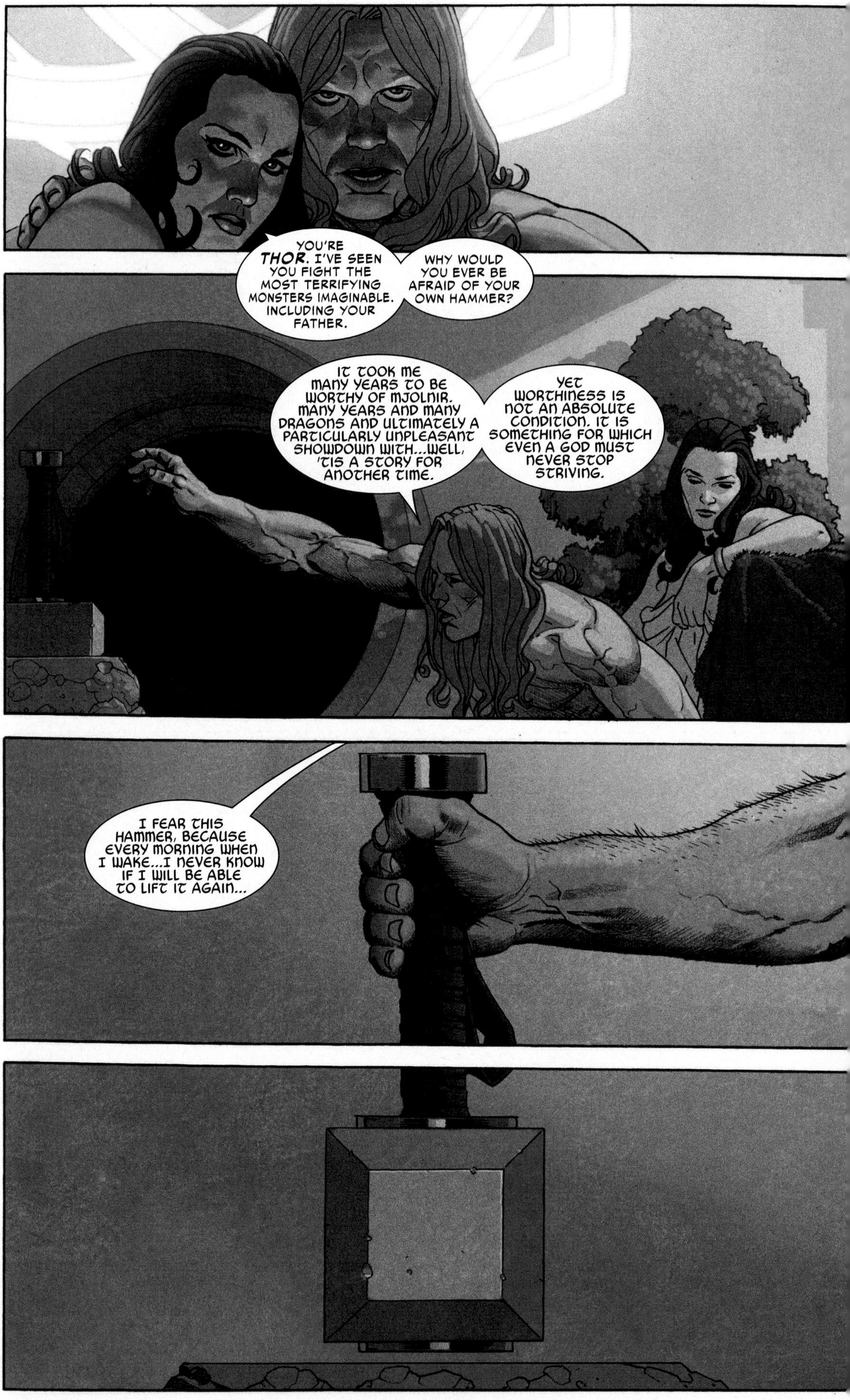
YOU'RE THOR. I'VE SEEN YOU FIGHT THE MOST TERRIFYING MONSTERS IMAGINABLE. INCLUDING YOUR FATHER.
WHY WOULD YOU EVER BE AFRAID OF YOUR OWN HAMMER?
IT TOOK ME MANY YEARS TO BE WORTHY OF MJOLNIR. MANY YEARS AND MANY DRAGONS AND ULTIMATELY A PARTICULARLY UNPLEASANT SHOWDOWN WITH...WELL, 'TIS A STORY FOR ANOTHER TIME.
YET WORTHINESS IS NOT AN ABSOLUTE CONDITION. IT IS SOMETHING FOR WHICH EVEN A GOD MUST NEVER STOP STRIVING.
I FEAR THIS HAMMER, BECAUSE EVERY MORNING WHEN I WAKE...I NEVER KNOW IF I WILL BE ABLE TO LIFT IT AGAIN...

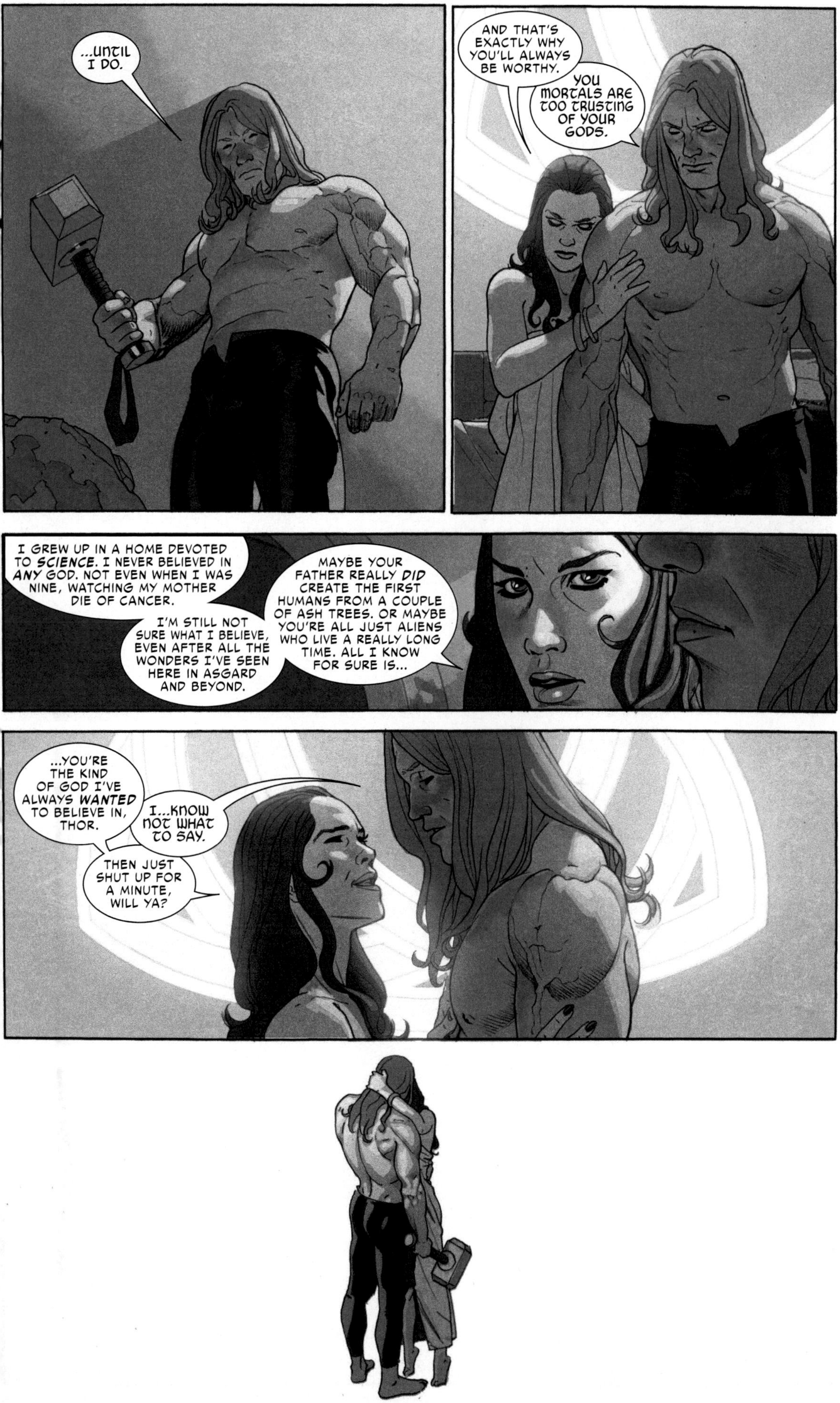
...UNTIL I DO.
AND THAT'S EXACTLY WHY YOU'LL ALWAYS BE WORTHY.
YOU MORTALS ARE TOO TRUSTING OF YOUR GODS.
I GREW UP IN A HOME DEVOTED TO SCIENCE. I NEVER BELIEVED IN ANY GOD. NOT EVEN WHEN I WAS NINE, WATCHING MY MOTHER DIE OF CANCER.
I'M STILL NOT SURE WHAT I BELIEVE, EVEN AFTER ALL THE WONDERS I'VE SEEN HERE IN ASGARD AND BEYOND.
MAYBE YOUR FATHER REALLY DID CREATE THE FIRST HUMANS FROM A COUPLE OF ASH TREES. OR MAYBE YOU'RE ALL JUST ALIENS WHO LIVE A REALLY LONG TIME. ALL I KNOW FOR SURE IS...
...YOU'RE THE KIND OF GOD I'VE ALWAYS WANTED TO BELIEVE IN, THOR.
I...KNOW NOT WHAT TO SAY.
THEN JUST SHUT UP FOR A MINUTE, WILL YA?

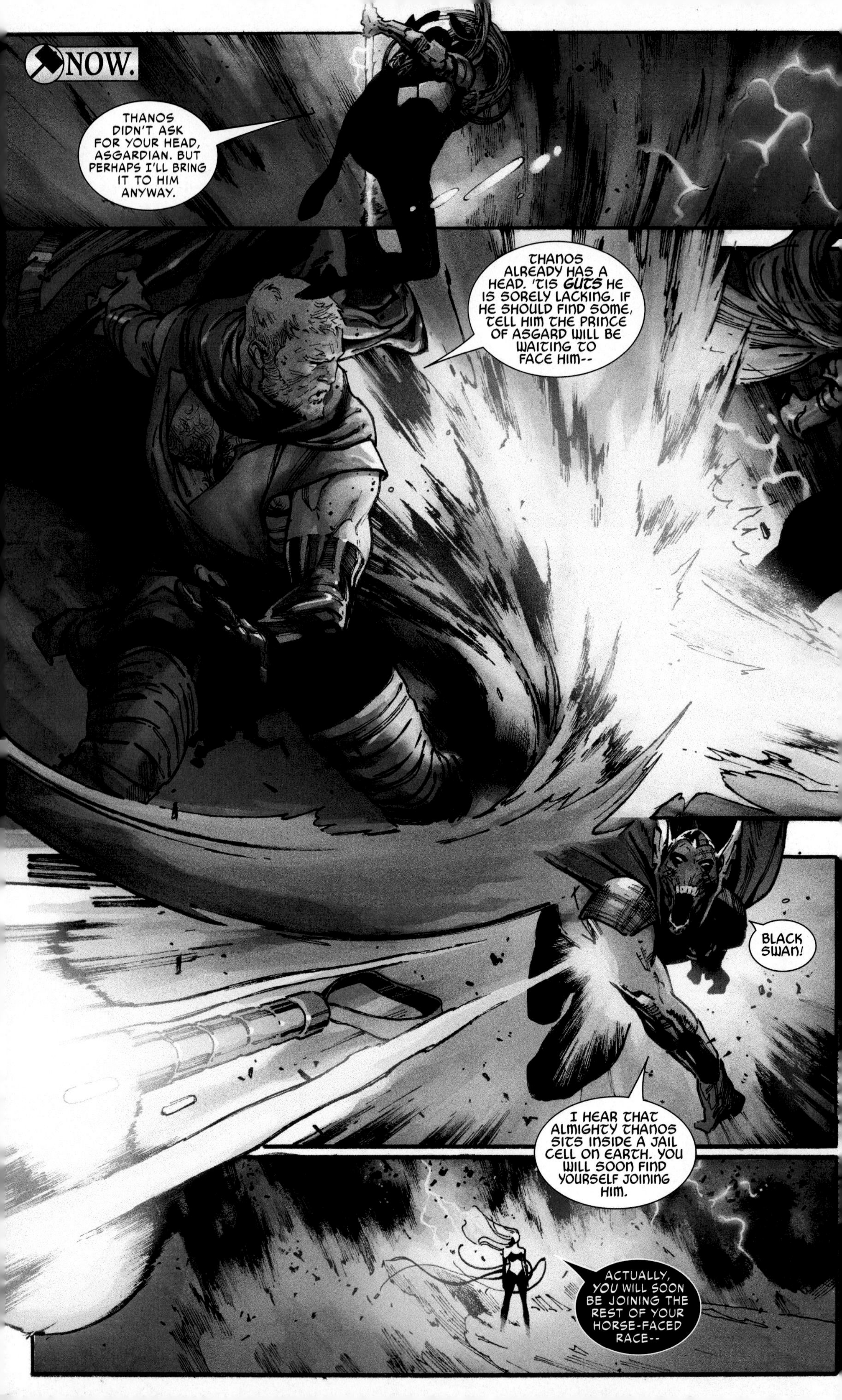
NOW.
THANOS DIDN'T ASK FOR YOUR HEAD, ASGARDIAN. BUT PERHAPS I'LL BRING IT TO HIM ANYWAY.
THANOS ALREADY HAS A HEAD. 'TIS GUTS HE IS SORELY LACKING. IF HE SHOULD FIND SOME, TELL HIM THE PRINCE OF ASGARD WILL BE WAITING TO FACE HIM--
BLACK SWAN!
I HEAR THAT ALMIGHTY THANOS SITS INSIDE A JAIL CELL ON EARTH. YOU WILL SOON FIND YOURSELF JOINING HIM.
ACTUALLY, YOU WILL SOON BE JOINING THE REST OF YOUR HORSE-FACED RACE--

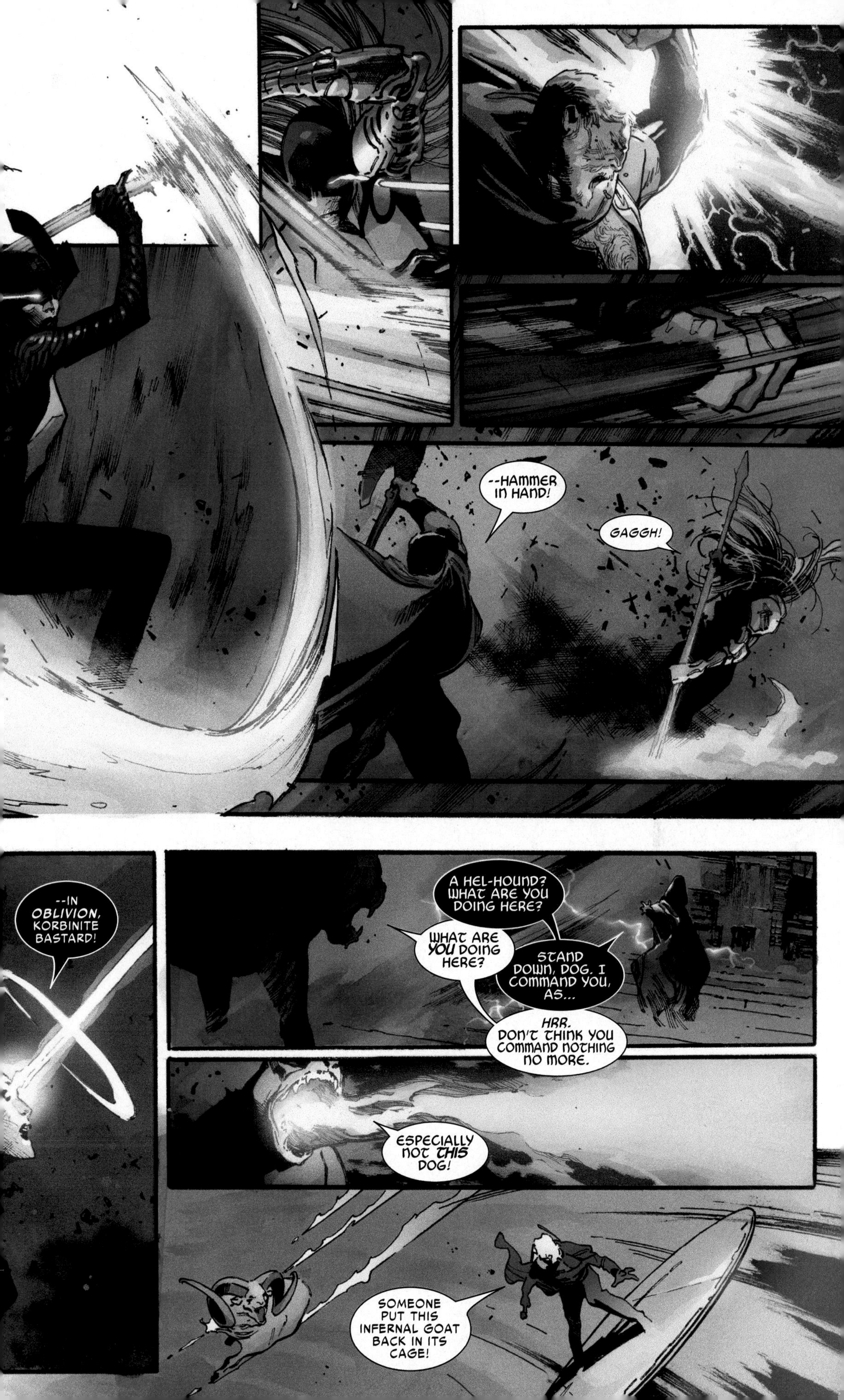
--HAMMER IN HAND!
GAGGH!
--IN OBLIVION, KORBINITE BASTARD!
A HEL-HOUND? WHAT ARE YOU DOING HERE?
WHAT ARE YOU DOING HERE?
STAND DOWN, DOG. I COMMAND YOU, AS...
HRR. DON'T THINK YOU COMMAND NOTHING NO MORE.
ESPECIALLY NOT THIS DOG!
SOMEONE PUT THIS INFERNAL GOAT BACK IN ITS CAGE!

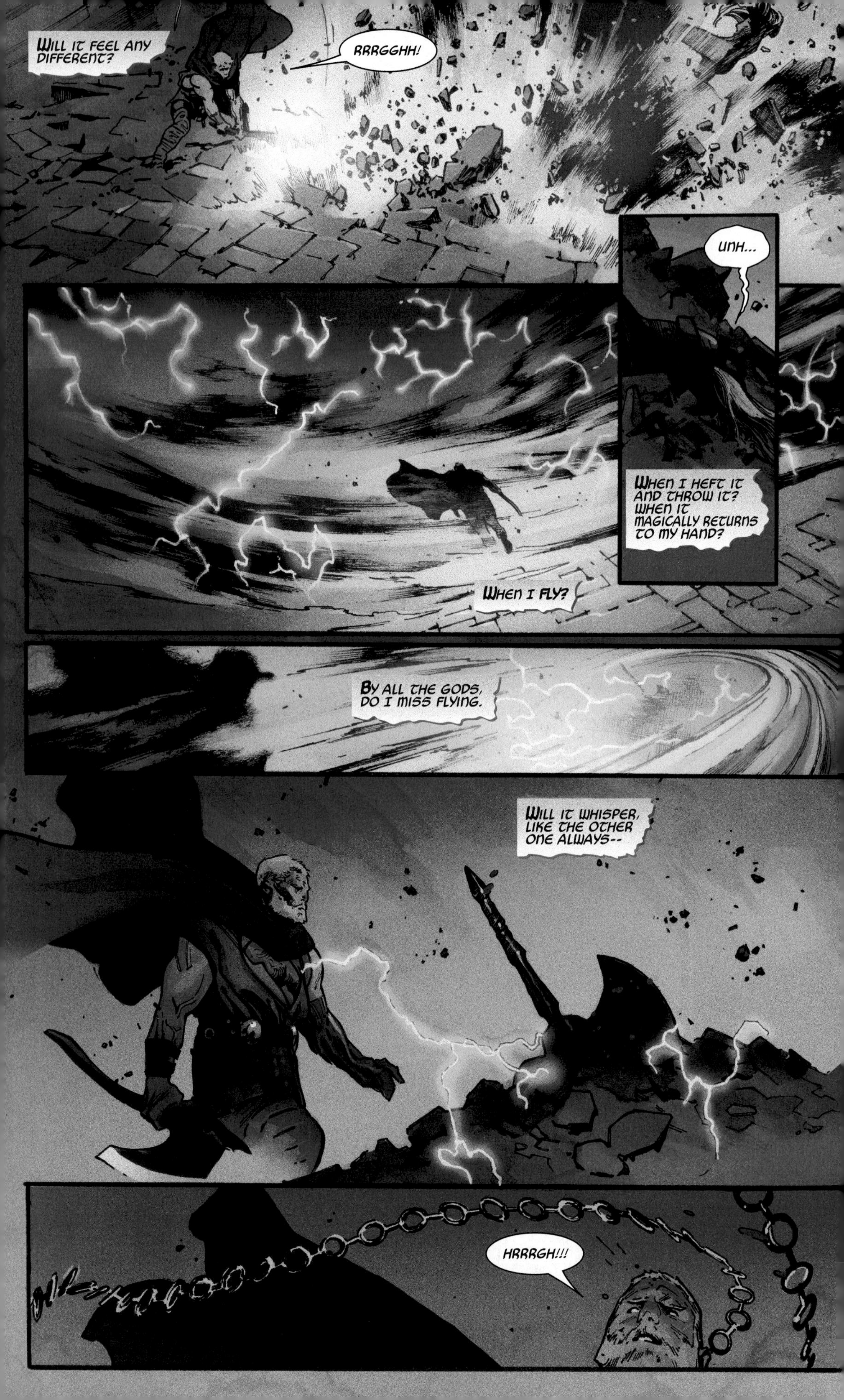
WILL IT FEEL ANY DIFFERENT?
RRRGGHH!
UNH...
WHEN I HEFT IT AND THROW IT? WHEN IT MAGICALLY RETURNS TO MY HAND?
WHEN I FLY?
BY ALL THE GODS, DO I MISS FLYING.
WILL IT WHISPER, LIKE THE OTHER ONE ALWAYS--
HRRRGH!!!

I TOLD YOU, YOU UNWORTHY WASTE OF A THOR... THAT HAMMER BELONGS TO ME!
YOU ALL BELONG TO ME!
No, 'tis not a whisper.
The hammer is SCREAMING. Screaming like thunder.
The same words over and over.
"Where is my Thor?"

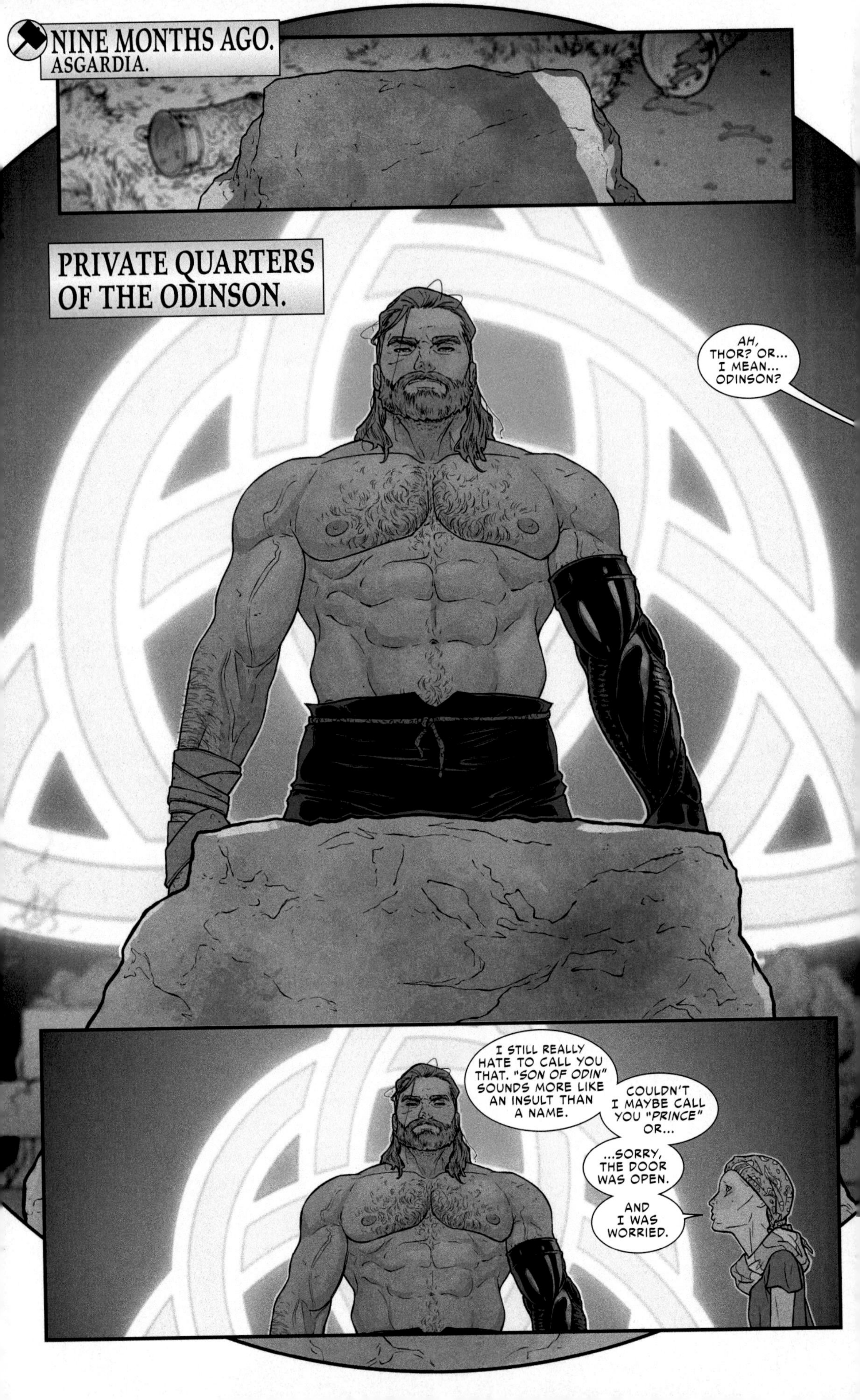
NINE MONTHS AGO.
ASGARDIA.
PRIVATE QUARTERS OF THE ODINSON.
AH, THOR? OR... I MEAN... ODINSON?
I STILL REALLY HATE TO CALL YOU THAT. "SON OF ODIN" SOUNDS MORE LIKE AN INSULT THAN A NAME.
COULDN'T I MAYBE CALL YOU "PRINCE" OR...
...SORRY, THE DOOR WAS OPEN.
AND I WAS WORRIED.

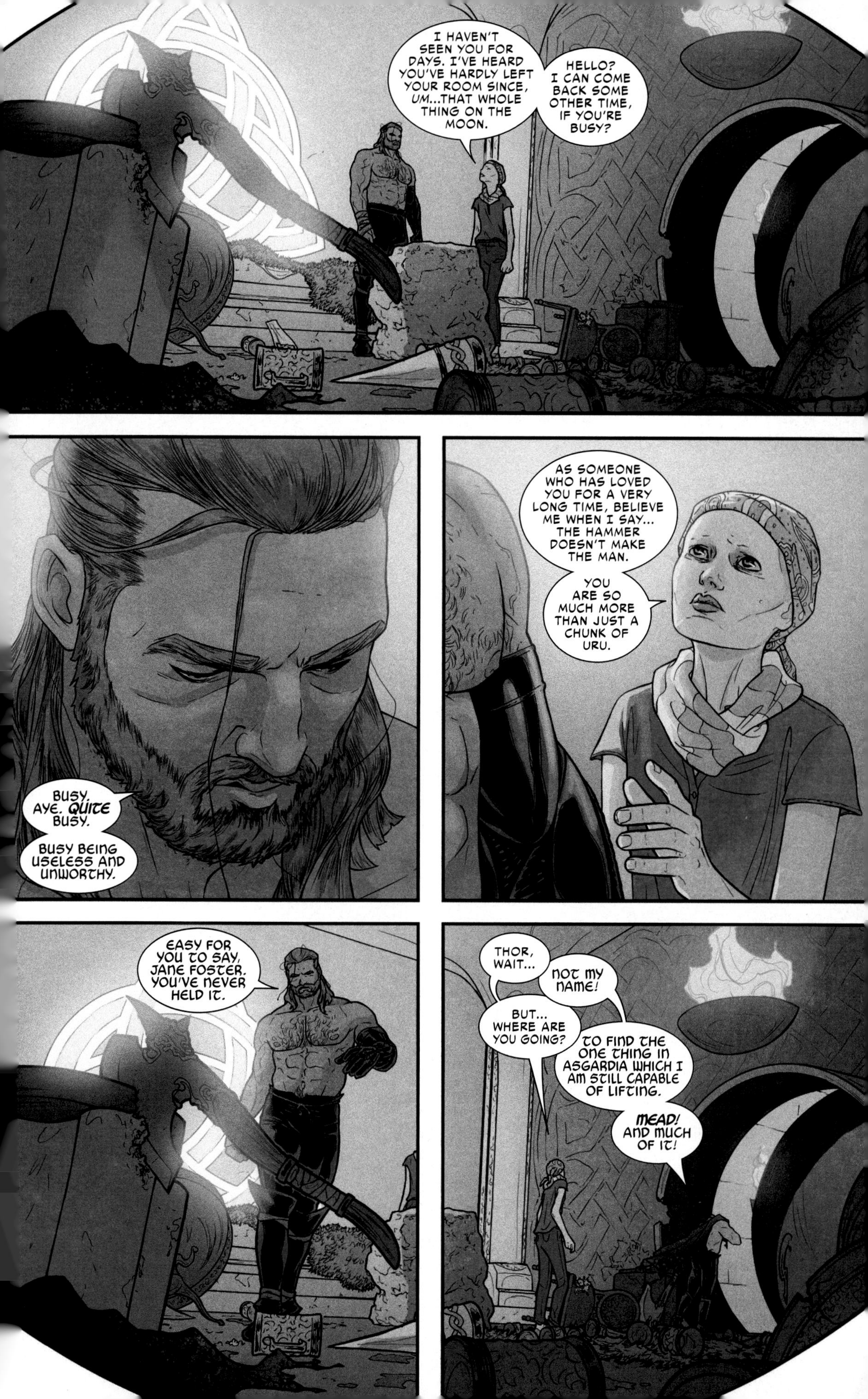
I HAVEN'T SEEN YOU FOR DAYS. I'VE HEARD YOU'VE HARDLY LEFT YOUR ROOM SINCE, UM...THAT WHOLE THING ON THE MOON.
HELLO? I CAN COME BACK SOME OTHER TIME, IF YOU'RE BUSY?
BUSY. AYE. QUITE BUSY.
BUSY BEING USELESS AND UNWORTHY.
AS SOMEONE WHO HAS LOVED YOU FOR A VERY LONG TIME, BELIEVE ME WHEN I SAY... THE HAMMER DOESN'T MAKE THE MAN.
YOU ARE SO MUCH MORE THAN JUST A CHUNK OF URU.
EASY FOR YOU TO SAY, JANE FOSTER. YOU'VE NEVER HELD IT.
THOR, WAIT...
NOT MY NAME!
BUT... WHERE ARE YOU GOING?
TO FIND THE ONE THING IN ASGARDIA WHICH I AM STILL CAPABLE OF LIFTING.
MEAD! AND MUCH OF IT!

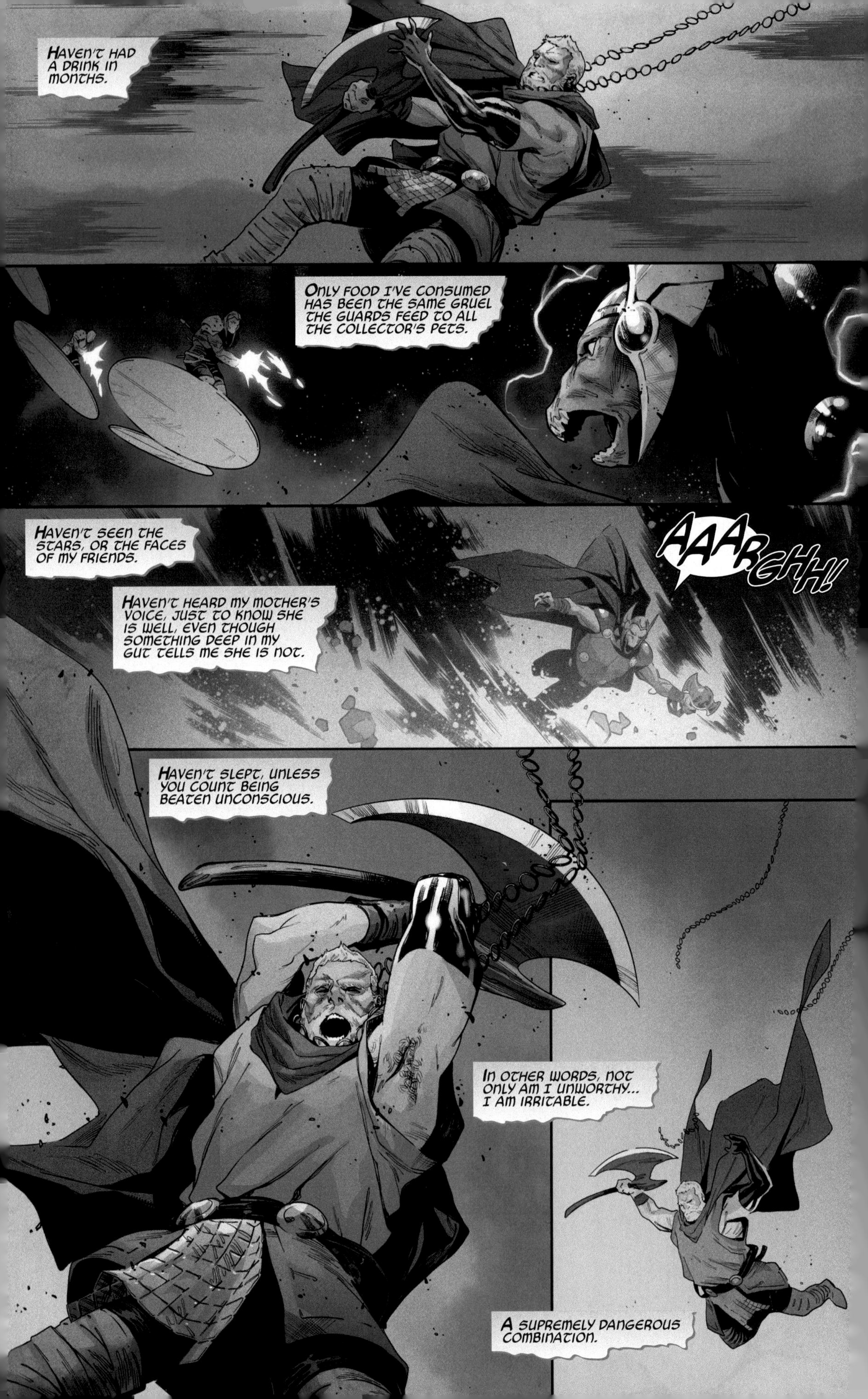
HAVEN'T HAD A DRINK IN MONTHS.
ONLY FOOD I'VE CONSUMED HAS BEEN THE SAME GRUEL THE GUARDS FEED TO ALL THE COLLECTOR'S PETS.
HAVEN'T SEEN THE STARS, OR THE FACES OF MY FRIENDS.
HAVEN'T HEARD MY MOTHER'S VOICE, JUST TO KNOW SHE IS WELL, EVEN THOUGH SOMETHING DEEP IN MY GUT TELLS ME SHE IS NOT.
AAARGHH!
HAVEN'T SLEPT, UNLESS YOU COUNT BEING BEATEN UNCONSCIOUS.
IN OTHER WORDS, NOT ONLY AM I UNWORTHY... I AM IRRITABLE.
A SUPREMELY DANGEROUS COMBINATION.

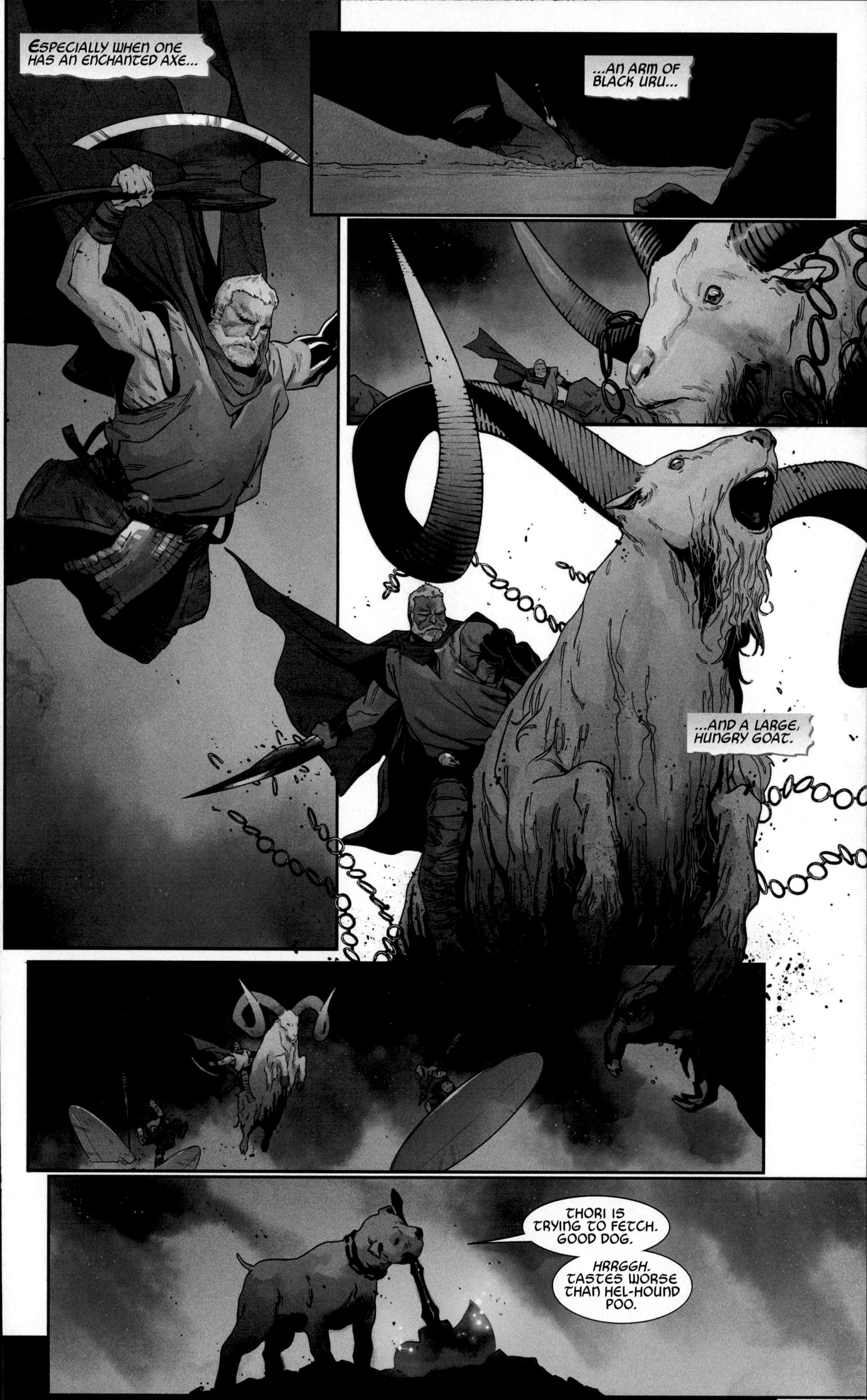
ESPECIALLY WHEN ONE HAS AN ENCHANTED AXE...
...AN ARM OF BLACK URU...
...AND A LARGE, HUNGRY GOAT.
THORI IS TRYING TO FETCH. GOOD DOG.
HRRGGH. TASTES WORSE THAN HEL-HOUND POO.

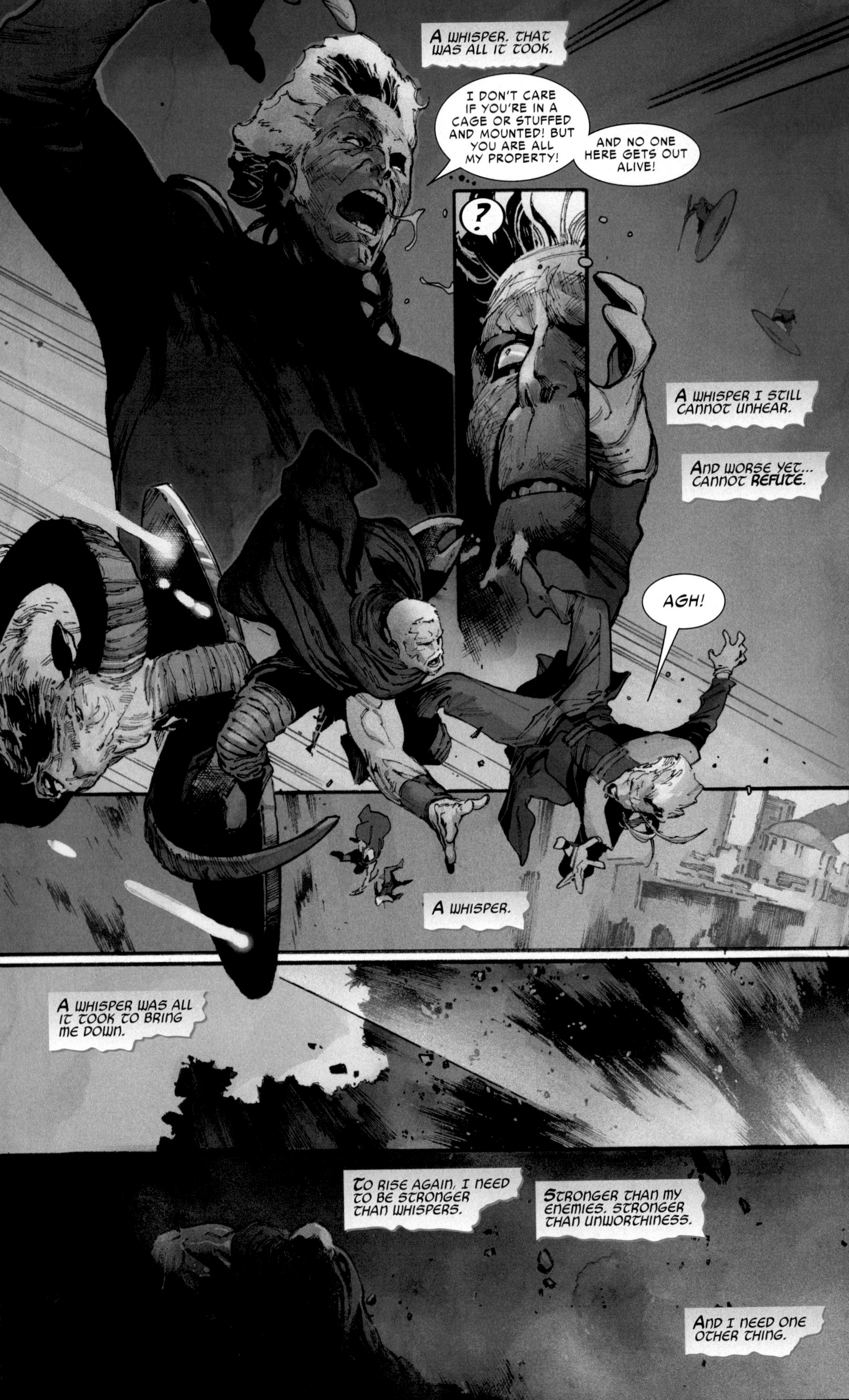
A WHISPER. THAT WAS ALL IT TOOK.
I DON'T CARE IF YOU'RE IN A CAGE OR STUFFED AND MOUNTED! BUT YOU ARE ALL MY PROPERTY!
AND NO ONE HERE GETS OUT ALIVE!
?
A WHISPER I STILL CANNOT UNHEAR.
AND WORSE YET... CANNOT REFUTE.
AGH!
A WHISPER.
A WHISPER WAS ALL IT TOOK TO BRING ME DOWN.
TO RISE AGAIN, I NEED TO BE STRONGER THAN WHISPERS.
STRONGER THAN MY ENEMIES. STRONGER THAN UNWORTHINESS.
AND I NEED ONE OTHER THING.

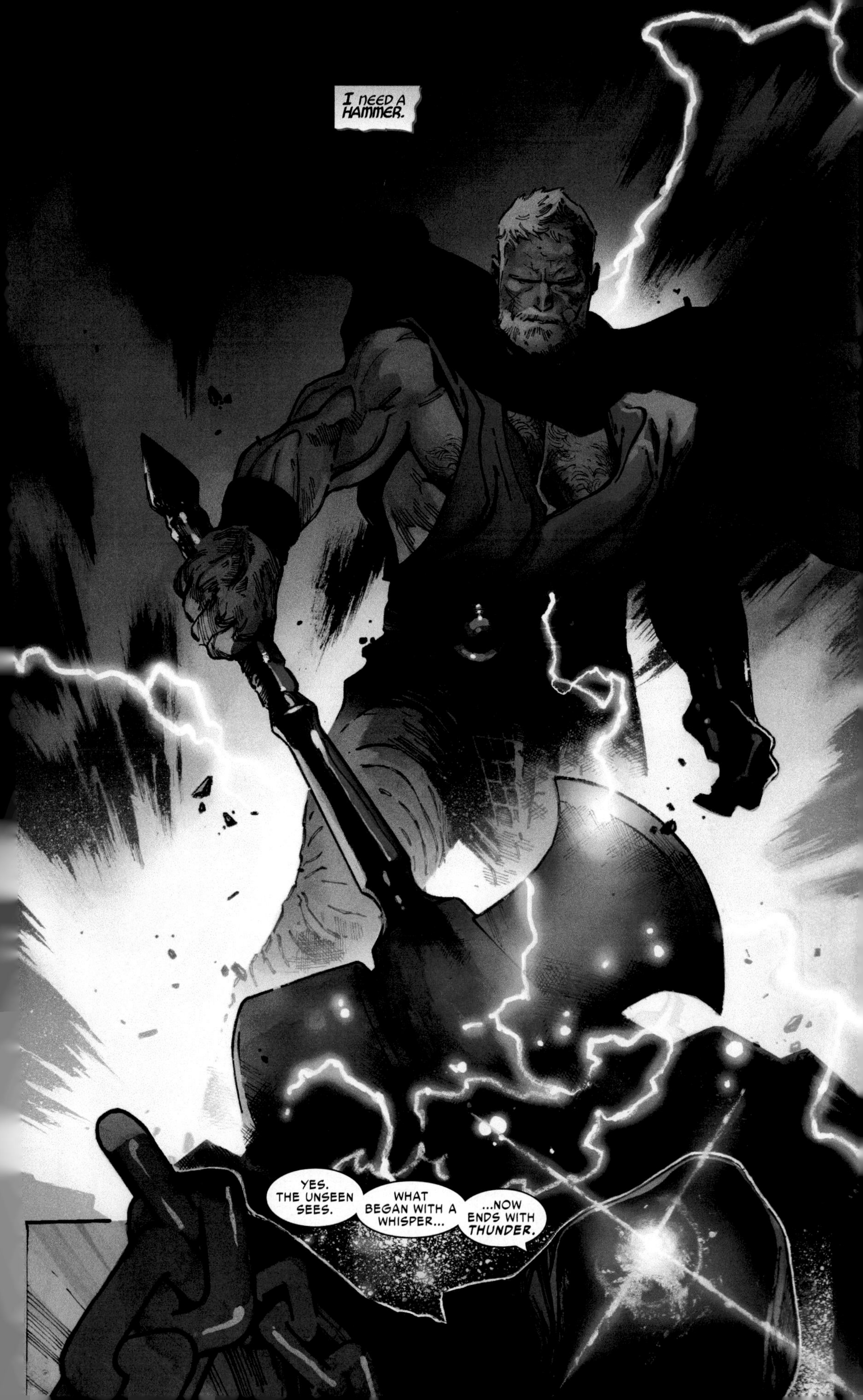
I NEED A HAMMER.
YES. THE UNSEEN SEES.
WHAT BEGAN WITH A WHISPER...
...NOW ENDS WITH THUNDER.

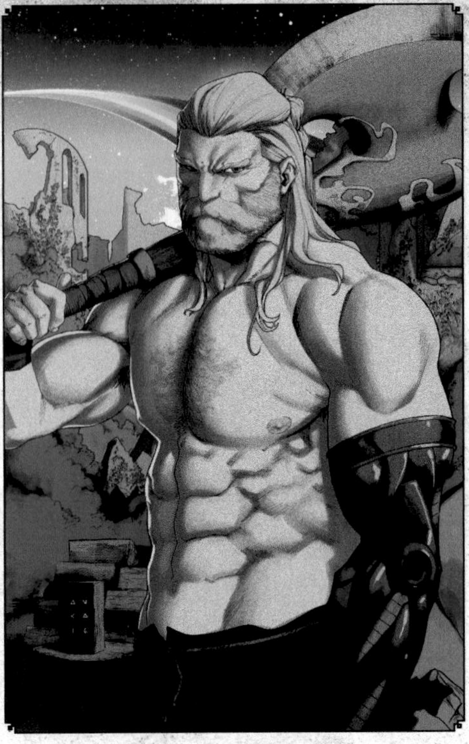

UNWORTHY THOR #2 VARIANT
BY **KRIS ANKA**

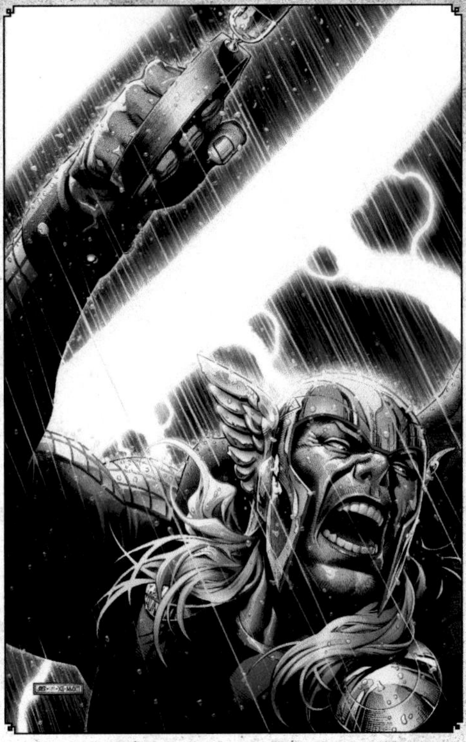

UNWORTHY THOR #2 VARIANT
BY **JIM CHEUNG** &
LAURA MARTIN

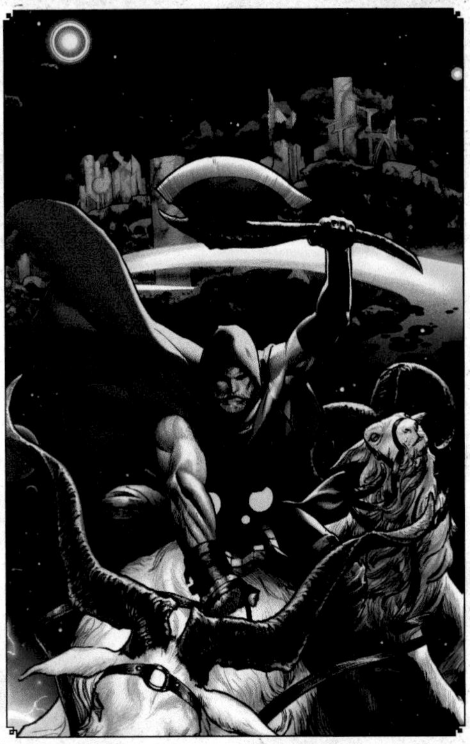

UNWORTHY THOR #3 VARIANT
BY **EMANUELA LUPACCHINO**
& **RICO RENZI**

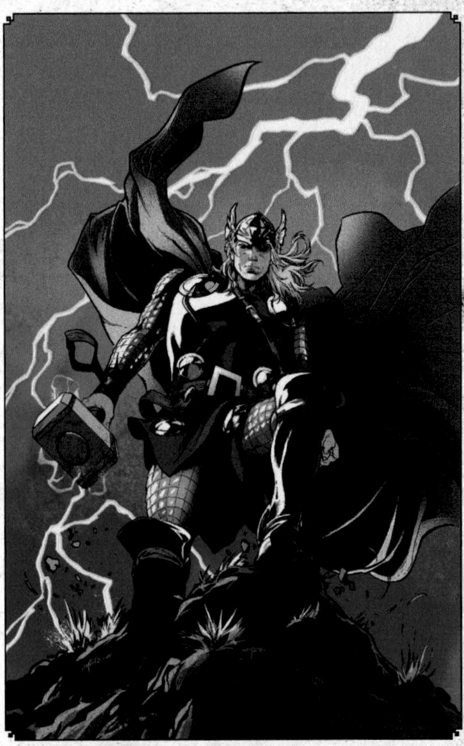

UNWORTHY THOR #3 VARIANT
BY **RYAN SOOK**

The Whisper

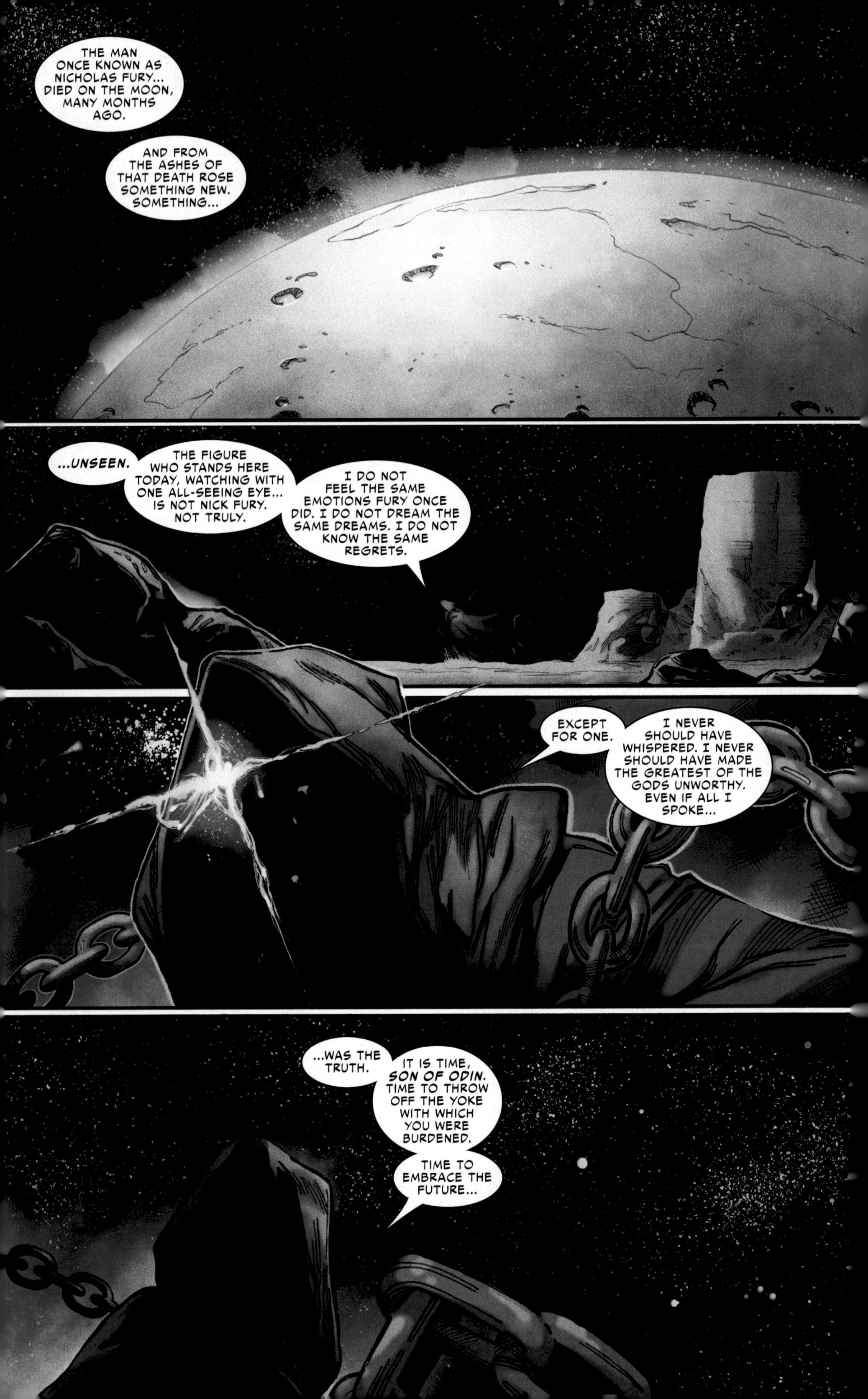
THE MAN ONCE KNOWN AS NICHOLAS FURY... DIED ON THE MOON, MANY MONTHS AGO.
AND FROM THE ASHES OF THAT DEATH ROSE SOMETHING NEW. SOMETHING...
...UNSEEN.
THE FIGURE WHO STANDS HERE TODAY, WATCHING WITH ONE ALL-SEEING EYE... IS NOT NICK FURY. NOT TRULY.
I DO NOT FEEL THE SAME EMOTIONS FURY ONCE DID. I DO NOT DREAM THE SAME DREAMS. I DO NOT KNOW THE SAME REGRETS.
EXCEPT FOR ONE.
I NEVER SHOULD HAVE WHISPERED. I NEVER SHOULD HAVE MADE THE GREATEST OF THE GODS UNWORTHY. EVEN IF ALL I SPOKE...
...WAS THE TRUTH.
IT IS TIME, SON OF ODIN. TIME TO THROW OFF THE YOKE WITH WHICH YOU WERE BURDENED.
TIME TO EMBRACE THE FUTURE...

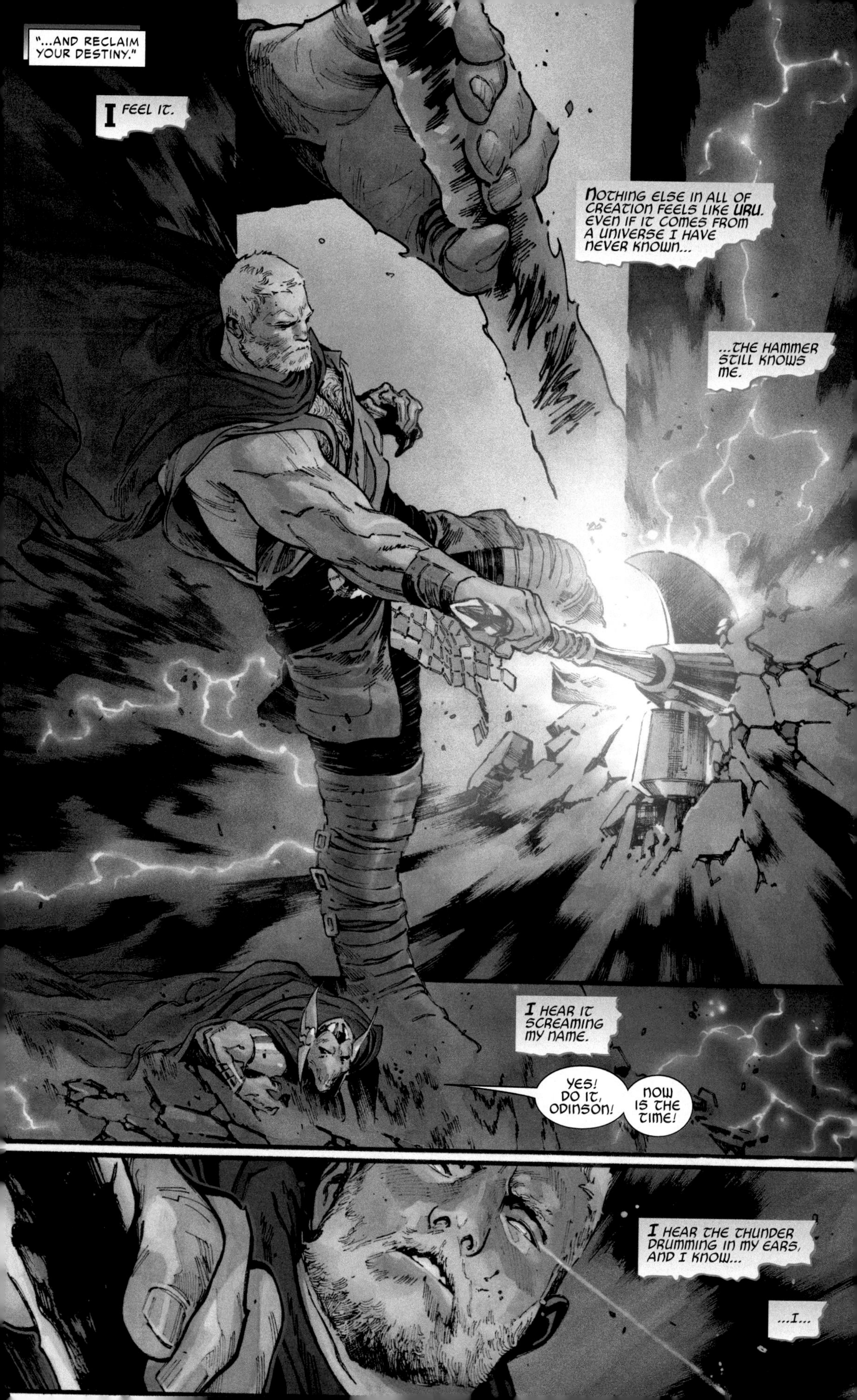
"...AND RECLAIM YOUR DESTINY."
I FEEL IT.
NOTHING ELSE IN ALL OF CREATION FEELS LIKE URU. EVEN IF IT COMES FROM A UNIVERSE I HAVE NEVER KNOWN...
...THE HAMMER STILL KNOWS ME.
I HEAR IT SCREAMING MY NAME.
YES! DO IT, ODINSON!
NOW IS THE TIME!
I HEAR THE THUNDER DRUMMING IN MY EARS, AND I KNOW...
...I...

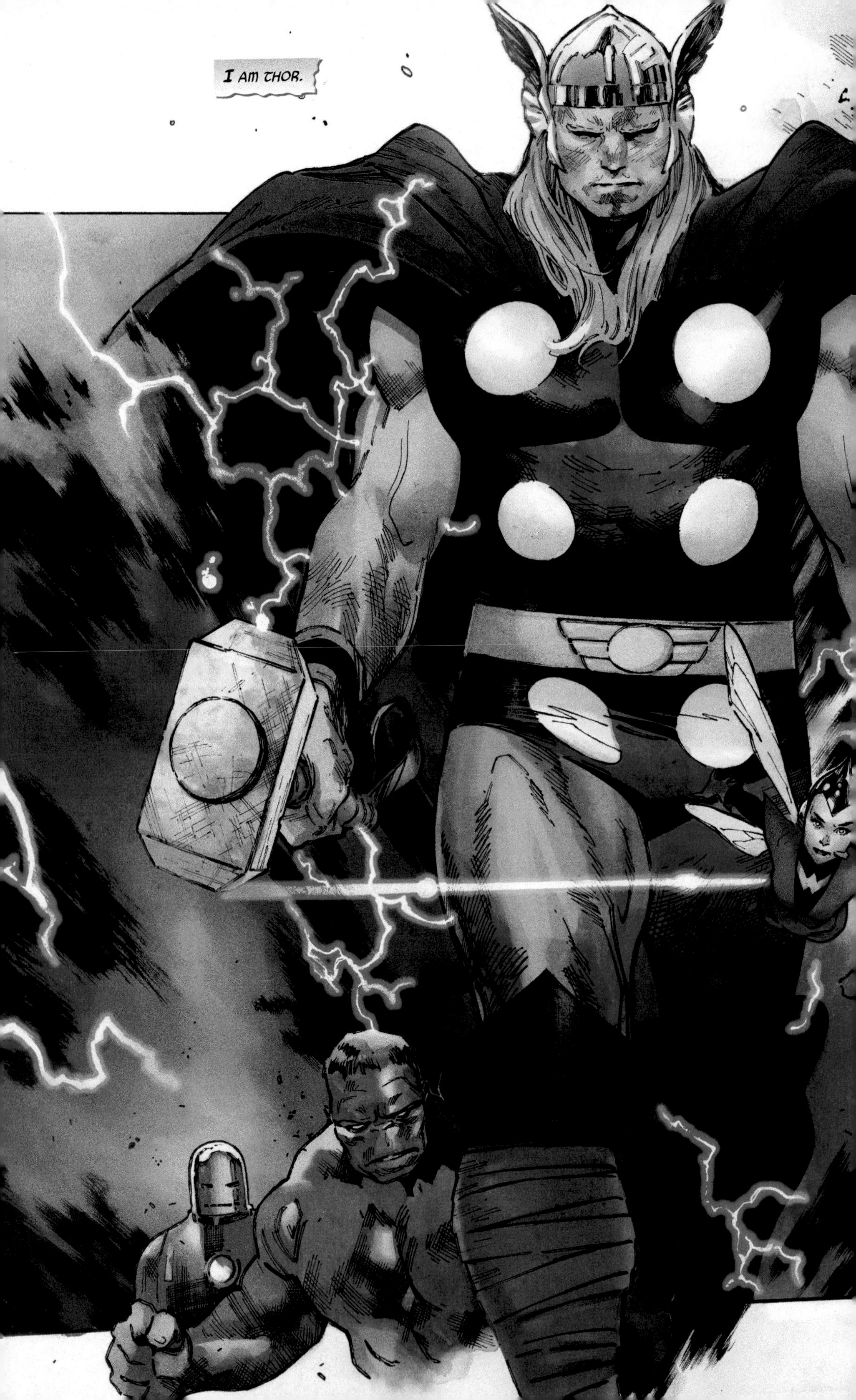
I AM THOR.

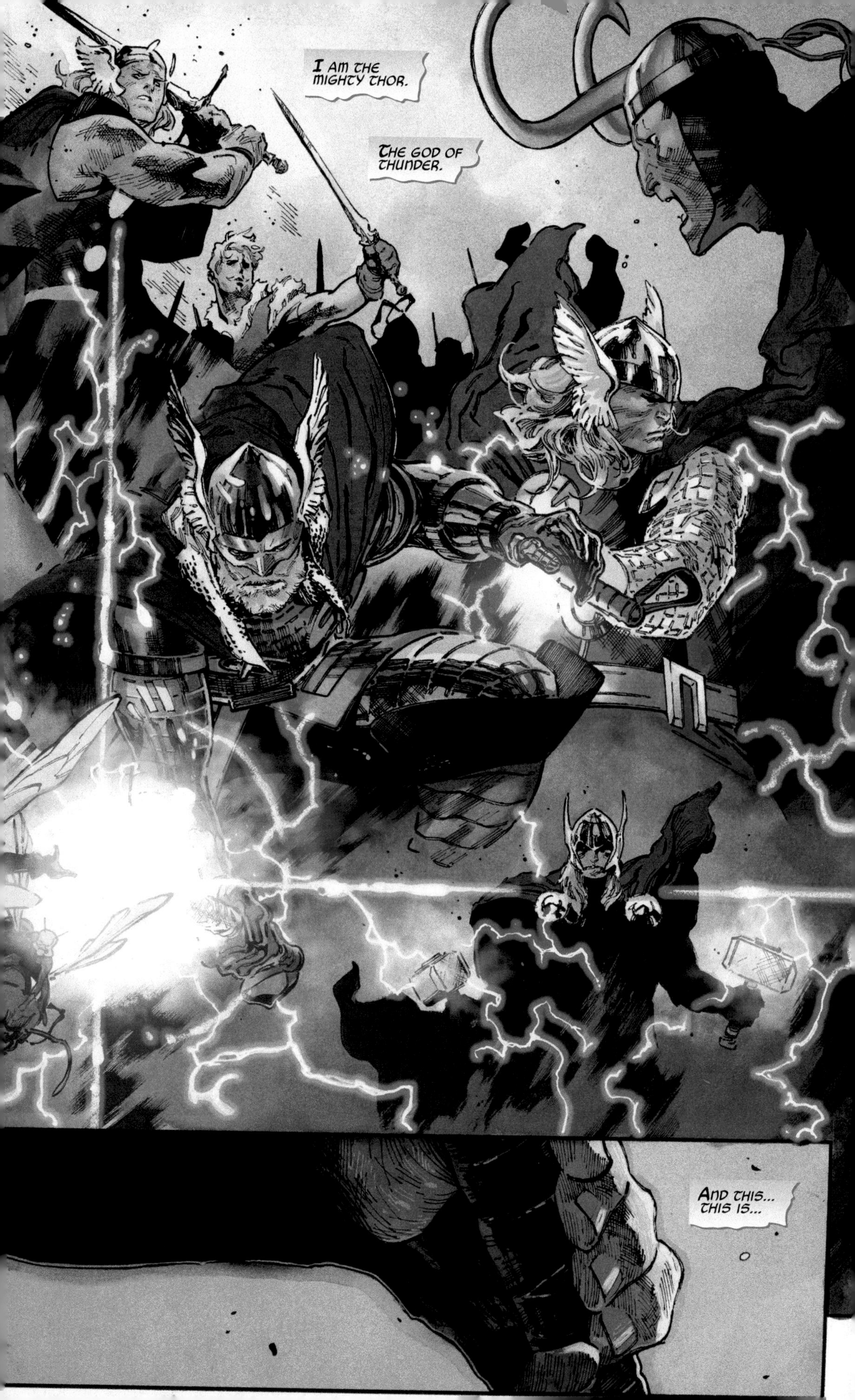
I AM THE MIGHTY THOR.
THE GOD OF THUNDER.
AND THIS... THIS IS...

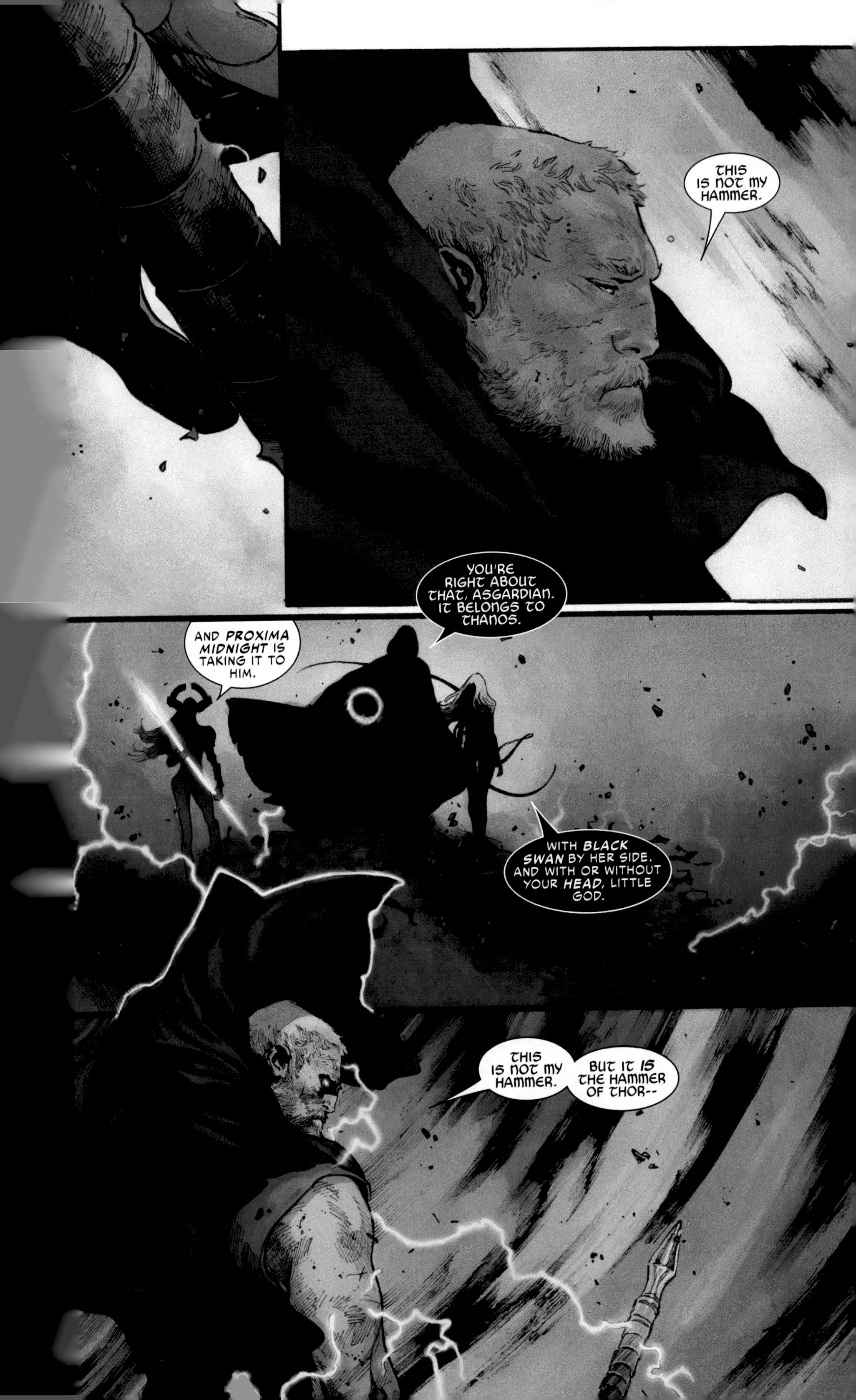
THIS IS NOT MY HAMMER.
YOU'RE RIGHT ABOUT THAT, ASGARDIAN. IT BELONGS TO THANOS.
AND PROXIMA MIDNIGHT IS TAKING IT TO HIM.
WITH BLACK SWAN BY HER SIDE. AND WITH OR WITHOUT YOUR HEAD, LITTLE GOD.
THIS IS NOT MY HAMMER.
BUT IT IS THE HAMMER OF THOR--

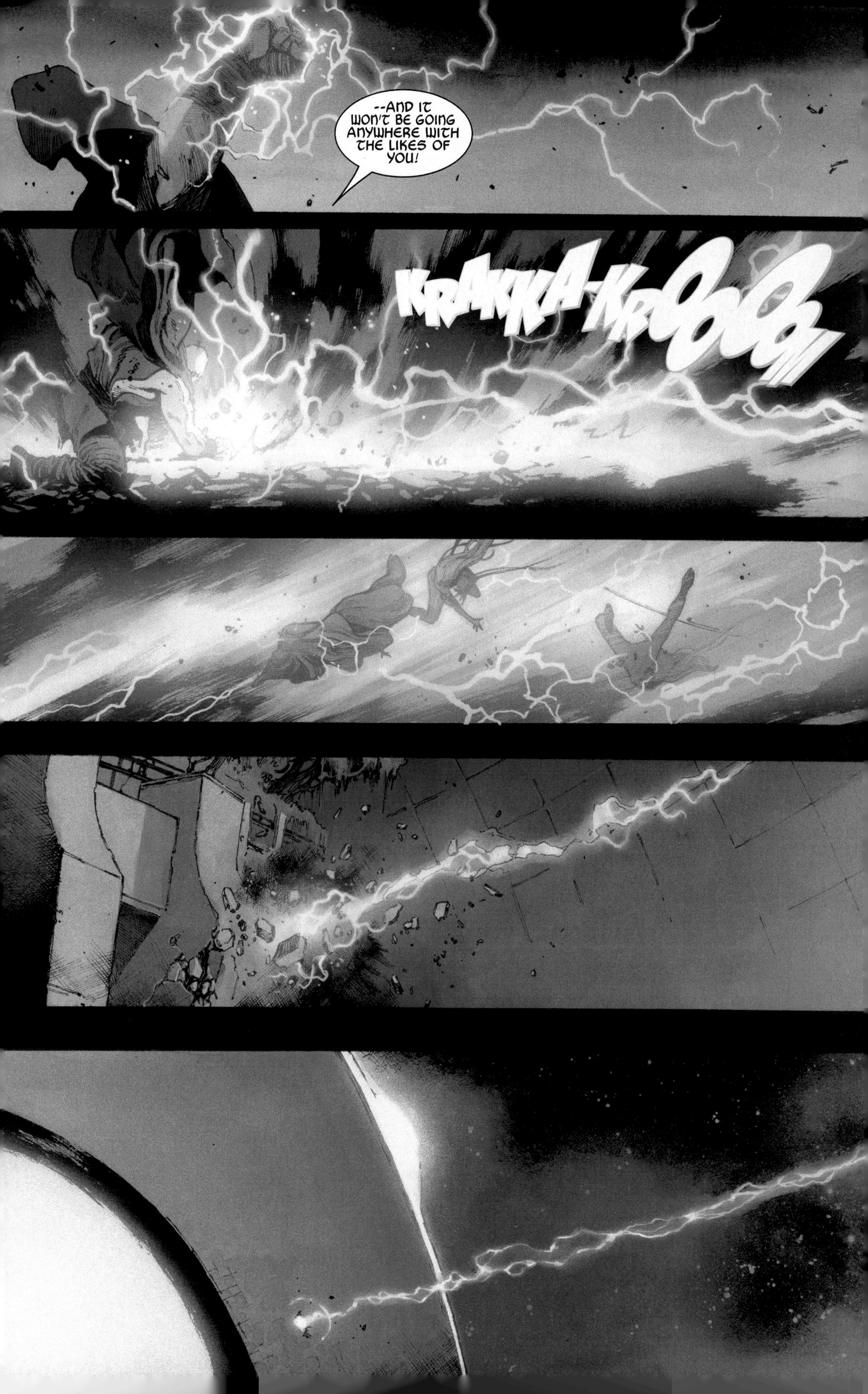
--AND IT WON'T BE GOING ANYWHERE WITH THE LIKES OF YOU!
KRAKKA-KROOOOM

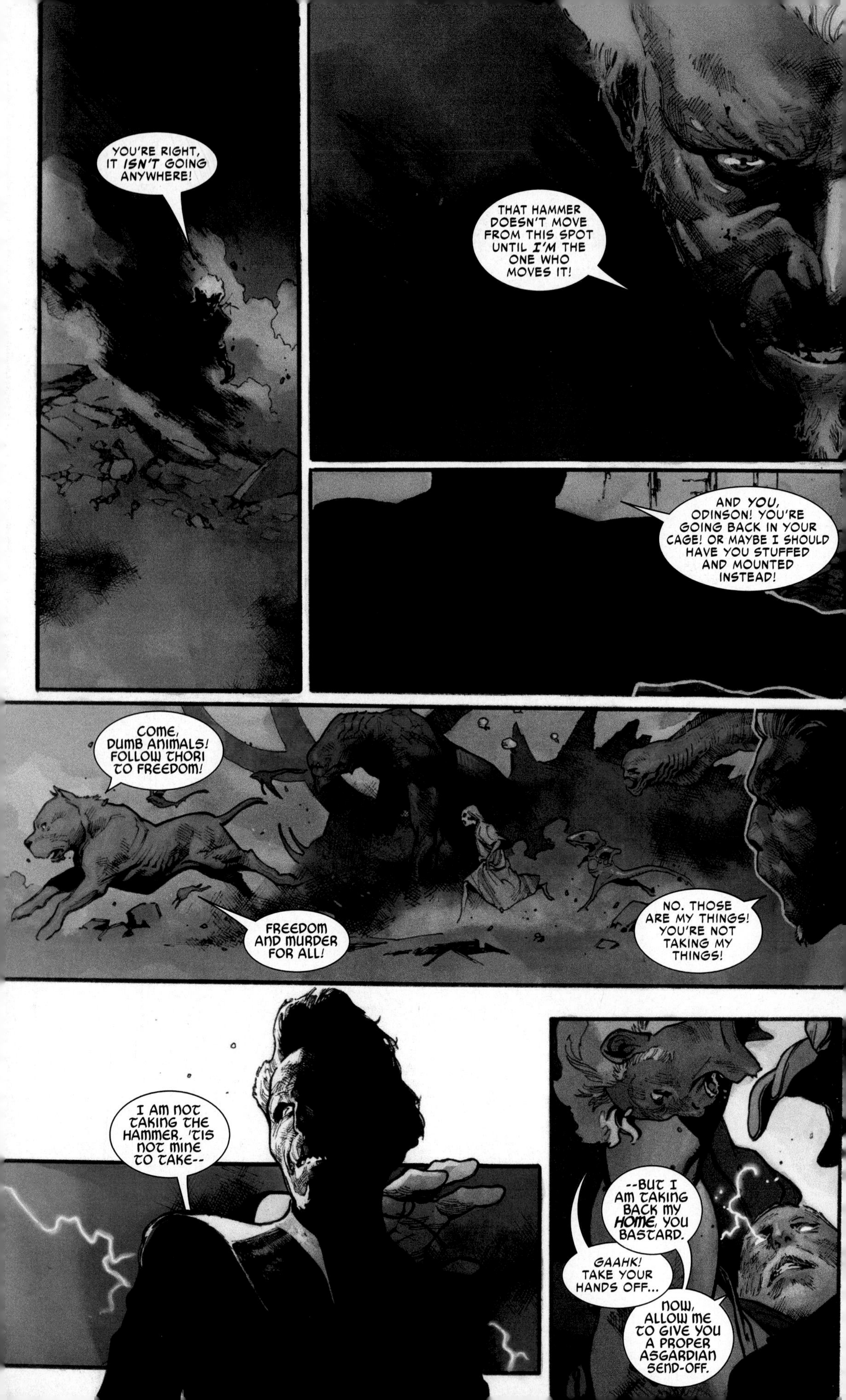
YOU'RE RIGHT, IT ISN'T GOING ANYWHERE!
THAT HAMMER DOESN'T MOVE FROM THIS SPOT UNTIL I'M THE ONE WHO MOVES IT!
AND YOU, ODINSON! YOU'RE GOING BACK IN YOUR CAGE! OR MAYBE I SHOULD HAVE YOU STUFFED AND MOUNTED INSTEAD!
COME, DUMB ANIMALS! FOLLOW THORI TO FREEDOM!
FREEDOM AND MURDER FOR ALL!
NO. THOSE ARE MY THINGS! YOU'RE NOT TAKING MY THINGS!
I AM NOT TAKING THE HAMMER. 'TIS NOT MINE TO TAKE--
--BUT I AM TAKING BACK MY HOME, YOU BASTARD.
GAAHK! TAKE YOUR HANDS OFF...
NOW, ALLOW ME TO GIVE YOU A PROPER ASGARDIAN SEND-OFF.

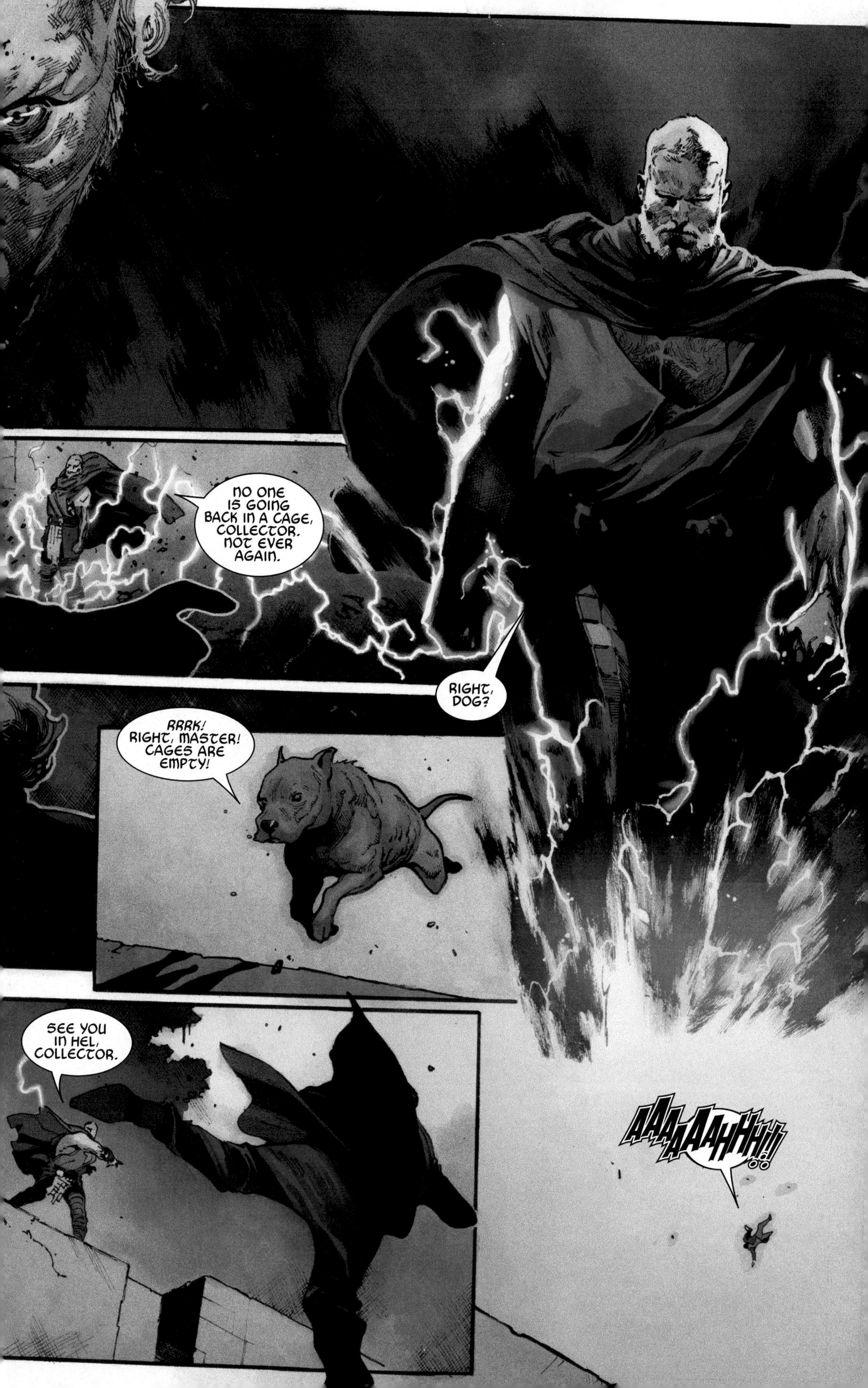
NO ONE IS GOING BACK IN A CAGE, COLLECTOR. NOT EVER AGAIN.
RIGHT, DOG?
RRRK! RIGHT, MASTER! CAGES ARE EMPTY!
SEE YOU IN HEL, COLLECTOR.
AAAAAAHHH!!!

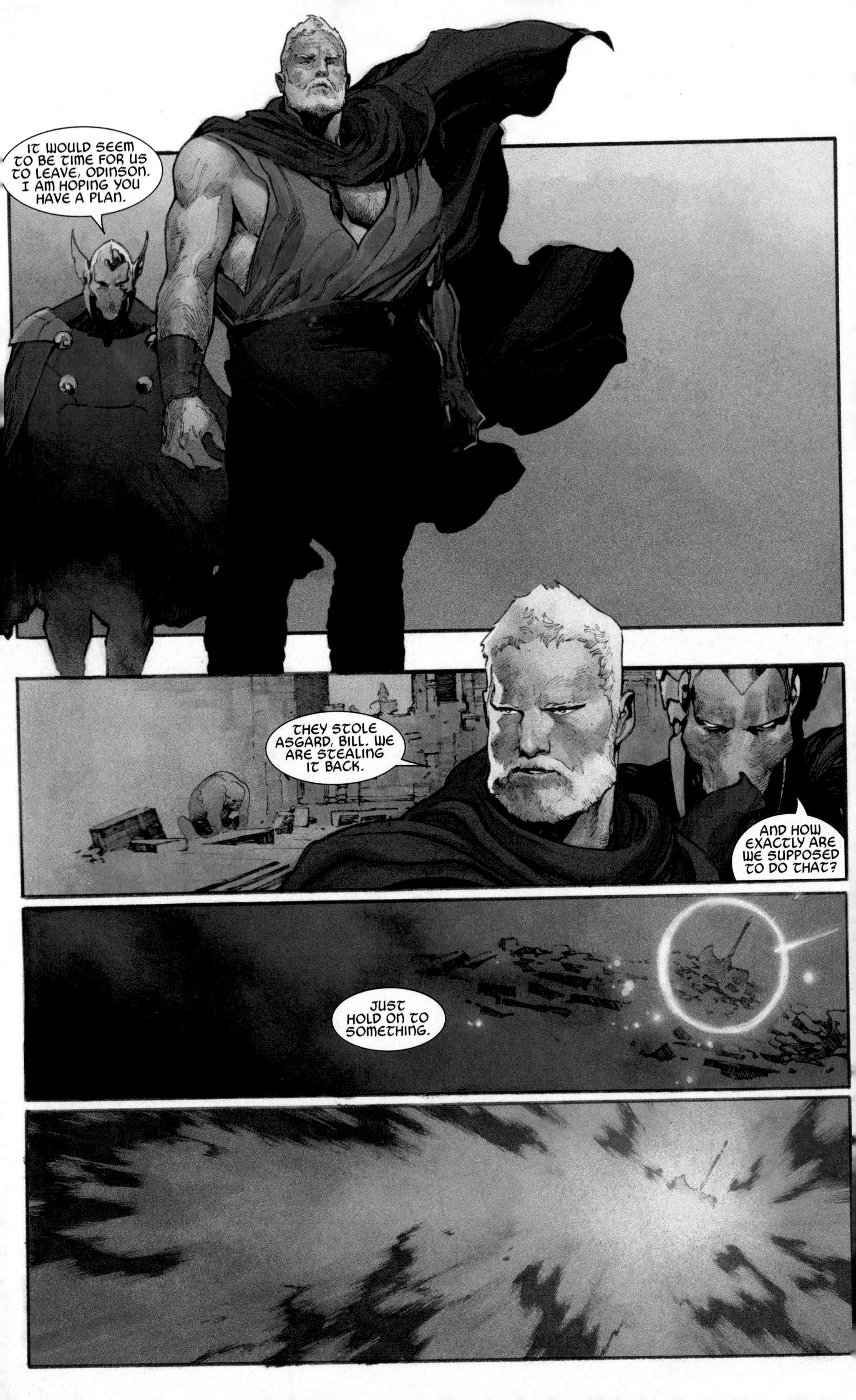
IT WOULD SEEM TO BE TIME FOR US TO LEAVE, ODINSON. I AM HOPING YOU HAVE A PLAN.
THEY STOLE ASGARD, BILL. WE ARE STEALING IT BACK.
AND HOW EXACTLY ARE WE SUPPOSED TO DO THAT?
JUST HOLD ON TO SOMETHING.

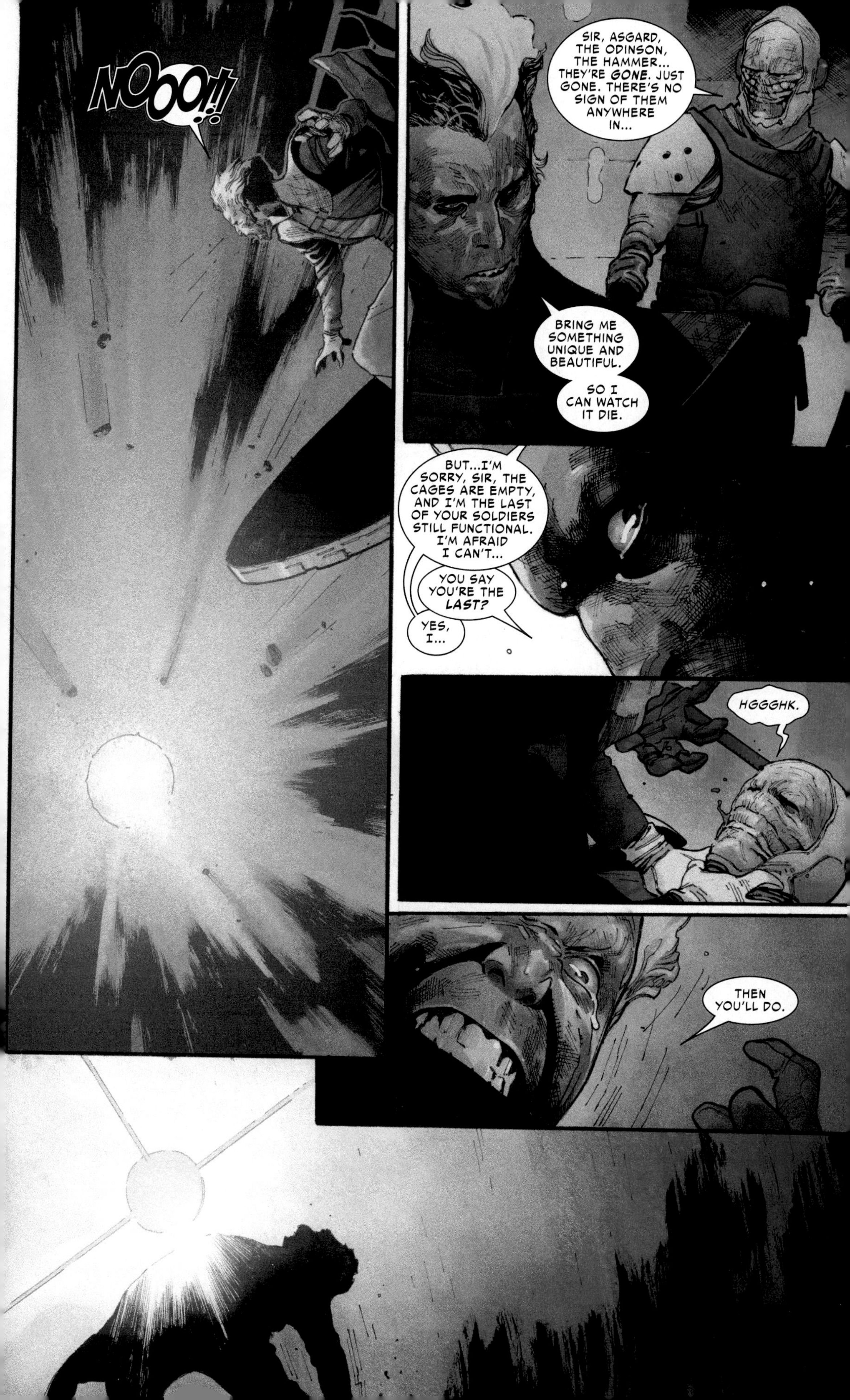
NOOOO!!!
SIR, ASGARD, THE ODINSON, THE HAMMER... THEY'RE GONE. JUST GONE. THERE'S NO SIGN OF THEM ANYWHERE IN...
BRING ME SOMETHING UNIQUE AND BEAUTIFUL.
SO I CAN WATCH IT DIE.
BUT...I'M SORRY, SIR, THE CAGES ARE EMPTY, AND I'M THE LAST OF YOUR SOLDIERS STILL FUNCTIONAL. I'M AFRAID I CAN'T...
YOU SAY YOU'RE THE LAST?
YES, I...
HGGGHK.
THEN YOU'LL DO.

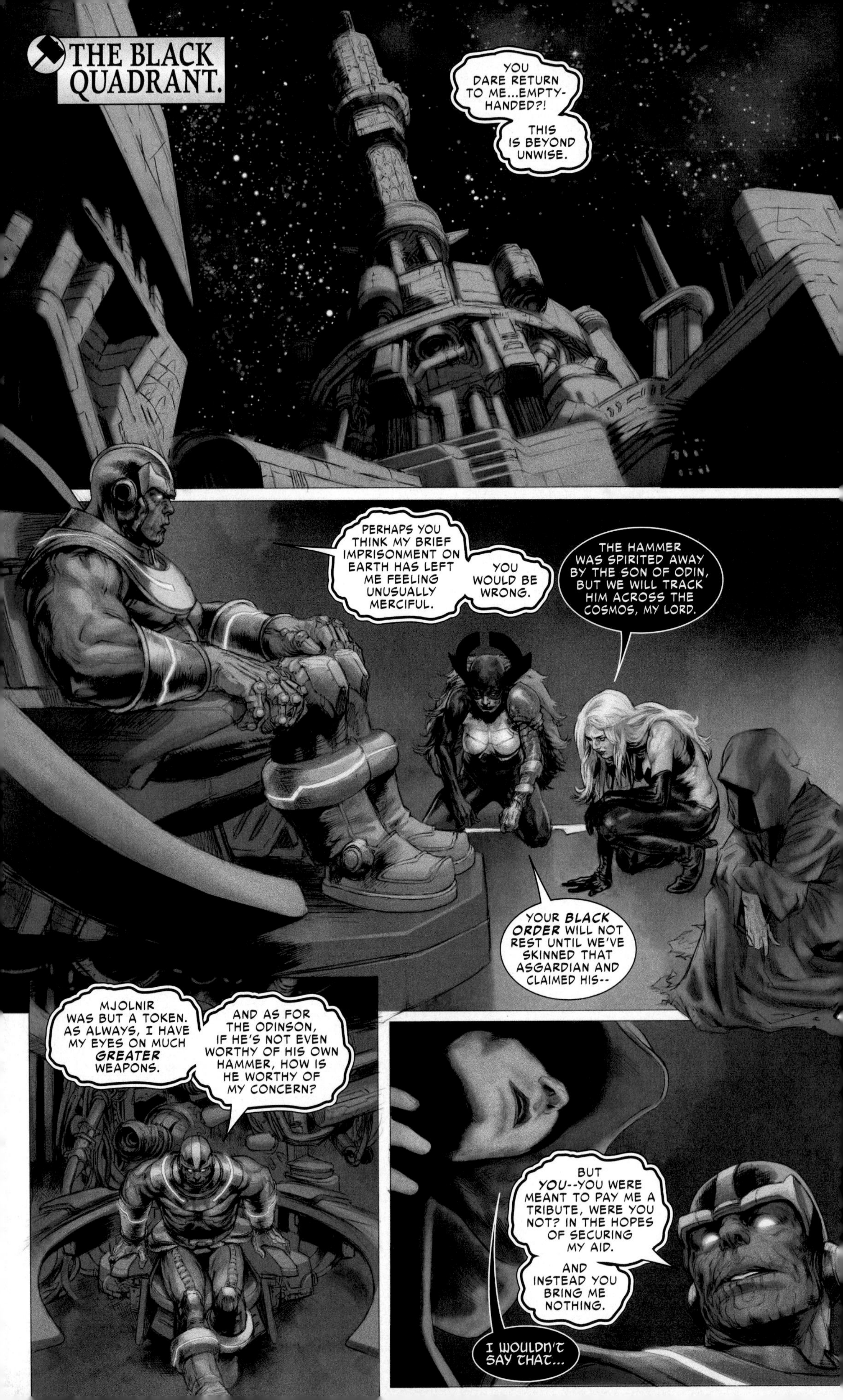
THE BLACK QUADRANT.
YOU DARE RETURN TO ME...EMPTY-HANDED?!
THIS IS BEYOND UNWISE.
PERHAPS YOU THINK MY BRIEF IMPRISONMENT ON EARTH HAS LEFT ME FEELING UNUSUALLY MERCIFUL.
YOU WOULD BE WRONG.
THE HAMMER WAS SPIRITED AWAY BY THE SON OF ODIN, BUT WE WILL TRACK HIM ACROSS THE COSMOS, MY LORD.
YOUR BLACK ORDER WILL NOT REST UNTIL WE'VE SKINNED THAT ASGARDIAN AND CLAIMED HIS--
MJOLNIR WAS BUT A TOKEN. AS ALWAYS, I HAVE MY EYES ON MUCH GREATER WEAPONS.
AND AS FOR THE ODINSON, IF HE'S NOT EVEN WORTHY OF HIS OWN HAMMER, HOW IS HE WORTHY OF MY CONCERN?
BUT YOU--YOU WERE MEANT TO PAY ME A TRIBUTE, WERE YOU NOT? IN THE HOPES OF SECURING MY AID.
AND INSTEAD YOU BRING ME NOTHING.
I WOULDN'T SAY THAT...

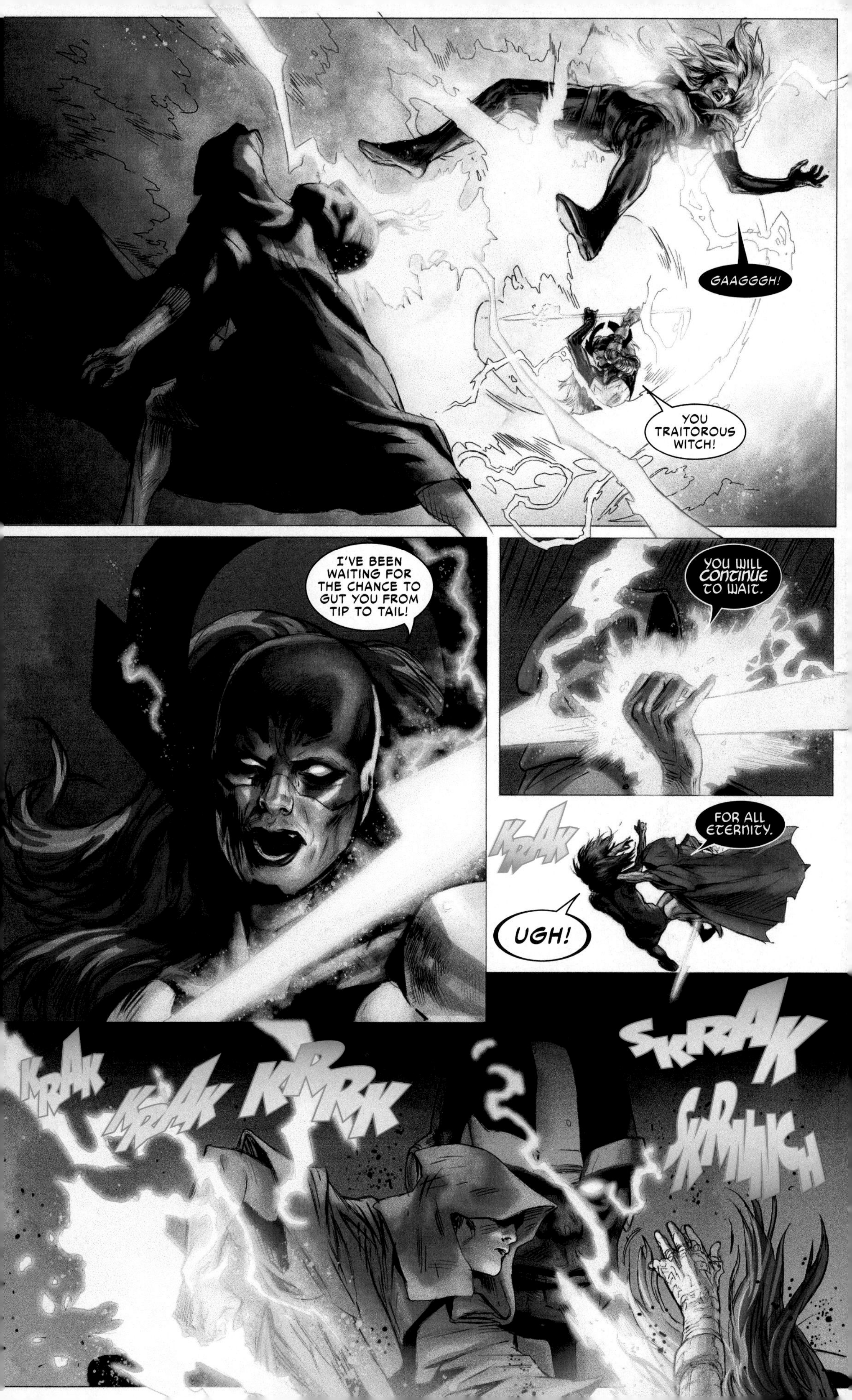
GAAGGGH!
YOU TRAITOROUS WITCH!
I'VE BEEN WAITING FOR THE CHANCE TO GUT YOU FROM TIP TO TAIL!
YOU WILL CONTINUE TO WAIT.
KRAK
FOR ALL ETERNITY.
UGH!
KRAK
KRAK
KRRK
SKRAK
SKRUNCH

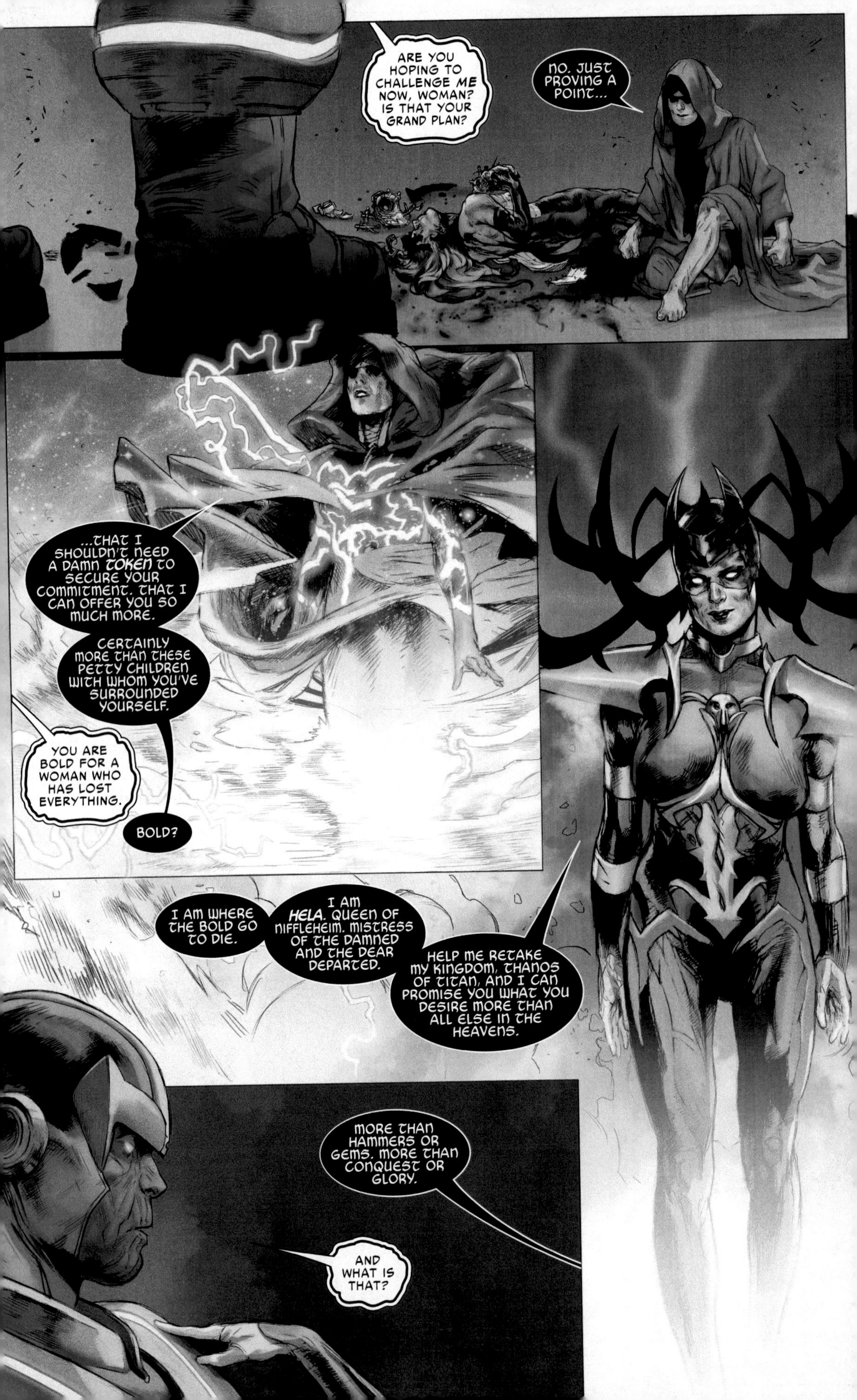
ARE YOU HOPING TO CHALLENGE ME NOW, WOMAN? IS THAT YOUR GRAND PLAN?
NO. JUST PROVING A POINT...
...THAT I SHOULDN'T NEED A DAMN TOKEN TO SECURE YOUR COMMITMENT. THAT I CAN OFFER YOU SO MUCH MORE.
CERTAINLY MORE THAN THESE PETTY CHILDREN WITH WHOM YOU'VE SURROUNDED YOURSELF.
YOU ARE BOLD FOR A WOMAN WHO HAS LOST EVERYTHING.
BOLD?
I AM WHERE THE BOLD GO TO DIE.
I AM HELA. QUEEN OF NIFFLEHEIM. MISTRESS OF THE DAMNED AND THE DEAR DEPARTED.
HELP ME RETAKE MY KINGDOM, THANOS OF TITAN, AND I CAN PROMISE YOU WHAT YOU DESIRE MORE THAN ALL ELSE IN THE HEAVENS.
MORE THAN HAMMERS OR GEMS. MORE THAN CONQUEST OR GLORY.
AND WHAT IS THAT?

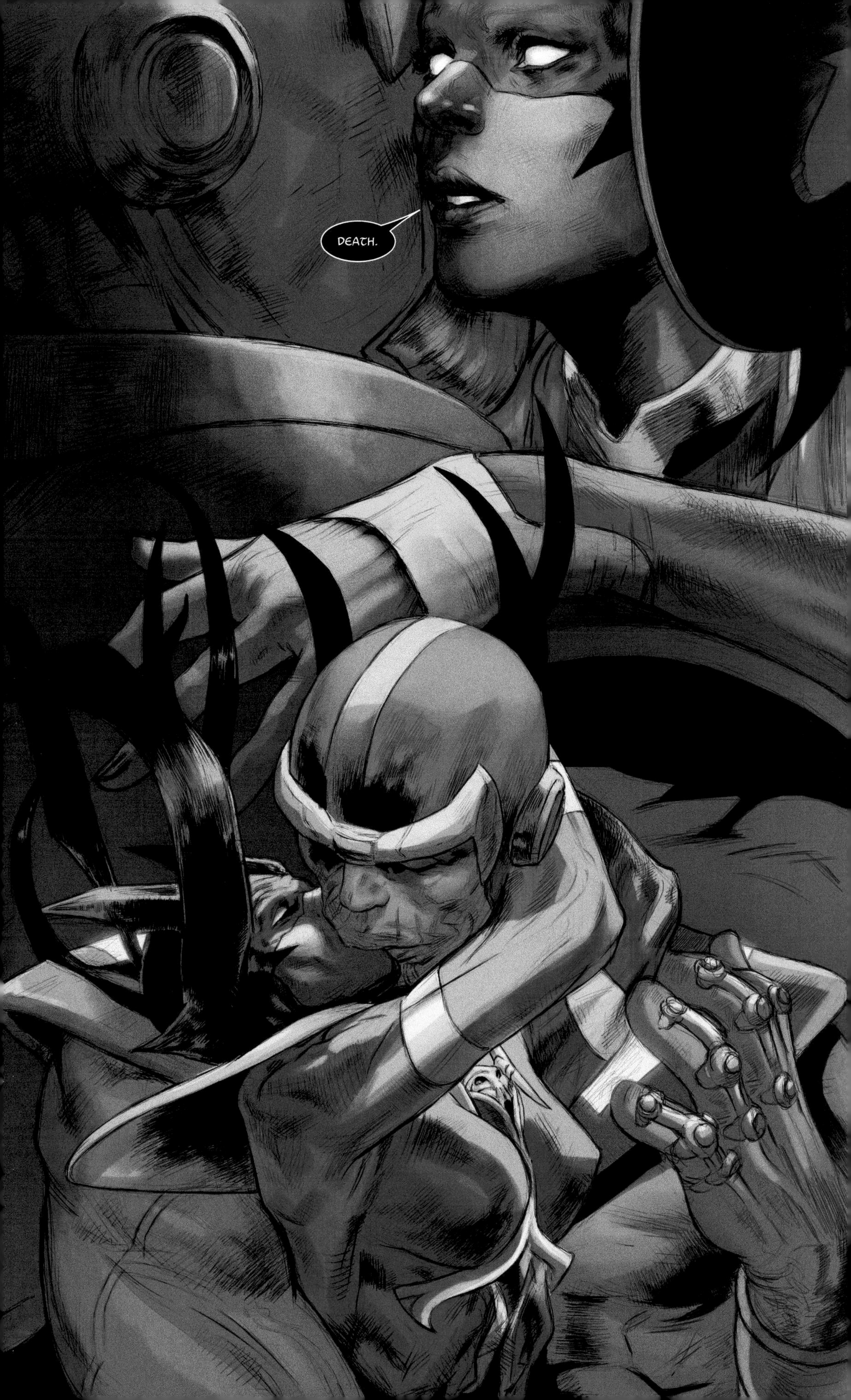
DEATH.

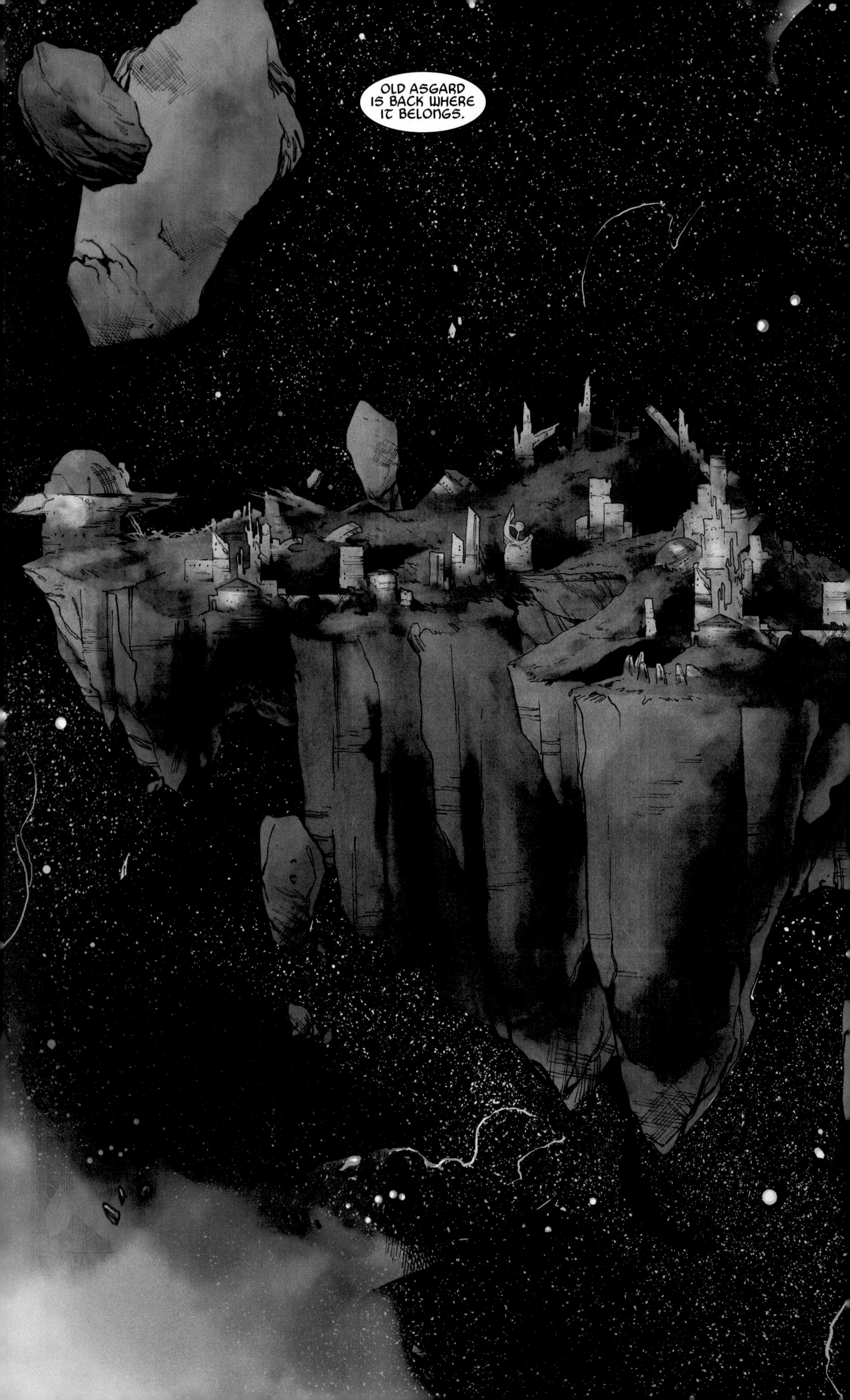
OLD ASGARD IS BACK WHERE IT BELONGS.

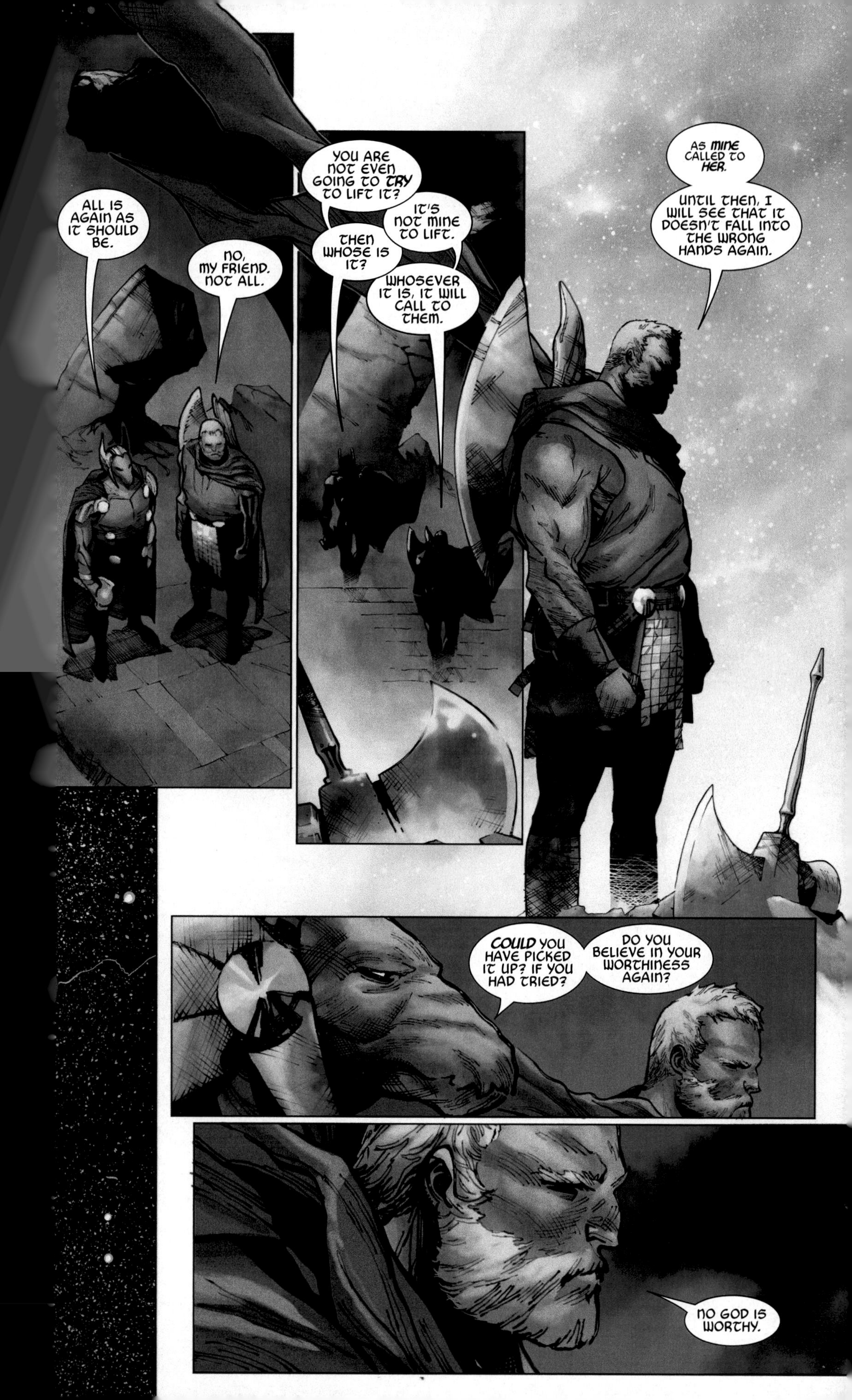
ALL IS AGAIN AS IT SHOULD BE.
NO, MY FRIEND. NOT ALL.
YOU ARE NOT EVEN GOING TO TRY TO LIFT IT?
IT'S NOT MINE TO LIFT.
THEN WHOSE IS IT?
WHOSEVER IT IS, IT WILL CALL TO THEM.
AS MINE CALLED TO HER.
UNTIL THEN, I WILL SEE THAT IT DOESN'T FALL INTO THE WRONG HANDS AGAIN.
COULD YOU HAVE PICKED IT UP? IF YOU HAD TRIED?
DO YOU BELIEVE IN YOUR WORTHINESS AGAIN?
NO GOD IS WORTHY.

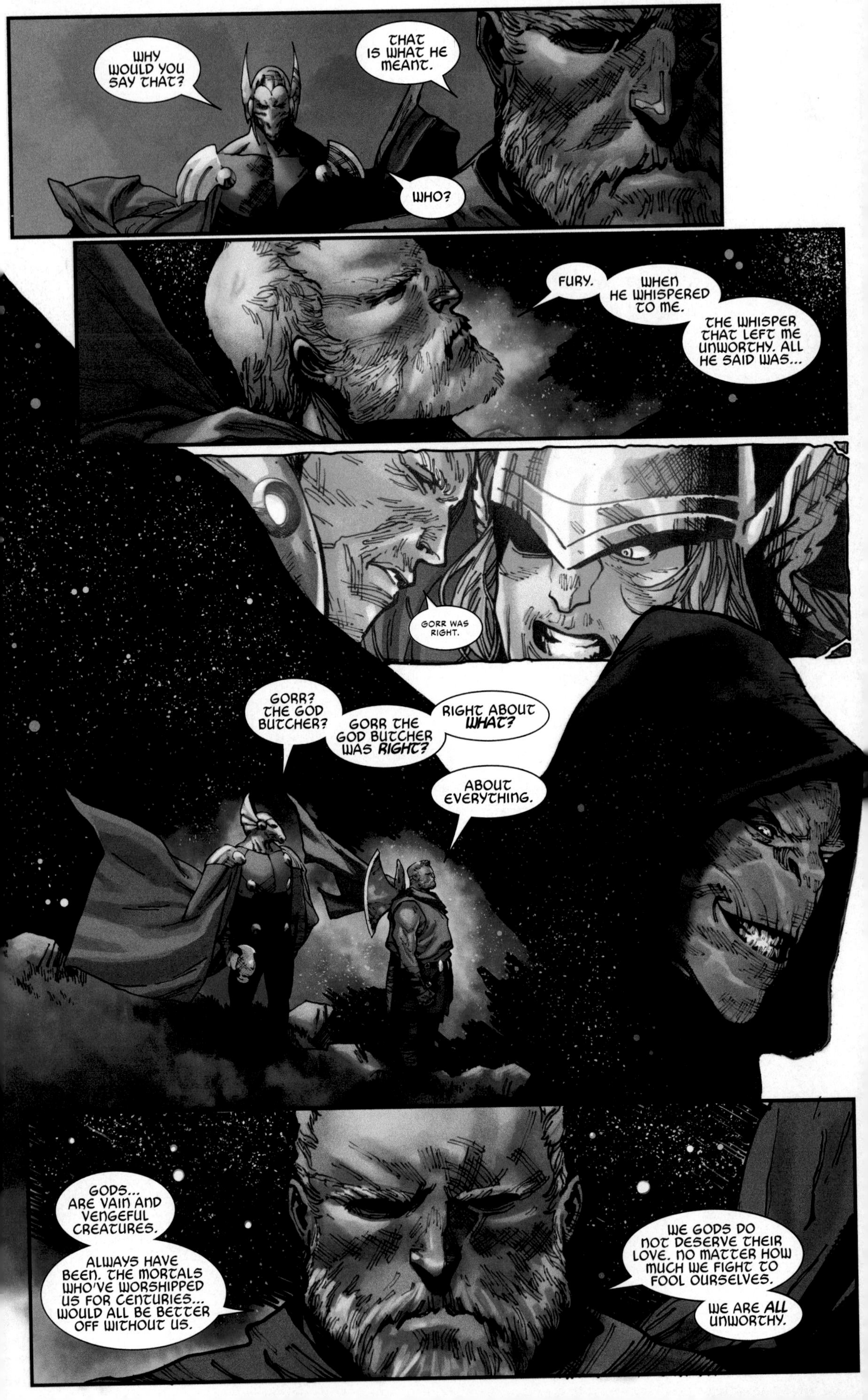

WHY WOULD YOU SAY THAT?
THAT IS WHAT HE MEANT.
WHO?
FURY.
WHEN HE WHISPERED TO ME.
THE WHISPER THAT LEFT ME UNWORTHY. ALL HE SAID WAS...
GORR WAS RIGHT.
GORR? THE GOD BUTCHER?
GORR THE GOD BUTCHER WAS RIGHT?
RIGHT ABOUT WHAT?
ABOUT EVERYTHING.
GODS... ARE VAIN AND VENGEFUL CREATURES.
ALWAYS HAVE BEEN. THE MORTALS WHO'VE WORSHIPPED US FOR CENTURIES... WOULD ALL BE BETTER OFF WITHOUT US.
WE GODS DO NOT DESERVE THEIR LOVE. NO MATTER HOW MUCH WE FIGHT TO FOOL OURSELVES.
WE ARE ALL UNWORTHY.

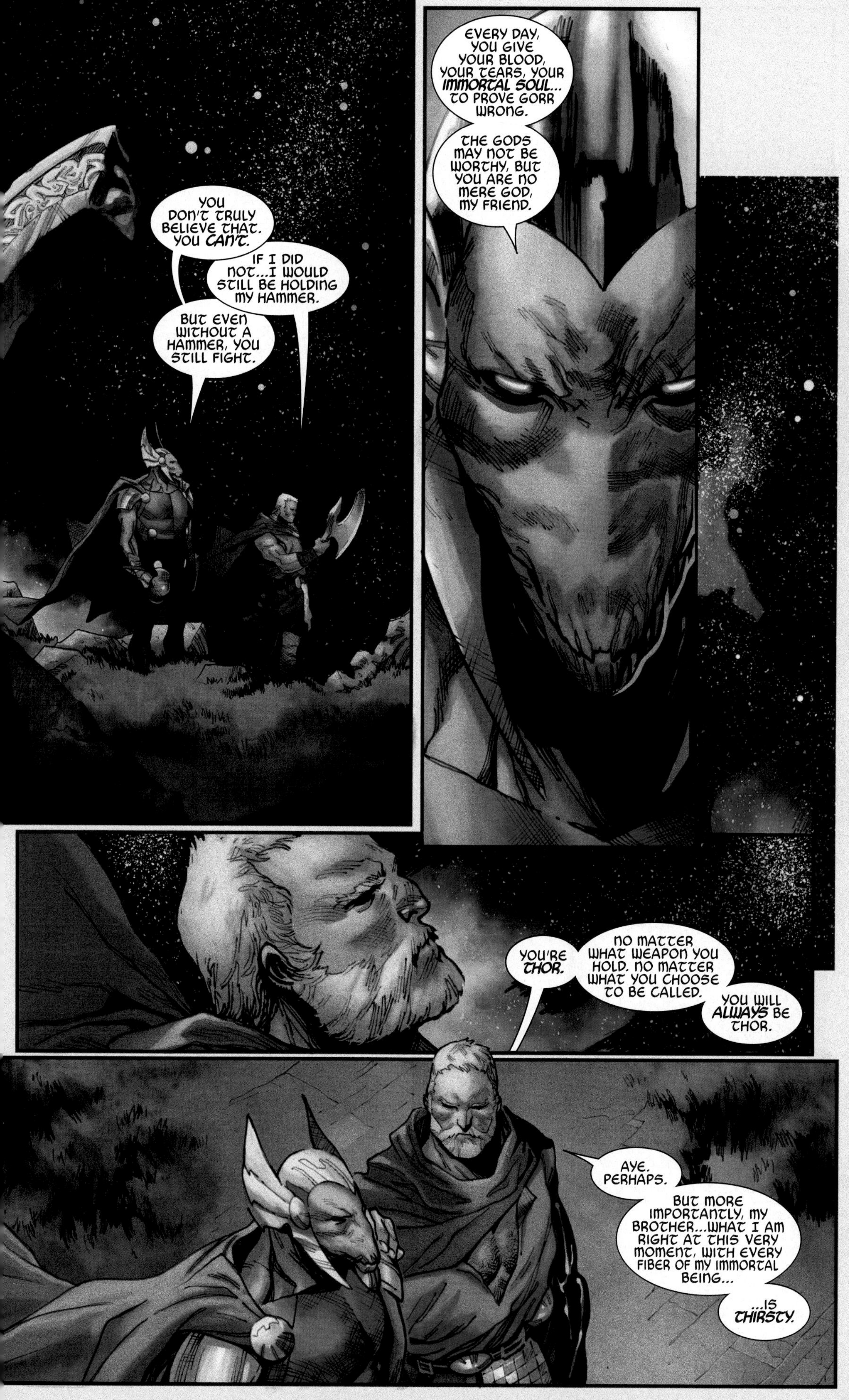
YOU DON'T TRULY BELIEVE THAT. YOU CAN'T.
IF I DID NOT...I WOULD STILL BE HOLDING MY HAMMER.
BUT EVEN WITHOUT A HAMMER, YOU STILL FIGHT.
EVERY DAY, YOU GIVE YOUR BLOOD, YOUR TEARS, YOUR IMMORTAL SOUL... TO PROVE GORR WRONG.
THE GODS MAY NOT BE WORTHY, BUT YOU ARE NO MERE GOD, MY FRIEND.
YOU'RE THOR.
NO MATTER WHAT WEAPON YOU HOLD. NO MATTER WHAT YOU CHOOSE TO BE CALLED.
YOU WILL ALWAYS BE THOR.
AYE. PERHAPS.
BUT MORE IMPORTANTLY, MY BROTHER...WHAT I AM RIGHT AT THIS VERY MOMENT, WITH EVERY FIBER OF MY IMMORTAL BEING...
...IS THIRSTY.

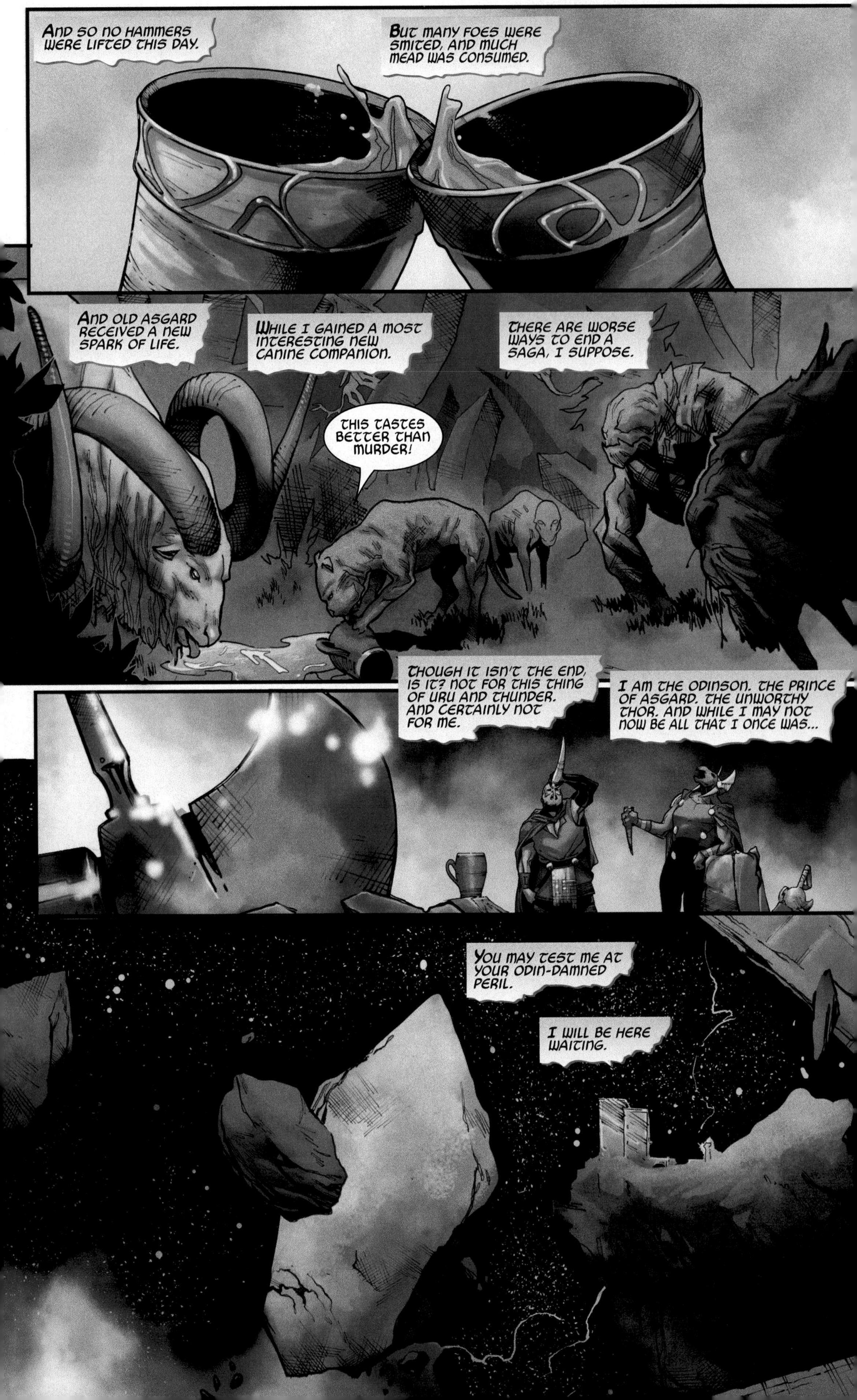
And so no hammers were lifted this day.
But many foes were smited, and much mead was consumed.
And old Asgard received a new spark of life.
While I gained a most interesting new canine companion.
There are worse ways to end a saga, I suppose.
This tastes better than murder!
Though it isn't the end, is it? Not for this thing of uru and thunder. And certainly not for me.
I am the Odinson. The prince of Asgard. The unworthy Thor. And while I may not now be all that I once was...
You may test me at your Odin-damned peril.
I will be here waiting.

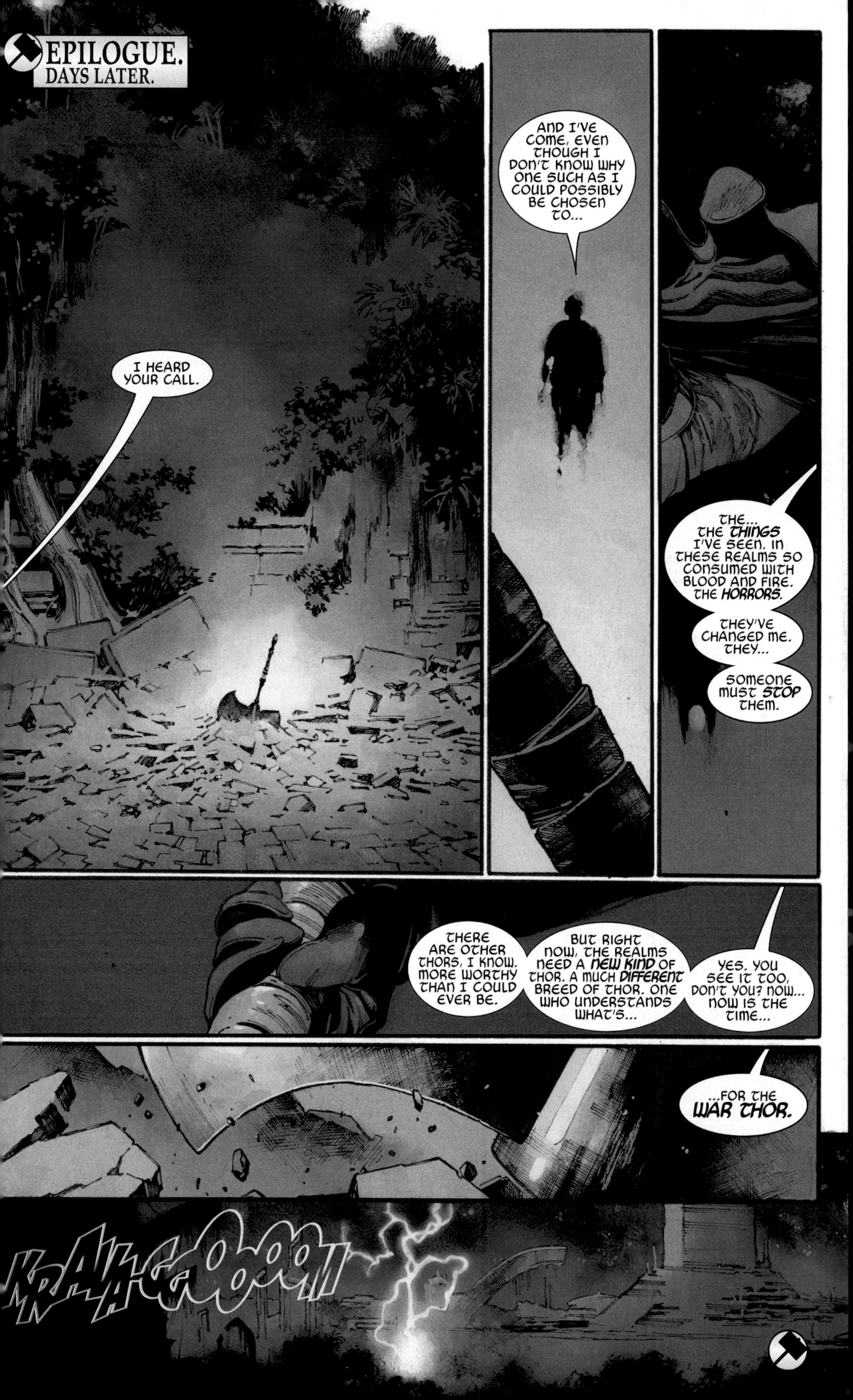

EPILOGUE.
DAYS LATER.
I HEARD YOUR CALL.
AND I'VE COME, EVEN THOUGH I DON'T KNOW WHY ONE SUCH AS I COULD POSSIBLY BE CHOSEN TO...
THE... THE THINGS I'VE SEEN. IN THESE REALMS SO CONSUMED WITH BLOOD AND FIRE. THE HORRORS.
THEY'VE CHANGED ME. THEY...
SOMEONE MUST STOP THEM.
THERE ARE OTHER THORS, I KNOW. MORE WORTHY THAN I COULD EVER BE.
BUT RIGHT NOW, THE REALMS NEED A NEW KIND OF THOR. A MUCH DIFFERENT BREED OF THOR. ONE WHO UNDERSTANDS WHAT'S...
YES. YOU SEE IT TOO, DON'T YOU? NOW... NOW IS THE TIME...
...FOR THE WAR THOR.
KRAKAGOOOM

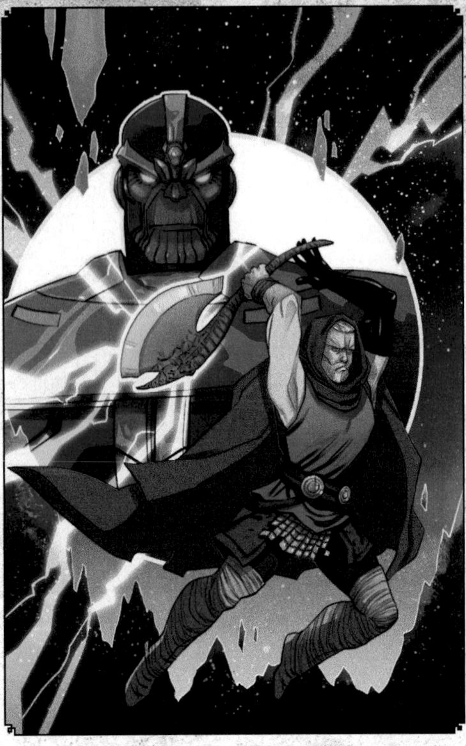

UNWORTHY THOR #4 VARIANT
BY **MARGUERITE SAUVAGE**

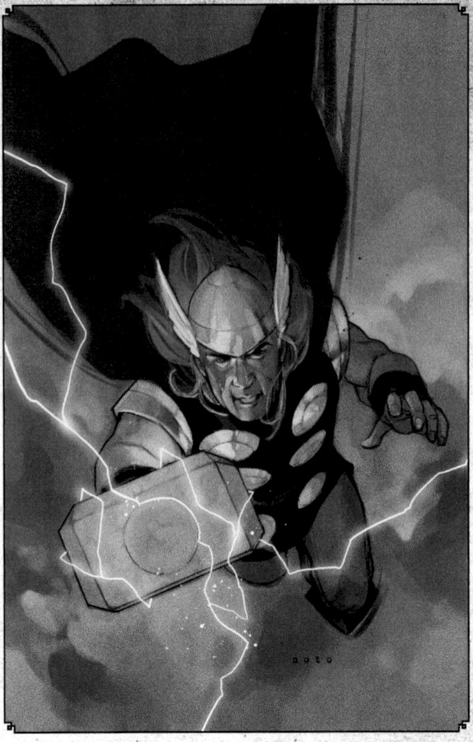

UNWORTHY THOR #4 VARIANT
BY **PHIL NOTO**

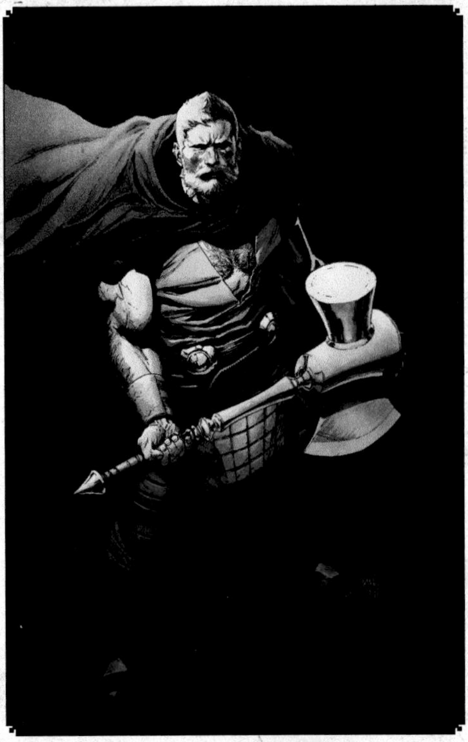

UNWORTHY THOR #5 VARIANT
BY **LEINIL FRANCIS YU**
& **MATTHEW WILSON**

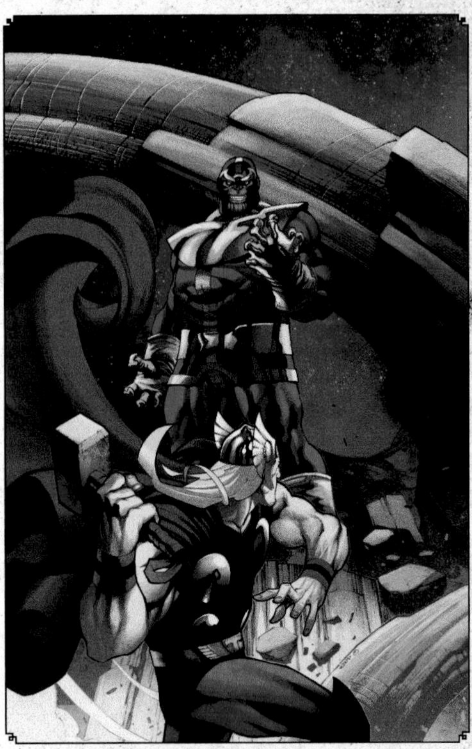

UNWORTHY THOR #5 VARIANT
BY **CHRIS STEVENS**
& **FRANK MARTIN**

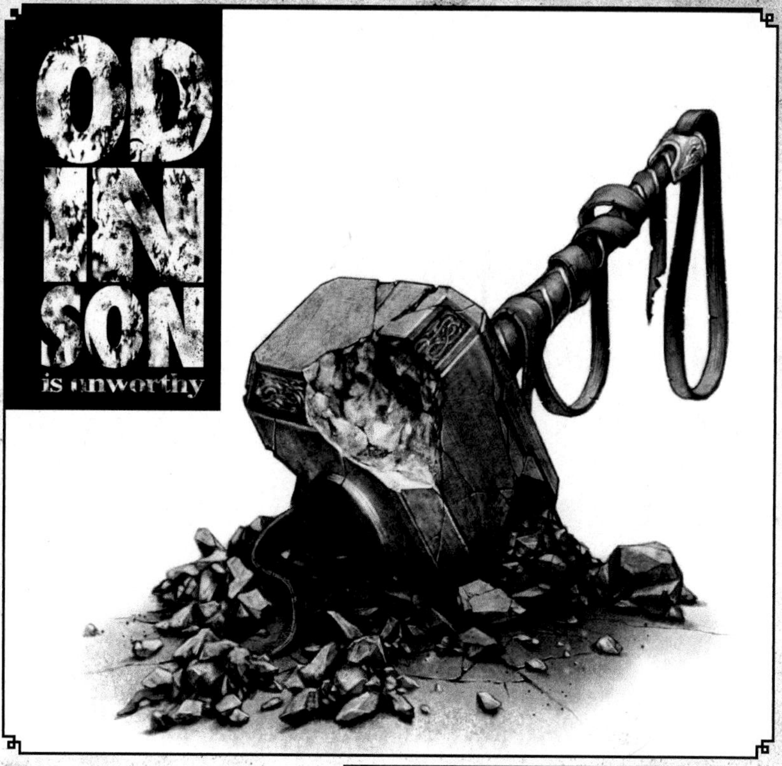
ODINSON
is unworthy

UNWORTHY THOR #1
HIP-HOP VARIANT
BY **STONEHOUSE**

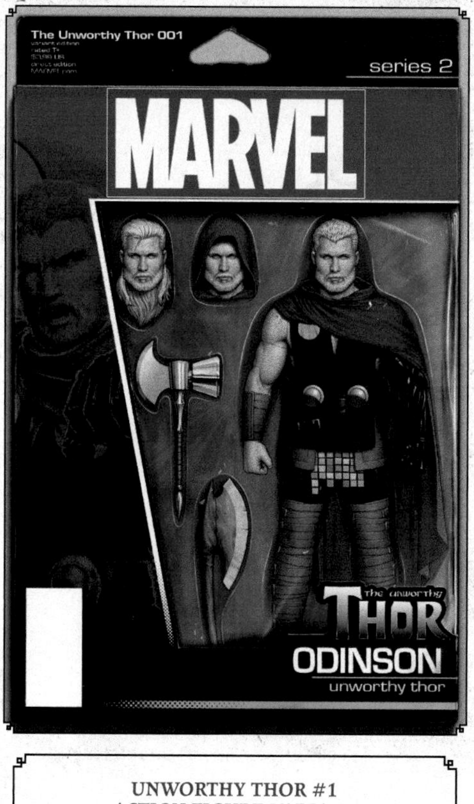
The Unworthy Thor 001
series 2
MARVEL
the unworthy THOR
ODINSON
unworthy thor

UNWORTHY THOR #1
ACTION FIGURE VARIANT
BY **JOHN TYLER CHRISTOPHER**

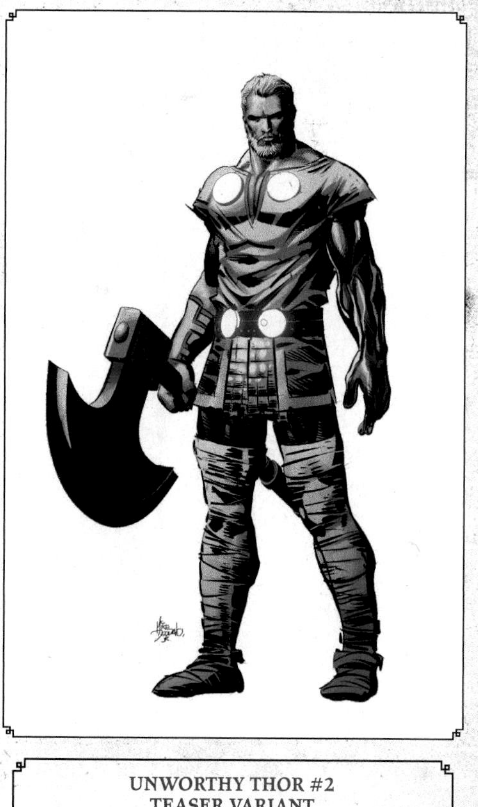

UNWORTHY THOR #2
TEASER VARIANT
BY **MIKE DEODATO**
& **FRANK MARTIN**

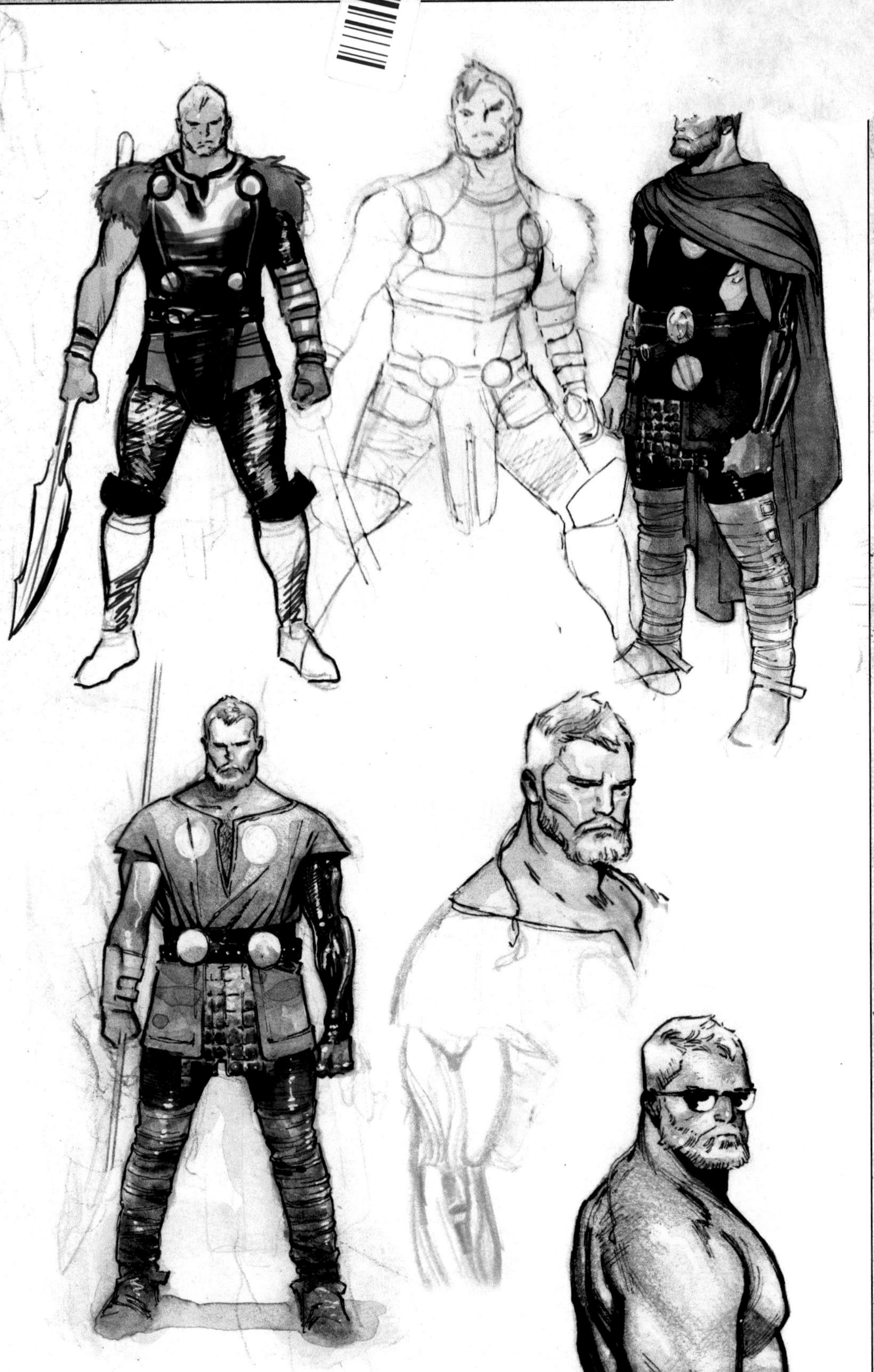

Sketchbook BY OLIVIER COIPEL